Critical Muslim 22

Utopias

Critical Muslim is published quarterly by C. Hurst & Co. (Publishers) Ltd. on behalf of and in conjunction with Critical Muslim Ltd. and the Muslim Institute, London. *Critical Muslim* acknowledges the support of the Aziz Foundation, London.

All correspondence to Muslim Institute, CAN Mezzanine, 49-51 East Road, London N1 6AH, United Kingdom

e-mail for editorial: editorial@criticalmuslim.com

The editors do not necessarily agree with the opinions expressed by the contributors. We reserve the right to make such editorial changes as may be necessary to make submissions to *Critical Muslim* suitable for publication.

C. Hurst & Co (Publishers) Ltd.,41 Great Russell Street, London WC1B 3PL

ISBN: 978-1-84904-824-8 ISSN: 2048-8475

To subscribe or place an order by credit/debit card or cheque (pounds sterling only) please contact Kathleen May at the Hurst address above or e-mail kathleen@hurstpub.co.uk

Tel: 020 7255 2201

A one year subscription, inclusive of postage (four issues), costs £50 (UK), £65 (Europe) and £75 (rest of the world).

Critical Muslim

Subscribe to Critical Muslim

Now in its sixth year in print, Hurst is pleased to announce that *Critical Muslim* is also available online. Users can access the site for just £3.30 per month – or for those with a print subscription it is included as part of the package. In return, you'll get access to everything in the series (including our entire archive), and a clean, accessible reading experience for desktop computers and handheld devices — entirely free of advertising.

Full subscription

The print edition of *Critical Muslim* is published quarterly in January, April, July and October. As a subscriber to the print edition, you'll receive new issues directly to your door, as well as full access to our digital archive.

United Kingdom £50/year
Europe £65/year
Rest of the World £75/year

Digital Only

Immediate online access to *Critical Muslim*

Browse the full *Critical Muslim* archive

Cancel any time

£3.30 per month

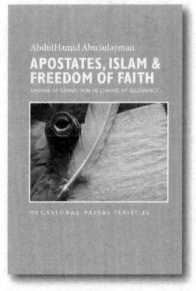

CM22

April–June 2017

CONTENTS

UTOPIAS

ARTS AND LETTERS

REVIEWS

ET CETERA

UTOPIAS

INTRODUCTION
THE COAST OF UTOPIA

Boyd Tonkin

From the kitchen window of my borrowed apartment in Cape Town, I can look up at the grandiose monument to a discredited Utopia. On his sprawling estate at Groote Schuur, below Devil's Peak on Table Mountain, Cecil John Rhodes hatched his plans for eternal white dominion in Africa – built on the sweat and blood of the Africans who mined the treasures of its earth. After his death in 1902, the architect Sir Herbert Baker designed a neo-classical memorial to the visionary imperialist. Flanked by eight bronze lions and guarded by the artist GF Watts's sculpture of a leaping horseman, the Rhodes Memorial commands spectacular vistas over two oceans – the Indian and Atlantic – and faces towards the planned starting-point of Rhodes's never-completed Cape-to-Cairo railway line.

On the nearby Upper Campus of the University of Cape Town – itself built on Rhodes-donated land – a statue of the arch-colonialist once stood. The Rhodes Must Fall campaign of late 2015, part of a broader tide of youthful protest across South Africa, toppled that stone tribute to conquest and control. The Memorial itself, much more imposing and conspicuous, still stands proud. On a sunny summer Sunday in December, diners crowd the adjacent restaurant while a Muslim family poses around Baker's Greek columns for wedding photographs. On the plinth of Watts's statue, a stanza from Rudyard Kipling's poetic homage to Rhodes lauds his 'immense and brooding spirit'. 'Living he was the land,' runs Kipling's fulsome elegy, 'and dead,/ His soul shall be her soul!' Sheer megalomania? In today's eyes, for sure. But for many decades Rhodes did preserve his name in the titles of two countries moulded in his image: Northern and Southern Rhodesia, now Zambia and Zimbabwe. Further down the hill, Rhodes's farmhouse headquarters at Groote Schuur became the Cape Town residence for South African presidents – a tradition that Nelson Mandela intermittently sustained. His successors found its use a concession to imperial history too far. Now it serves as a little-visited museum.

In almost all its historic iterations, utopia for some implies dystopia for others. Rhodes's stratified paradise of plunder saw all wealth and power flow upwards from the 'native' toilers through intermediate classes of 'coloured' subalterns, Muslim and Jewish traders, and Afrikaner farmers, until it reached the narrow apex of the Anglo overlords. When, in 1948, Anglo-Boer antagonism finally ripped up this segmented blueprint for South Africa, the more nakedly racist ideology of apartheid took its place. With its rigid demarcations of identity and community, and its punctilious top-down planning to dictate where you lived, how you worked, and whom you loved, apartheid belongs firmly on one, twisted branch of the Utopian family tree.

Utopia still haunts the best, and the worst, of our dreams of social change. And South Africa gives a special vantage-point from which to observe the evolution of this stubbornly evergreen desire. After the apartheid state set out on its journey towards a dreamworld of 'separate development' guaranteed by whip and gun, it took more than four decades of struggle before, in 1994, a nation founded on non-racial ideals came into being on this soil. Only in late 1996 did South Africa acquire its exemplary constitution: arguably, the most 'Utopian' document of its type since that of the United States in 1787. As 2016 closed, the retired constitutional judge Albie Sachs — one of its principal architects and interpreters — took to the local media to promote a new book and defend the tarnished record of his 'rainbow nation'. Meanwhile, a never-ending tide of political scandal joined deepening inequality and persistent insecurity to present a distinctly dystopian picture of South Africa to the outside world.

Favoured in its landscape, its climate, its resources, the Cape Peninsula has attracted the carpenters of ideal communities since the Dutch coloniser Jan van Riebeeck made landfall here in 1652. Even then, one man's field of dreams proved another's killing-ground around the Cape of Good Hope. That, by the way, is a Utopian euphemism; in 1488, the Portuguese explorer Bartolomeu Dias had first named it the Cape of Storms. Harassed, persecuted and enslaved, the indigenous Khoikhoi people of the Cape lost their lands to the agents of the Dutch East India Company who carved out splendid estates on the lush slopes of Table Mountain. Soon after his arrival, van Riebeeck began to plan a 'protective barrier' (that giveaway feature of almost all divisive Utopias), planted with bitter almond trees to separate European settlers from displaced Africans. A stretch of his supremacist hedge survives in the gorgeous grounds of the Kirstenbosch Botanical Gardens: a strip of pain in a landscape of bliss. The Gardens' own curators define its importance: 'For many, this hedge marks the first step on the road to apartheid and symbolises how white South Africa cut itself off from the rest of Africa, dispossessed the indigenous people and kept the best of the resources for itself.'

Not far from Kirstenbosch, Cape Town even boasts its own 'garden city' suburb. Pinelands is a charming green enclave laid out in 1919 on the pattern of pioneer developments such as Letchworth in Hertfordshire. In the 1920s, only a minority of Capetonians could have hoped to lived there. Even now, according to the 2011 census, Pinelands remains 63 per cent white (and 15 per cent Coloured, 14 per cent Black African and 5 per cent Asian: a fairly typical distribution for upmarket suburban Cape Town).

On the borders of Pinelands, a variant type of utopianism thrives among the 45 micro-enterprises of the Oude Molen Eco-Village. From playgroups to elderly care by way of organic smallholdings and livery stables (run by a former gangster), the social entrepreneurs of Oude Molen have transformed an abandoned hospital site into a classic self-managing 'intentional community' of hard work and high ideals. Remember that Gandhi first endeavoured to put his communal precepts into practice in South Africa – on Tolstoy Farm in the Transvaal. In this issue of *Critical Muslim*, Hassan Mahamdallie investigates a celebrated example of another such project: the Findhorn Community in Scotland. Whereas outposts of enlightenment such as Findhorn often stand apart, the Rhodes Memorial looks straight down from its imperial heights on Pinelands and the eco-village. Few other cities give as powerful a sense as Cape Town of what happens when incompatible versions of the good place, and the good life, converge on a single patch of fiercely contested ground.

II

Torn and stitched, ripped and sewn, the social fabric of Cape Town affirms that ideas of Utopia – and its dystopian shadow – still live in the mind and on the ground. By no means does Thomas More's 'good place' and 'nowhere' (his Greek title hints at both meanings) belong to a vanished past of system-building folly. When More published his teasing tract, in 1516, Utopian cities and islands – and their possible deficiencies – already had a literary history that stretched back for 1800 years. The mythical Atlantis invoked in two of Plato's dialogues, *Timaeus* and *Critias*, figures as both an abode of virtue and a barbarian antagonist to the authentic great polis: Athens. In Plato's earlier *Republic*, the philosopher-kings preside over a bureaucratic city of order that later critics of Utopia would read as the sinister prototype for modern tyranny. Writing from a tradition that More hardly knew, Ibn Tufayl's twelfth-century philosophical tale *Hayy ibn Yaqdhan* sets the self-education of its young castaway on another island, where thought flowers and wisdom blooms (Marco Lauri explores Tufayl's work in this volume). After More, landmarks of the genre – such as Tomasso Campanella's *City of the Sun* and Francis Bacon's *New Atlantis*, both in the early seventeenth century – refined the rules of the Utopian game.

In literature and politics, Utopian narratives revived in the mid-nineteenth century. Not coincidentally, this was another epoch – like More's Renaissance – marked both by intellectual upheaval, and the aggressive overseas expansion of European powers. Quarrels between the 'Utopian socialism' of Fourier, Owen or Saint-Simon and the anarchist or Marxian insistence on class conflict and direct action as the motor of revolution defined the terms of a debate that persists to this day. Set among Russian thinkers and activists of this time, Tom Stoppard's trilogy of plays *The Coast of Utopia* (2002) pits the moderate reformism of Herzen against the incendiary militancy of Bakunin. Stoppard pretty clearly sides with Herzen – but, as with other champions of gradualist reform, he has trouble making his hero match the dangerous charisma of the Utopian firebrand.

In the age of HG Wells, Jules Verne and William Morris, the positive and negative sides of Utopian dreams weighed fairly evenly on the scales of fiction. For every regimented technocracy, as in Edward Bellamy's Boston-set *Looking Backward* (1888), a post-industrial Eden of leisure and creativity

beckoned – most famously, in Morris's vision of a socialist 'epoch of rest',
News from Nowhere (1890). Wells himself spanned the spectrum of attitudes
to Utopia, from the dystopian hell of *The Time Machine* (1895) – with its
apartheid-like segregation of toiling Morlocks from pampered Eloi – to
the more benign paternalism envisaged in *A Modern Utopia* (1905). The
genre spread far beyond the West. In 1905, the Bengali Muslim women's
rights activist Rokeya Sakhawat Hossein first published her novel *Sultana's
Dream*, about a crime-free, hi-tech 'Ladyland' run entirely by women. In
Begum Rokeya's feminist wonderland (discussed in this issue by Yasmin
Khan), men now undergo the seclusion of purdah.

Yet, for much of the twentieth century, the crimes of modern
totalitarianism hijacked almost all Utopian discourse. The tradition of
speculative social architecture fixed by More in his riddling yarn found
itself swamped, first by the brazen horrors enacted in the name of an ideal
state by Fascist and Communist regimes. After their fall, dystopian fiction
switched its attention to the more insidious coercion enforced by intrusive
technology and obligatory consumerism. Global war, and the ideologies of
mass manipulation that flourished in its wake, had destroyed the dialectical
balance between liberation and subjugation, freedom and order, in the
imagination of a conflict-free community.

For Utopia, the twentieth century by and large read Dystopia. It thrilled
to the literary nightmares of George Orwell or Aldous Huxley, of JG
Ballard or Margaret Atwood. In his pioneering dystopian satire *We* (1921),
which Orwell acknowledged as an inspiration for *Nineteen Eighty-Four*, the
Russian author Evgeny Zamyatin not only conceived a Stalinesque
surveillance-led dictatorship. He dramatised the absolute division of
insiders from outsiders, citizens from barbarians, that marks almost all
negative Utopias. Around Zamyatin's all-controlling One State, a 'Green
Wall' – think of Trump as well as Van Riebeeck – protects the supervised
subjects of the 'Benefactor' from the untamed wilderness beyond.

Huxley himself was capable of a Wellsian ambivalence about the ideal
state. His (relatively) benign story of a Utopian community, *Island* (1962),
has far fewer readers than the prophetic glimpse of shopping-and-sedatives
passivity in *Brave New World* (1932). Meanwhile, Orwell's *Nineteen Eighty-
Four* (1949) became the skeleton key that turned the lock on any despotic
system. The Algerian writer Boualem Sansal has recently paid one of the

most original of countless fictional homages to Orwell, in his novel *2084*. Unlike the more conventionally-minded Michel Houellebecq, with his teasing tale of a future France in thrall to Saudi-financed Islamic fundamentalism, *Submission*, Sansal brings to life the underlying logic of obedience and resistance in any tyrannical theocracy. True, his oppressive 'Abistan' has strong echoes of Khomeini's revolutionary Iran. Still, this divinely-ordained dystopia breaks free of its topical moorings.

Many of Sansal's readers will assume that such ghastly visions of control refer exclusively to distant lands and alien creeds. In the West, the critique of Utopia became a cost-free default position for anyone immune to the temptations of totalitarian dogma, whether secular or sacred, and repelled by the artificial paradises promised by supermarkets, junk entertainment and social media. Of course, ran this consensus view, no sane and humane person could ever fall for the sinister and nonsensical master plans satirised by our literary flesh-creepers. Civilised societies rested exclusively on pluralism, pragmatism, and modest, ameliorative reform.

As I write, during the final days of 2016, this anti-Utopian orthodoxy has itself come to resemble an idealist's cloud-cuckoo-land. Ever since the attacks of 9/11, scholars and reporters have tracked the undeniably Utopian impulses behind certain strands of jihadi fundamentalism. In this issue, Sadek Hamid interrogates these themes. The city of Raqqa in Syria, taken by Isil fighters in 2014, turned into the unhappy laboratory for the creation of a perfect godly state. Its theology would have baffled earlier religious Utopians – for example, the American Puritans of the seventeenth century – but not its patriarchal machinery of domination. In literature, the finest dystopias can leap boundaries of context or culture. Read Atwood's *The Handmaid's Tale* to understand the blood-washed masculinist playground lately erected by Isil in parts of Iraq and Syria.

So the Grand Guignol of Islamist utopianism may have left Western reformers with illusions of immunity intact. History, in the West, had not quite ended as Francis Fukuyama and the free-market Utopians had dreamed as Soviet Communism crashed. Marginal zealots might still spread fear, and inflict death, in sporadic acts of doctrine-driven violence. Overall, however, the mass enslavement of majority populations in the West to irrational, all-consuming ideologies had surely run its course. After the year of Trump and Brexit, such complacency has swiftly evaporated.

Feelings of loss, alienation, resentment and prejudice may well have stoked isolationist movements in the US and UK alike. Both political earthquakes, however, drew energy from a kind of Utopian nostalgia; from the fantasy of a better yesterday. These nativist insurgencies not only clamoured to build walls and barriers – against Muslims, Mexicans, migrants, refugees, even (in the case of Brexit) against wealthy, white fellow-Europeans. However fancifully, they also hankered after collective solidarity and mutual welfare – the togetherness of a gated community. Their world-shaking success poses in stark terms the questions that have shadowed every Utopian project, whether literary or political, since the age of More himself. Does the ideal state of justice and harmony presuppose a homogeneity of culture, race or faith? Can its elect and its elite enjoy their comfort and fraternity solely on the back of suffering endured by an underclass of servants, helots or outcasts? And will Utopia only work if restricted to – in the phrase once invoked by apologists for the white supremacist state in Southern Rhodesia – our own kith and kin?

Contributors to this issue of *Critical Muslim* show from their different perspectives that thinkers, activists and visionaries have never ceased to ask questions, and seek answers, about the good place or the ideal state. Nazry Bahrawi and Marco Lauri remind us that the Islamic legacy of Utopian thought stretches as far back as the speculations of Abu Nasr Muhammad Al-Farabi in the early tenth century and, of course, ibn Tufayl, the twelfth-century Andalusian philosopher. Bruce Wannell explains that the fabled Qur'anic gardens of delight resemble 'a utilitarian market garden and fruit orchard and date-palm grove' rather than some luxurious leisure centre – as do More's own strictly practical allotments, in his *Utopia*. Yasmin Khan shows that the quest for Utopia is alive in contemporary, and not so contemporary, Arabic and Muslim literature. For Sadek Hamid, the Islamic revolutionary state – the 'Khilafatopia' – envisaged by the militants of Hizb ut-Tahrir finds expression only in 'ahistorical, idealised terms that do not bear serious scrutiny'. More hopefully, Naomi Foyle locates in her ordeal of illness and recovery the materials for a truly Utopian practice of care and solidarity through which we may 'overcome differences and unite in the face of a shared threat'. And, among the contemporary Utopians of the Findhorn Community, Hassan Mahamdallie identifies the varied ideological springs that nourish its idealists today as 'the old streams of

Christian dissenters, Rosicrucians, occultists and theosophists now flow into the broader river of New Age eclecticism and alternative lifestyle consumerism.' Practical or fanciful, traditional or futuristic, dogmatic or holistic: Utopia seems to offer a personalised micro-climate for every traveller who yearns to make landfall there.

III

Return to the source, and it muddies rather than clarifies the waters. Playful, ironic and elusive, More's *Utopia* dances so nimbly between genres and tones that it has for centuries defeated all efforts to catch its 'message' in the net of a coherent ideology. His enigmatic fantasia 'concerning the best state of a commonwealth and the new island of Utopia' can be read plausibly, and simultaneously, as a parodic traveller's tale, an ethical treatise, a political satire and a philosophical dialogue. Opt for one interpretation – Communist Utopia, Catholic Utopia, Colonial Utopia, Green Utopia – and some smart authorial ruse will trip up the most confident critic. Allegedly brought back to Antwerp from the new-found Americas by the voyager 'Raphael Hythloday', More's story of a paternalistic island state balances the ideals of common ownership and radical equality with punctilious social discipline and stifling conformism. More makes sure that his Utopia offers something for everyone to love – and loathe. These days, we may warm to his defence of animal rights and environmental stewardship, and cheer his (or maybe Raphael's) vehement denunciations of personal wealth and competitive inequality in any unjust system where 'by far the largest and the best part of the human race will be oppressed by a heavy and inescapable burden of cares and anxieties'.

On the other hand... (and More always deals his cards from two hands), cheerleaders for Utopia must embrace those features of its landscape less attractive to liberal, modern eyes. That means its slavery (although limited in hardship and duration), its colonialism (justified, as in Europe's colonial heyday, 'wherever the natives have plenty of unoccupied and uncultivated land') and its fussily microscopic regulation of everyday behaviour. Perhaps you would enjoy the jolly fruit-and-veg competitions staged between the spacious garden estates of More's airy, well-planned cities – a kind of Great Utopian Grow-Off. The provisions for divorce 'by mutual consent' sound enlightened enough. But adultery carries the penalty of 'the strictest form of slavery'. A second offence incurs capital punishment.

More, of course, never intended his mischievous treatise as a manifesto, a route-map – still less as an application for planning permission. Ursula Le Guin, whose own speculative fiction has updated the Utopian impulse for a less patriarchal and rationalistic cultural climate, calls the original text 'a blueprint without a building-site'. 'Utopia is uninhabitable', as she argues. 'As soon as we reach it, it ceases to be Utopia.' Nonetheless, More's account of the ethnic and religious make-up of his island clarifies the practical task that later Utopians would face when they tried to imagine the optimum conditions for mutual trust and collective harmony.

Since this is (purportedly) a tale shipped from the Americas, More's Raphael explains that Utopia owes its foundation to the invasion of 'Abraxa' – the island's original name – by the warlord Utopus: a sort of conquistador. He forcibly civilised its 'rude and uncouth inhabitants' and lifted them 'to such a high level of culture and humanity'. So this free and noble people descend from the victims of imperial occupation. Most slaves in Utopia are either prisoners of war, or condemned criminals bought by the authorities from foreign states as cheap labour. A third category, 'hardworking penniless drudges' from abroad, enter voluntarily as migrant workers and are treated 'almost as well as citizens'. Since slavery cannot be inherited, Utopia's citizen population has presumably grown more mixed. In Utopia's own colonies, easy intermarriage seems to be the norm, as 'the two peoples gradually and easily blend together'.

More's commonwealth looks much more multi-ethnic than many of its later heirs and offshoots. Crucially, this human diversity ceases to matter much thanks to the island's cultural uniformity. We learn that its 54 cities are 'identical in language, customs, institutions and laws'. It sounds a little like the French republican ideal, now so battered and beleaguered: superficial diversity above an unshakeable bedrock of shared civic values.

As for the Utopians' religious beliefs, More again permits plurality but celebrates an underlying unity. The island hosts a variety of faiths, with Christianity a late and moderately popular arrival. Some folk worship prophets or planets. A few even profess a kind of atheism and materialism. This weird eccentricity bars the dissident from public office and attracts censure as a 'low and torpid' outlook. 'Yet they do not afflict him with punishments, because they are persuaded that no one can choose to believe by a mere act of will.'

'The vast majority', however, believe in 'a single power, unknown, eternal, infinite, inexplicable.' The Utopians call this supreme being Mithra: More borrows the name of the Persian spirit of light. Their minimal monotheism – along with a belief in the afterlife – binds together the various confessions. In keeping with the 'natural religion' of Renaissance philosophy, the Utopians unite around two simple principles – an abstract divinity, and a soul that survives death – and agree to differ on almost everything else. So their tolerance has its limits (although no one jails or burns those poor materialists) but extends far further than the mainstream Christianity of More's day. Moreover, the laws strongly penalise the feuding of sects and factions, and 'anyone who fights wantonly about religion is punished by exile or enslavement'. Fuss-free and de-cluttered, More's reasonable religion has some affinities with the faith depicted by ibn Tufayl and his Muslim counterparts.

Composed in Latin in 1515 and 1516, after happy sojourns with his literary friends in Antwerp and Bruges, *Utopia* enshrines a Utopian moment in the life both of More himself and that of the European intellect. Although prompted by high-spirited conversations with Pieter Gillies, the learned city clerk of Antwerp, More's story has its roots in his fifteen years of comradeship and collaboration with the boldest, broadest mind in the Christian Europe of their time: Erasmus of Rotterdam. In 1516, More, Erasmus and their pan-European humanist network could justly think of themselves as a vanguard of scholar-reformers with history on their side. Hence the witty assurance with which, in *Utopia*, More dares to bracket or suspend much of Catholic doctrine without bothering to question it. In this zero-gravity environment of fantasy and speculation, conscious doubt and heresy would feel as boring as conventional piety.

Reality soon crashed into this idyll of unchained thought. By the end of 1517, Martin Luther had begun his public challenge to the church. Soon, the semi-secret garden of ideas that More and Erasmus had cultivated would wither away. Reformation and Counter-Reformation drew ever-harder lines across the mental map of Europe. To the acute distress of Erasmus, the free-spirited author of *Utopia* would become Henry VIII's hard-line, heretic-burning Chancellor. Finally, the king's ambitions pushed

St Thomas More through the door of (entirely orthodox) sacrifice and martyrdom. It might be that the most enduring models of Utopia not only take shape around fictional islands, peninsulas and oases. To bloom, they may need to grow on the most privileged islands and enclaves of history: those brief spells when everything seems possible – and nothing inevitable. Likewise, the varied Utopian ecology of the decades prior to 1914 failed to survive the toxic shock of the First World War and the Russian Revolution.

IV

In futuristic or revolutionary forms, the road to Utopia can merge with the pathway to paradise. In nostalgic and escapist guises, it can resemble a trail leading back towards a Golden Age. In Cape Town, the latter yearning also finds its place. Close to the inner city, Cape Town's District Six Museum remembers in an affectionate – if somewhat rose-tinted – fashion the multi-cultural neighbourhood that for generations flourished near here. Then, in 1966, the apartheid state declared it 'white' under the notorious Group Areas Act and planned to expel its residents. The District Six commemorated here fits neatly into the Utopian template of unity in diversity now adopted by liberal urbanists around the world. Mixed in race, religion and income, a place where black, brown and white, Muslim, Jew and Christian lived, worked, and traded, the area glows in memory as a wrecked idyll. Much of this is largely true: from its 'Cape Malay' (i.e. Muslim) choirs and cuisine to its jazz scene and sports clubs, District Six did form, if not a melting-pot, then a well-functioning patchwork. It also had its gangsters, its poverty, and its class fractures. The former resident who showed us round, Noor Ebrahim, came from a family that owned a successful ginger-beer factory. This was never just a hybrid slum.

Fitfully, through the 1970s, ethnic cleansing swept up 60,000 residents of District Six and dumped them in the grim townships of Cape Flats. Its lattice of crowded streets between dockside and mountain was bulldozed, with only the mosques and churches left standing as a hollow gesture of respect. By this time, however, even the city council – not to mention global public opinion – had begun to protest against the most glaring outrages of apartheid. Objectors managed to block the government's plans for development, which means that, even today, much of District Six remains a windswept wasteland. The relocated residents and their children now have a notional right of return. As yet, far too few new houses have risen on the empty lots criss-crossed by urban freeways. Both practical and sentimental, the long fight to rebuild this flattened arcadia continues.

In the townships themselves, the Utopian – or dystopian – racial geography of apartheid becomes hideously clear. Contrary to lurid cliché, they vary enormously in prosperity, in atmosphere, in architecture. Many neat suburban homes will sport the same minatory metal shields, announcing that the owner has signed up with an 'armed response' security firm, as in the plushest avenues of Newlands or Bishopscourt. At the other extreme, the 'informal settlements' of Langa or Khayelitsha proclaim in their dense tangle of corrugated-iron shacks a level of poverty and desperation that fuels the crime that keeps the private police of South Africa in business.

On the nation's 'Day of Reconciliation', 16 December, I attended a classical concert in Mitchells Plain: the mainly Coloured township, close to the coast of False Bay. This is where most of the dispossessed people of District Six ended up after their forcible eviction. It happened to be a Friday, and along the broad, monotonous streets groups of men in white thawbs were walking to the mosque. Mitchells Plain has areas of relative affluence as well as acute deprivation, with tracts of solid bourgeois homes in addition to stretches of frail shanties. But it has suffered even more than other Cape Flats communities from the social blight of gangsterism, with its simultaneous cause and consequence: crystal-meth addiction. The area counted as a 'model township', designed by the apartheid regime as a well-regulated showcase for the virtues of ethnic separation. One could argue that, twenty-two short years after the advent of democracy, every young life cursed by drugs or violence here still ranks as the victim of a distorted utopianism – the coercive urge to lock down humankind into fenced reserves, divided by iron laws of hierarchy and inequality.

Once inside Yellowwood Primary School, though, a more positive utopianism found its voice. After the Cape Town Philharmonic's first-class youth orchestra had played Mozart and Bartók, school principal Donovan Senosi spoke with passion about the value of art and culture in opening to every learner the prospect of a wider, richer life. Around the walls of the school hall, joyful works of art by pupils showed that his ideals had borne fruit. In 2013, Mitchells Plain gained unwelcome headlines as the area with South Africa's worst crime statistics. Cape Town itself, according to a 2016 survey, ranks as the ninth most violent city in the world, with a homicide rate of 65.53 for every 100,000 people. For some communities, imagining Utopia may be not so much a luxury as a necessity.

In any case, the peoples of this peninsula have a long history of transforming sites of exile and loss into homes of solidarity and hope. In a broad ring around the city and its mountain stand the twenty-three kramats of the Cape. Some ornate, others austere, scattered over hillside, farmland and shoreline, dotted among the renowned vineyards of Constantia and even planted near the former prison-camp on Robben Island, these shrines to Muslim holy men compose the much-mythologised Circle of Saints.

Several stand on Signal Hill above the old Muslim quarter of Bo-Kaap, with its homes – and places of worship – photogenically painted in a riot of sweetshop colours. Where else would you find a turquoise mosque? According to legend, the kramats protect the Cape from disaster with a ring of spiritual steel. Once a strictly local cult, the kramats have now found wider fame. The Cape Mazaar Society tends to them, researches their history, and invites people of all faiths to visit. Incidentally, it chooses to describe the forefathers of Islam in the Cape as Saints (capital S).

Many of these shrines owe their existence to an earlier wave of persecution and expulsion. The first Saints to land at the Cape, in 1667, arrived as political exiles deported from the Dutch colonies of the East Indies. As the Mazaar Society's guide puts it, after the Dutch colonisation of parts of Java and Sumatra, 'Very soon, the inhabitants began to resist and united to form defences against the imperialist tyranny. The men to lead the people were of a high calibre; men of great spiritual intellect who commanded a great deal of respect from the communities. They were however cunningly captured, and together with their followers, banished to the Cape.'

Sheikh Abdurahman Matebe Sha and Sheikh Sayed Mahmud, now buried on the oak- and vine-swathed slopes of Constantia, had ruled as princes in Malacca and Sumatra. Near Cape Flats stands the tomb of Sheikh Yussuf of Macassar, the pioneer leader of the peninsula's Muslim community. When the Mecca-educated Yussuf arrived as a political exile in 1694, governor Simon van der Stel welcomed him, even granted him a stipend, but insisted that he and his party — imams included — stay at a safe distance from the Dutch settlement. Sheikh Yussuf, perhaps, enjoyed the last laugh. The area around his shrine is now known as Macassar. Cape Muslims flock to his kramat during an annual Easter Pilgrimage. Some mistake, surely? Not at all: under Dutch colonial rule, all slave labourers (many of them Muslims) had the right to an Easter-tide holiday. The Muslims used it to visit shrines.

Colourful, syncretic, 'superstitious', the folkways of Islam in the Cape might horrify a purist. From the sacred daisy-chain of guardian kramats to the sweet-and-spicy flavours of Cape Malay food, they also feed the springs of a shared popular culture. Dislocated, even enslaved, the sheikhs and their followers grew their Utopian hopes on the harsh terrain of exile. The prophecy says that the Circle of Saints preserves from calamity everyone within its compass. Treat it, perhaps, as an alternative myth of the good, safe place to that bitter almond hedge of segregation planted by Jan van Riebeeck. Not only in Cape Town, but around the world, utopianism still shows its double face: inclusive and exclusive; open and closed; the broad circle, and the high hedge. The voyage continues.

GARDENS OF PARADISE

Bruce Wannell

Without doubt, the gardens of paradise are the ultimate utopias of Muslim consciousness. But what does the Qur'an say about gardens, landscapes and the promise of paradise? In this essay, I give longer extracts from the Qur'an, to show the context in which garden or nature imagery are used in that text, and to trace those images and expressions back to the natural landscape of the area in which that text was revealed, the history of agriculture and the social use of gardens before the rise of historical Islam in the seventh century. My aim is to sketch the sort of landscape and agricultural practices and horticultural models that informed the Qur'anic vision, with the essential caveat that the Qur'an is a religious and moral text, not a manual of gardening, and that any reference it makes to 'realia' is by and large metaphorical, striking similes and exempla (*aya/ayat, mathal/amthal*) for the edification of the faithful.

The *longue durée* – the survival over hundreds of years, if not millennia, of historical echoes persisting over time, embedded in landscape or language, in typical significant gestures, modes of visual representation, lexical items, legends, folklore or proverbs – is apparent in the Qur'an's text, and places that revelation firmly within the context of the historical cultures that flourished between the Nile valley and Mesopotamia, Yemen and Syria over the course of two millennia before the great Arab conquests of the mid seventh century. These cultures are indebted not only to the continuing self-conscious tradition of Jewish and Christian lore, but also to the chronologically and geographically more distant models from the Eastern Mediterranean, Egypt and Babylon, as well as Assyria and Iran. It remains to disentangle elements that are observed within the Hijaz or the Arabian Peninsula from those that have been incorporated along with the stock of inherited stories and exempla from further afield. In any case, the extrapolation of detail regarding gardens must be done with caution and humility: there is always a danger of over- or mis-interpreting textual evidence.

CRITICAL MUSLIM 22, APRIL–JUNE 2017

The Semitic area provides the geographical frame of reference for the Qur'an, with its geology apparent on the surface with bare rocks, volcanic lava flows, stony and sandy deserts, its precarious hydrology with occasional oases and seasonal water courses and few, crucial rivers, and its hot arid climate and progressive desertification. The Hijaz, rocky and infertile Mecca and the oasis Madina, the volcanic Harra, the fertile strip of the Wadi al-Qura, the oases in Najd and towards the eastern coast at al-Ahsa and Qatif, and in the north at Ha'il, are the core of the Qur'anic culture of the Arabian Peninsula. Further afield, the fertile Yemen highlands and the Tihama coastal strip, and the great valley of the Hadramaut to the south, the Jordanian, Palestinian and Syrian landscape of desert and oases and cultivated areas in the Fertile Crescent to the north feed into the culture of the Qur'an. Further still, the Egyptian balance of Nile and desert and the Delta, Mesopotamia, Babylon, Assyria, and – on the remotest horizon – the Iranian plateau, the Mediterranean, the Horn of Africa and Ethiopia where the first Muslim refugees sought sanctuary before the Hijra of 622 – all these are relevant to the world-view and range of geographic and cultural reference of the Qur'an.

The invention of agriculture, hoeing by hand, ploughing with oxen, cereal cultivation, date palm groves, grapes and the making of wine, salad and herb gardens; irrigation by wells, canals, flash-flood control, managing and maximising the benefits of rainfall or snow-melt; the invention of land-surveying; improving soil quality, minimising erosion or invasive sand; pollinating date palms, sowing grain seeds; the domestication of animals; the exploitation of ecological niches of seasonal verdure by transhumance; the interdependence and mutual exchange and frequent rivalries between settled agriculturalists and nomad pastoralists: all these developments underlie the stories and lessons of the Torah and the Qur'an. The need of agriculturalists for fixed and regular calendars, established by observation of the movements of sun and moon, and attempts at foretelling the future by observing the twelve signs of the zodiac and the movements of the seven known planets, the tendency to conciliate the elements and life forces in the form of a multiplicity of divinities; the more egalitarian warrior ethos of the nomads and their keen awareness of the night sky: all this underlies much of the teaching and poetic language of the texts of revelation.

What are gardens for? How did they originate? Do they cease to be gardens when they become too big? In what sense are the accidental geometries of a surveyed and demarcated or irrigated agricultural landscape different from the intentionally and aesthetically-planned geometries of formal gardens? These are all questions that must be asked in the attempt to elucidate the concept and typology of gardens implicit in the Qur'anic revelation. Reference must be made to a possible origin of gardens in sacred groves, with their taboos on cutting down trees or hunting animals, with their shade, mystery and symbolism; but also to the more mundane domestic vegetable and herb patch adjacent to dwellings in towns and villages, the sphere of women as nurturers and cooks; at a level of greater social elaboration and magnificence are formal gardens for receptions, parks for hunting and sport, and the typical combination of later Islamic culture, the royal enclosures of gardens with walkways, kiosks, palaces giving privacy, views, shade, water, coolness in the heat of the summer, as palace complexes. As noted by Ibn Khaldun, the nomad origin of warrior and aristocratic elites of the Islamic world guarantees the importance of tents as a relic of nomadism – well suited to the climate – which is scarcely diminished even in the modern era. The tent can have one or all of its sides raised and opened to the breeze and the view, and this aesthetic of lightness and openness has influenced the style of construction of garden pavilions and kiosks through most of Islamic architectural history.

In Sura al-An'am VI, aya 95–99, we read:

'Inna Llaha faliqu l-habbi wa n-nawa … la ayatin li qaumin yu'minun'

In AJ Arberry's translation (*The Qur'an Interpreted*), which I have used throughout:

إِنَّ اللَّهَ فَالِقُ الْحَبِّ وَالنَّوَىٰ يُخْرِجُ الْحَيَّ مِنَ الْمَيِّتِ وَمُخْرِجُ الْمَيِّتِ مِنَ الْحَيِّ ذَٰلِكُمُ اللَّهُ فَأَنَّىٰ تُؤْفَكُونَ
فَالِقُ الْإِصْبَاحِ وَجَعَلَ اللَّيْلَ سَكَنًا وَالشَّمْسَ وَالْقَمَرَ حُسْبَانًا ذَٰلِكَ تَقْدِيرُ الْعَزِيزِ الْعَلِيمِ
وَهُوَ الَّذِي جَعَلَ لَكُمُ النُّجُومَ لِتَهْتَدُوا بِهَا فِي ظُلُمَاتِ الْبَرِّ وَالْبَحْرِ قَدْ فَصَّلْنَا الْآيَاتِ لِقَوْمٍ يَعْلَمُونَ
وَهُوَ الَّذِي أَنْشَأَكُم مِّن نَّفْسٍ وَاحِدَةٍ فَمُسْتَقَرٌّ وَمُسْتَوْدَعٌ قَدْ فَصَّلْنَا الْآيَاتِ لِقَوْمٍ يَفْقَهُونَ
وَهُوَ الَّذِي أَنزَلَ مِنَ السَّمَاءِ مَاءً فَأَخْرَجْنَا بِهِ نَبَاتَ كُلِّ شَيْءٍ فَأَخْرَجْنَا مِنْهُ خَضِرًا نُّخْرِجُ مِنْهُ حَبًّا مُّتَرَاكِبًا وَمِنَ النَّخْلِ مِن
طَلْعِهَا قِنْوَانٌ دَانِيَةٌ وَجَنَّاتٍ مِّنْ أَعْنَابٍ وَالزَّيْتُونَ وَالرُّمَّانَ مُشْتَبِهًا وَغَيْرَ مُتَشَابِهٍ انظُرُوا إِلَىٰ ثَمَرِهِ إِذَا أَثْمَرَ وَيَنْعِهِ إِنَّ فِي ذَٰلِكُمْ
لَآيَاتٍ لِّقَوْمٍ يُؤْمِنُونَ

It is God who splits the grain and the date-stone, brings forth the living from the dead; He brings forth the dead too from the living. So that then is God; then how are you perverted? He splits the sky into dawn, and has made the night for a repose, and the sun and moon for a reckoning. That is the ordaining of the Almighty, the All-knowing. It is He who appointed for you the stars, that by them you might be guided in the shadows of land and sea. We have distinguished the signs for a people who know. It is He who produced you from one living soul, and then a lodging place, and then a repository. We have distinguished the signs for a people who understand. It is He who has sent down out of heaven water, and thereby We have brought forth the shoot of every plant, and then We have brought forth the green leaf of it, bringing forth from it close compounded grain, and out of the palm-tree, from the spathe of it, dates thick-clustered, ready to hand, and gardens of vines, olives, pomegranates, like each to each, and each unlike to each. Look upon their fruits when they fructify and ripen! Surely in all this are signs for a people who believe.

This extended passage, a beautifully observed evocation of nature and agriculture, is a typical example of the use of natural imagery in the Qur'an to emphasise God's power as creator of all life and life-forms; and to underline the doctrine of the resurrection as an essential part of the faith. From the smallest seed to the furthest star, the natural order ideally serves mankind, and the life-giving quality of water, coming as rain from heaven, recalls God's practical mercy to His creature Mankind; the landscape evoked is in strong contrast to the black calcined lava-flows of the Harra or the sandy and stony deserts of Najd, rather it is one of arable fields of cereals, date-palm groves, vineyards, olive groves, gardens of pomegranates: an agricultural landscape, made fruitful by the cooperation of husbandry and ever-renewed creation, a transparent message to those with eyes to see and ears to hear.

As in any literary or artistic representation, there are highlights: choices are made in this text. It is an evocation for the purposes of orally delivered spiritual and moral lessons, not an exhaustive seed-catalogue or farmer's manual. It is a moot point where the olive *zaitun*, olive oil *zait*, the vine *karma*, grapes *a'nab*, and the pomegranate *rumman*, grow best – do these plants represent some Eastern Mediterranean location north of the Hijaz? Syria was a major exporter of olive oil during the Roman Empire, as testified by the many 'dead cities' around Aleppo.

The germination of seeds, as a miracle of renewed life after apparent death, a symbol of the resurrection, has recently been shown to be possible even after 2,000 years lying dormant, in the case of cereal grains buried in the palace of Herod at Masada. This helps elucidate the twelfth century Persian mathematician 'Umar Khayyam's sceptical quatrain, calling into doubt the reality of heaven and the resurrection: 'Would that there were a place to rest, or a destination to reach on this distant road, or that, after a hundred thousand years in the belly of the earth, like wheat-grass, we might hope to spring up once again!'

The sceptical materialist view of life is briefly encapsulated in the Qur'an, sura al-Jathiya XLV, aya 24: 'They say, there is nothing but our present life; we die, and we live, and nothing but Time destroys us.' The tyranny of time, identified as *Zurvan* by the Sasanian Iranian Zoroastrians, dominates even the gods, the forces of good and evil; this *dahri* heresy, denying divine agency or the resurrection and life after death, was the reductionist materialist hopelessness against which, as also against polytheism, the preaching of the Qur'an was addressed, insisting on the absolute power of the one transcendent creator God, and the reality of resurrection and judgement. The Book of the Prophet Ezekiel (chapter 37 'and shall these bones live?') is echoed in the heart of the Qur'an, sura Yasin XXXVI, aya 78–83:

> '*Qala man yuhyi l-'idama wa hiya ramim? Qul yuhyi-ha l-ladhi ansha'a-haawwala marratin … al-ladhi bi yadi-hi malakutu kulli shai'in wa ilai-hi turja'un*'

> He says, 'Who shall quicken the bones when they are decayed?' Say: 'He shall quicken them who originated them the first time; He knows all creation, who has made for you out of the green tree fire and lo, from it you kindle.' Is not He, who created the heavens and the earth, able to create the like of them? Yes indeed; He is the All-creator, the All-knowing. His command, when He desires a thing, is to say to it 'Be' and it is. So glory be to Him, in whose hand is the dominion of everything, and unto whom you shall be returned.

The cultivation of date-palms (*nakhla*) is as old as civilisation throughout the hot and arid areas of Arabia, North Africa and the Middle East, wherever irrigation is to be had. There is a beautiful Hadith commanding respect for the date palm, to be treated as 'family' as it was created of the same clay as Adam. But in the *Sira*, the biography of the Prophet, as recorded in the Hadith, there is also the incident of the prohibition of artificial pollination of date-palms, until the ensuing sterility threatened to bring famine. Like types of cereals that need human cooperation to

flourish, dates are best produced with human help in pollination of the
female palms, which is only marginally more extraordinary than
pollination by bees, moths, flies or bats. The Prophet's initial scruples
about apparently unnatural interference with the divine processes of
nature gave way to the professional expertise of the agriculturalists, in
realism and humility, the Prophet acknowledging 'I am just a man like
you.' The words *tamr* or *rutab* or *'ajwa* for dates fresh or dry feature
frequently in Qur'an, Hadith and Sira, for example in the Hadith (Bukhari
chapter of foods 63, section 15) of breaking fast with seven dried dates as
a recommended diet. Dates were the main sweetener along with honey
and figs, *tin*, before the introduction of cane sugar after the great Islamic
conquests of the seventh century. Techniques such as supporting plants on
trellises or columns, such as the vine *karma* and grapes *'anab*, plural *a'nab*,
are referred to in the Qur'an, sura al-An'am VI, aya 141 as ma'rushat, as
can still be seen today with short stone columns in Yemen to support vines
for the production of eating grapes and dried raisins.

Hadiqa plural *hada'iq*, an enclosed garden, occurs only three times in the
Qur'an, always in the plural, as in sura 'Abasa LXXX, aya 24–32:

'*Fa-l-yanzuri l-insanu … wa li-an'ami-kum*'

Let Man consider his nourishment. We poured out the rains abundantly, then
we split the earth in fissures and therein made the grains to grow and vines,
and reeds, and olives, and palms, and dense-treed gardens, and fruits and
pastures, an enjoyment for you and your flocks

Jannat is the most frequently used word for a garden, orchard or an oasis
in the Qur'an; the word is Aramaic in origin, already present in the Torah,
in the Book of Genesis's account of the creation of the 'Garden' of Eden,
which was not so much a small enclosed garden space, but rather an
extensive area of cultivation, even a microcosm of the known world; the
word is also attested in the Gospel account of the 'garden' of Gesthemane;
also in Ethiopic names, such as the church of Genneta Maryam near Lalibela;
also in Sabaean inscriptions of South Arabia, including a fine Minaean bronze
plaque from the temple of Wadd in Qaryat al-Faw, where the site is referred
to as Gannatun, the oasis. The proof case, where textual reference in the
Qur'an can be checked against the physically surviving archaeological

record is in the account of Sabaean irrigated agriculture and the final destruction of the dam at Ma'rib, the ceremonial capital of Saba in Yemen. Qur'an sura Saba XXXIV, aya 15–16:

'laqad kana li-Saba'i fi maskani-him aya: jannatani 'an yaminin wa shimal ... wa athlin wa shai'in min sidrin qalil'

For Sheba (Saba) also there was a sign in their dwelling place – two gardens, one on the right and one on the left: 'Eat of your Lord's provision, and give thanks to Him; a good land, and a Lord All-forgiving.' But they turned away; so We loosed on them the Flood of 'Arim, and we gave them in exchange for their two gardens two gardens bearing bitter produce and tamarisk bushes (athl) and here and there a few lote-trees (sidr, Zizyphus Spina Christi, jujube).

The notable dam at Ma'rib, and its two irrigated areas of oases north and south of the torrent bed, can be used as a reality check for the use of the word *jannat* in the Qur'an and elsewhere. The usual translation of the word *jannat* as 'garden', or here the dual form *jannatan* as 'two gardens', is rather overtaxed as a description of 10,000 hectares of irrigated, cultivated land, or 5,000 hectares per 'garden'; it is more adequately translated as oases, irrigated cultivated areas – unless 'garden' is used in a specific sense, such as the English counties Kent or Herefordshire being described as the 'garden of England' because of their many apple orchards; certainly this use of 'garden' is far from any concept of landscape architecture or formal garden design.

The ancient civilisations of Arabia Felix, South Arabia, the Yemen, the blessed land, were based on trade networks dealing mainly in aromatics and gum incenses collected wild, and on a thriving agriculture characterised by extremely skilful terracing and irrigation to maximise the agricultural potential of often marginal lands in the mountains or on the edge of the desert. Whereas the mountains to the west attracted the remnants of monsoon rains, and gave rise to an extraordinary system of terraced agriculture, the land further east, as the land mass of Arabia shelves down towards the Gulf and flattens out, is more arid. In order to support food production for their capital city Ma'rib, situated on the edge of the Rub' al-Khali desert, the Sabaeans had to harness the spate of twice yearly rains from the surrounding mountains and channel them to the productive land north and south of the torrent of Wadi Dhana, as it emerged from the limestone mountains of the Jabal Balaq. A remaining sluice gate of the old

dam of Ma'rib dates from almost 3,000 years before the present, and the
first Sabean inscriptions date from the mid-eighth century BC; the kingdom
grew to its greatest strength under Karrib'il Watar around 685 BC when he
conquered Najran, 'Aden, and the Tihama. Both the northern 'Arab nomad
migrations of the second century BC, and the growth of the new power of
Himyar which had its capital further west in the mountains at Zafar, caused
a gradual decline of the state of Saba. Ma'rib remained, however, an
important ceremonial centre, and attempts were made to counteract the
effects of silting, up to thirty metres deep upstream from the dam, and
those of ruptures in the dam walls. The rise of Judaism and Christianity in
the area led to a decline of the great pagan temples that had coordinated
regular irrigation maintenance and repair. The last inscriptions recorded
attempted repairs to the dam date to 549 under the rule of the Ethiopian
conquerors of the Yemen and their viceroy Abraha. Thereafter, uncontrolled
silting and flash-flood damage destroyed the central masonry-clad
earthwork barrage but left standing the north and south sluice-gates and
diversion channels, built directly onto the rock, of solid, beautifully cut
masonry. Whereas these had, at their peak, channelled up to two million
cubic metres of water annually during the spate, and had irrigated up to
10,000 hectares and fed a population of up to 50,000, the land now
reverted to semi-desert of acacia and tamarisk scrub (athl, sidr); and the
population migrated to San'a. This was finally the case after almost one and
a half millennia – an impressive record for a masonry-clad earthwork
barrage coping with huge annual accumulations of silt: the Sail al-'Arim,
the seventh century flood, swept away the working dam.

Another destruction is recorded in the Qur'an, sura al-Fajr LXXXIX, aya
6–8: 'Hast thou not seen how thy Lord did with Ad, Iram of the pillars, the
like of which was never created in the land?' Iram, the legendary lost
garden, with pillars dhat al-'imad clearly also belonging to the south of
Yemen or the Hadramaut, where the grave of their Prophet Hud is still
venerated. In the Qur'an, it actually refers more to a former city-state on
the incense route, destroyed and abandoned, and thus an example of the
precariousness of human civilisation, exposed to the blasts of fate and
divine displeasure. There were historical reasons too for such decay: the
economic near-collapse of the Roman Empire, major importer of Yemeni
incense to burn on its temple altars, in the fourth century; the development

of the maritime route up the Red Sea for oriental luxury trade, which rendered the camel-borne trade across the Arabian deserts too slow, expensive and dangerous; the Ethiopian invasion of the Yemen in the sixth century to avenge the martyrdom of the Himyarite Christians of Najran at the hands of an Arab king converted to Judaism; the destructive wars of the early seventh century between Heraclius of Byzantium and Khusrau/ Chosroes of Iran, which ravaged Syria and severely weakened both empires, while establishing a Persian hold on Yemen and Oman. But the romantic allure of the doomed city and its gardens gripped the later imagination, with the result that the name Iram has been given to many later gardens, notably the beautiful garden of the nineteenth century Qashqai tribal chiefs, now the Botanical Institute of Shiraz University in Fars, Iran.

Caution should also be applied in dealing with the Garden of Eden: the text in the Book of Genesis has 'God planted a garden in Eden in the east', Eden being a larger place than the 'garden' and the name echoing the South 'Arabian port of 'Aden – though that particular calcined waste of volcanic lava hardly evokes the land of pleasure, which is what Eden means! *Jannat 'adn* is a place of pleasure, paralleled by *jannat al-na'im* delight in another common Qur'anic compound for the paradise garden; or by *jannat al-firdaus*, paradeisos, pardis – a large royal hunting enclosure, the Persian word referring to the enclosed hunting grounds or paradises of the ancient Persian kings, whose empire included the southern portions of the Arabian peninsula until the seventh century. All these Qur'anic compounds are expressed typically as *jannat 'adn, jannat al-na'im, jannat al-firdaus*, and also *jannat al-ma'wa*, the garden of eternal abode; whereas the formulation with *rauda*, plural *riyad/raudat*, is *raudat al-jannat* (Qur'an sura al-Shura XLII, aya 22) a green area which can also be a wide expanse for cavalry exercises and other sports; later, *rauda* was also applied to funerary gardens, notably the Prophet's tomb in his mosque, originally built with the palm-tree columns in the courtyard of his house in Yathrib/Medina. The Qur'anic compounds are used more or less interchangeably, as indeed are singulars and plurals.

The most frequently repeated phrase descriptive of the Qur'anic paradise, contrasted with the apocalyptic ending of the world and the torments of Hell, is in Qur'an sura al-Baqara II, aya 25, and passim, 'gardens underneath which rivers flow'. Precisely what that means is not always

Harvest scene from the Tomb of Sennedjem

clear, especially when a similar phrase is used about rivers flowing beneath buildings as in Qur'an, sura al-Zumar XXXIX, aya 20. Are they small irrigation channels of water flowing through palm grove oases, or larger rivers, as the Barada at Damascus flowing below tower houses scattered through orchards and parkland, as depicted in the famous Umayyad mosaics of the Great Mosque? There is however a distinct, if distant, reminiscence in this phrase of the early Egyptian paradise, the fields of peace or of Yaru/ Ialou, which are entirely surrounded by water, as in the thirteenth century BC depictions of agriculture and gardens as a setting for the afterlife in the Tomb of Sennejem, Dair al-Madina, Luxor, Egypt.

Sennejem, a craftsman for the royal tombs, lived and was buried in the craftsmen's village, and is shown with his wife, in their finest clothes, working in the fields of paradise, the fields of Yaru/Ialou: this agricultural landscape is surrounded and intersected by flowing water canals drawn off the Nile. The lower levels show water plants such as papyrus, then date palms and doum palms, then persea and sycamore fig, then a scene of the blessed departed ploughing with oxen, sowing seed, pulling flax and harvesting tall-standing wheat before sailing to meet the gods.

Agricultural work in the afterlife is another Egyptian echo in the Book of Genesis account of Eden (chapter 2, verse 15) where the first man is put to work in the garden, in order not to sit eternally idle. This is also echoed in the Hadith recounted by Abu Huraira in Bukhari's collection the 'Sahih' (chapter 61 section 20), which seems to echo some disquiet with the apparent idleness of the feasting dear departed in the Qur'anic paradise: 'One of the inhabitants of Paradise asked his Lord permission to plough and sow seed. "Do you not have all that you desire?" "Yes, but I would like to start sowing." So he sowed, and in the blinking of an eyelid, the plants grew and ripened, giving a mountainous harvest. "O son of Adam, nothing will satisfy you!" An Arab nomad listening to the Prophet exclaimed, "That must have been one of the Quraish or a Helper from Medina – these oasis-dwellers like ploughing and sowing, whereas we nomads have nothing to do with agriculture!" And the Prophet laughed.'

Many other fragments of visual evidence survive to inform us about the ancient Egyptians' attitudes to and practice of agriculture and horticulture: the fifteenth century BC temple of the female Pharaoh Hatshepsut at Dair al-Bahri shows the transport of incense trees, with their roots encased in their original soil, all the way from the land of Punt (Somalia or East Africa), by ship back to Luxor – the avenue to the temple still shows the holes where these trees were planted. The Temple of Karnak has a courtyard with linear bas-reliefs of a variety of mostly Near Eastern plants, currently known as the 'Botanic Garden', deriving from the military campaigns of Thutmose III in Palestine, also fifteenth century BC. The early fourteenth-century-BC tomb of the scribe Menna shows the land being surveyed and measured to estimate the cereal crop for taxation. Nearby, the tomb of Immenenheb shows a rectangular orchard planted with three concentric alignments of thirty-two sycamore fig trees, twenty-four date and doum palms, and twenty perseas, with a rectangular lotus pool in the centre; this is similar in design to the now destroyed floor painting at al-Amarna recorded by Petrie, where the rectangular pool was surrounded by concentric beds of flowering plants. Among the most striking instances of Egyptian survivals into the Biblical canon, and thence recognisably into the nature imagery of the Qur'an, is the version of Akhenaten's hymn of praise to the Aton, the unique solar divinity, the first historically attested monotheism of circa 1350 BC, which appears as Psalm 104:

> My God, how great you are! Clothed in majesty and glory, wrapped in a robe of light! You stretch the heavens out like a tent, you build your palace on the waters above; using the clouds as your chariot, you advance on the wings of the

wind; you use the winds as messengers and fiery flames as servants. You fixed
the earth on its foundations, unshakeable for ever and ever; you wrapped it
with the deep as with a robe, the waters overtopping the mountains. You set
springs gushing in ravines, running down between the mountains, supplying
water for wild animals, attracting the thirsty wild donkeys; near there the birds
of the air make their nests and sing among the branches. From your palace you
water the uplands until the ground has had all that your heavens have to offer;
you make fresh grass grow for cattle and those plants made use of by man, for
them to get food from the soil: wine to make them cheerful, oil to make them
happy and bread to make them strong. You made the moon to tell the seasons,
the sun knows when to set: you bring darkness on, night falls, all the forest
animals come out: savage lions roaring for their prey, claiming their food from
God. Earth is completely full of things you have made: among them vast
expanse of ocean, teeming with countless creatures, creatures large and small,
with the ships going to and fro. All creatures depend on you to feed them
throughout the year; you provide the food they eat, with generous hand you
satisfy their hunger. You turn your face away, they suffer; you stop their breath,
they die and revert to dust. You give breath, fresh life begins, you keep
renewing the world. Glory for ever to God! May God find joy in what He
creates, at whose glance earth trembles, at whose touch the mountains smoke!

Other Egyptian survivals are the victor's characteristic gesture of taking
his defeated foe by the forelock, so often seen on Egyptian bas-relief
sculpture from the 5,000 year-old palette of Narmer onwards, and echoed
in the Qur'an's account of God taking the sinner by the forelock nasiya
plural nawasiy, in Qur'an sura al-Rahman LV, aya 41: 'The sinners shall be
known by their mark, and they shall be seized by their forelocks and their
feet.' The recurring phrase 'He makes the night to enter into the day and
makes the day to enter into the night', as for example in Qur'an sura
al-Fatir XXXV, aya 13, can be understood as referring to the lengthening
of the hours of daylight during the summer and the lengthening of the
hours of darkness during winter against the ideal standard of equal
duration of each (day and night) in traditional Egyptian time-keeping.

Archaeo-botany has allowed the identification of many plants, especially
food plants from ancient Egypt, including peas, beans, lentils, onions, garlic,
leeks, radishes and cucumbers – thus confirming the Torah's Book of
Numbers (chapter 11, verse 5) 'We recall the fish that we used to eat in
Egypt for free, the cucumbers, the watermelons, the green leeks, the onions,

and the garlic!' and Qur'an sura al-Baqara II, aya 61: 'Pray to the Lord for us
that He may bring forth for us of that the earth produces – green herbs,
ridged cucumbers, corn, lentils, onions.' These are accounts of the regrets of
the wandering Israelites on their long – forty year – trek from well-fed
Egyptian captivity through the deserts with its divine but unvarying diet of
manna. An after-echo of Egypt's reputation for fertility is the lovely mosaic
preserved at Palestrina in Italy, showing the lush landscape of the Nile Delta.

Many edible plants and vegetables have names going back to ancient
Babylon and its ancient Semitic Akkadian texts, some from over 3,500
years before the present – many are preserved in modern Semitic
languages such as Arabic: *na'na'* mint; *kuzbara* coriander; *kammun* cumin;
thum garlic; *simsim* sesame; *kam'a* desert truffle; *karma* vine; as well as other
words to do with eating such as: *akl* food; *samn* clarified butter; *arnab* hare;
nun fish; *dam* blood; *ma* water; *tannur* clay oven. If language can have such
a long memory, it is not surprising that gesture and visual culture can also
present continuities over many hundreds of years.

Qur'an Sura al-Rahman LV, aya 46–78:

'*Wa li man khafa maqama rabbi-hi … dhi l-jalali wa l-ikram*'

But such as fears the Station of his Lord, for them shall be two gardens – O
which of your Lord's bounties will you and you deny? abounding in branches
– O which of your Lord's bounties will you and you deny? therein two
fountains of running water – O which of your Lord's bounties will you and you
deny? therein of every fruit two kinds – O which of your Lord's bounties will
you and you deny? reclining on couches lined with brocade, the fruits of the
garden nigh to gather – O which of your Lord's bounties will you and you
deny? therein maidens restraining their glances, untouched before them by any
man or jinn – O which of your bounties will you and you deny? lovely as
rubies, beautiful as coral – O which of your Lord's bounties will you and you
deny? Shall the recompense of goodness be other than goodness? O which of
your Lord's bounties will you and you deny?

And besides these shall be two gardens – O which of your Lord's bounties will
you and you deny? green, green pastures – O which of your Lord's bounties
will you and you deny? therein two fountains of gushing water – O which of
your Lord's bounties will you and you deny? therein fruits and palm-trees and
pomegranates – O which of your Lord's bounties will you and you deny?
houris, cloistered in cool pavilions – O which of your Lord's bounties will you
and you deny? untouched before them by any man or jinn – O which of your

Lord's bounties will you and you deny? reclining upon green cushions and
lovely druggets – O which of your Lord's bounties will you and you deny?

Blessed be the Name of thy Lord, majestic and splendid

This richly ornate passage, in hypnotically beautiful Arabic, is an
extended example of the other most typical and frequent use of nature
imagery in the Qur'an, to evoke the timeless and ineffable bliss of the
afterlife in paradise. It is one of the texts most often quoted about Islamic
gardens, paradise conceived in terms of a series of 'gardens', graded
according to the merits of the blessed. The first two gardens are orchards
of fruit trees with thick canopies of branches filtering the light, and with
springs of water channelled into runnels and rivulets irrigating the ground;
in this setting are placed rich textiles, carpets and cushions, where the
blessed recline to take their ease.

The mention of the garden 'abounding in branches' calls to mind Roman
gardens, such as the frescoed room representing the Empress Livia's
garden arboretum, now in the Roman Museum, Rome, with exotic
imported trees, fountains and birds and enclosure of trellis fences – though
this is a different tradition of gardening, with the pedestal fountains and
jets of water implying a level of sophistication not discernible in the
Qur'an's account of paradise gardens.

Qur'an, sura al-Waq'ia LVI, aya 10–40:

'*Wa s-sabiqun as-sabiqun: ula'ika l-muqarrrabun ... wa thullatun min al-akhirin*'

And the Outstrippers: the Outstrippers, those are they brought nigh the
Throne, in Gardens of Delight (a throng of the ancients, and how few of later
folk) upon close-wrought couches, reclining upon them, set face to face,
immortal youths going round about them with goblets and ewers, and a cup
from a spring (no brows throbbing, no intoxication) and such fruits as they
shall choose, and such flesh of fowls as they desire, and wide-eyed houris as the
likeness of hidden pearls, a recompense for that they laboured. Therein they
shall hear no idle talk, no cause of sin, only the saying 'Peace, Peace!'

The Companions of the Right (O Companions of the Right!) mid thornless
lote-trees and serried acacias, and spreading shade and outpoured waters, and
fruits abounding unfailing, unforbidden, and upraised couches. Perfectly We
formed them, perfect, and We made them spotless virgins, chastely amorous,

like of age for the Companions of the Right. A throng of the ancients and a throng of the later folk.

Here, the previous account of heavenly bliss is further clarified and elaborated in the grading of paradise gardens according to the merits of the deceased, and the divine garden party is furnished with ever more elaborate paraphernalia of royal entertainments: bejewelled young wine-servers (Arberry's 'immortal' chooses the association with khuld rather than to catch the specific association of mukhalladun with khilda, precious stones, as pointed out by the French translator of the Qur'an, Jacques Berque), the guests reclining on luxurious couches as in a classical symposium or Assyrian or Persian royal feast. Couches or benches or *takht* or *charpoy* – *arika* plural *ara'ik* or *sarir* plural *surur* – were used to express royal or aristocratic ease out of doors in parkland or palm grove, as can be seen as far back as the Nineveh bas-reliefs.

An Assyrian bas-relief from Nineveh (circa 645 BC) (now in the British Museum Assyrian basement) shows date-palms and vines and the king Ashurbanipal on a couch and his queen on a throne, each ceremonially drinking out of a shallow bowl in one hand, holding a flower in the other hand, to the sound of music. This prefigures the Qur'an's promise of the blessed departed reclining on couches, attended by young wine servers and virginal girls – BUT not the shrivelled head of the Elamite king killed in battle some twelve years previously, hanging upside down in the pine-tree, which is more in accord with Assyrian blood-thirstiness than with the Qur'an's promise of mercy. The servants with fly-whisks, the incense burners, garland necklace, rich textiles and bolsters, palm-trees and vine arbour hung with bunches of grapes close at hand, birds flitting between the trees, altogether could be a foretaste of the Qur'anic paradise. That imagery is ultimately based on such royal precedents, which were perhaps known in seventh-century Arabia in the form of luxury Sasanian silver imported from Iran which often showed similar feasting – it should be remembered that the Sasanian Iranians ruled the Yemen and Oman until the great 'Arab conquests of the mid seventh century. In the Qur'an this imagery is not literal description, but is used to give an intimation of the ineffable bliss of the afterlife.

The paradisiac party is different in that there are no headaches or brawls or vulgarity such as are too often caused by alcohol at worldly parties. Fresh fruit and roasted game birds or chickens accompany the drinking, with, again, the virginal girls ready to pleasure the dear departed. The idealised nature of this imagery is evident in the sufficient space enjoyed by each of the facing couches, which could, if realistically described, become a cause of over-crowding worse than a summer beach full of deck-chairs or a coach-park or a supermarket parking lot ... luckily such prosaic considerations do not seem to have exercised the poetic genius of the Qur'an.

Qur'an, sura al-Insan LXXVI, aya 5 -22:

'Inna al-abrara yashrabuna min ka'sin ... wa kana sa'iu-kum mashkur'

إِنَّا أَعْتَدْنَا لِلْكَٰفِرِينَ سَلَٰسِلَا۟ وَأَغْلَٰلًا وَسَعِيرًا ۝ إِنَّ الْأَبْرَارَ يَشْرَبُونَ مِن كَأْسٍ كَانَ مِزَاجُهَا كَافُورًا ۝ عَيْنًا يَشْرَبُ بِهَا عِبَادُ اللَّهِ يُفَجِّرُونَهَا تَفْجِيرًا ۝ يُوفُونَ بِالنَّذْرِ وَيَخَافُونَ يَوْمًا كَانَ شَرُّهُ مُسْتَطِيرًا ۝ وَيُطْعِمُونَ الطَّعَامَ عَلَىٰ حُبِّهِ مِسْكِينًا وَيَتِيمًا وَأَسِيرًا ۝ إِنَّمَا نُطْعِمُكُمْ لِوَجْهِ اللَّهِ لَا نُرِيدُ مِنكُمْ جَزَاءً وَلَا شُكُورًا ۝ إِنَّا نَخَافُ مِن رَّبِّنَا يَوْمًا عَبُوسًا قَمْطَرِيرًا ۝

Surely the pious shall drink of a cup whose mixture is camphor, a fountain whereat drink the servants of God, making it to gush forth plenteously. They fulfil their vows, and fear a day whose evil is upon the wing; they give food, for love of Him, to the needy, the orphan, the captive: 'We feed you only for the Face of God; we desire no recompense from you, no thankfulness; for we fear from our Lord a frowning day, inauspicious.' So God has guarded them from the evil of that day, and has procured them radiancy and gladness, and recompensed them for their patience with a Garden, and silk; therein they shall recline upon couches, therein they shall see neither sun nor bitter cold; near them shall be its shades, and its clusters hung meekly down, and there shall be passed around them vessels of silver, and goblets of crystal, crystal of silver that they have measured very exactly. And therein they shall be given to drink a cup whose mixture is ginger, therein a fountain whose name is called Salsabil. Immortal youths shall go about them: when thou seest them, thou supposest them scattered pearls, when thou seest them then thou seest bliss and a great kingdom. Upon them shall be green garments of silk and brocade; they shall be adorned with bracelets of silver, and their Lord shall give them to drink a pure draught. 'Behold, this is a recompense for you, and your striving is thanked.'

Wine tempered with camphor – an Iranian royal taste, which a modern oenophile might regard with dismay! A ginger-flavoured drink is more enticing. Sura al-Waqi'a LVI, aya 89 adds '*fa rauhun wa raihanun wa jannatu na'imin*' which Arberry translates as 'There shall be repose and ease and a Garden of Delight', which fails to catch the additional sensory delight of fragrant herbs '*raihan*' normally identified as sweet basil. These are among the very few allusions to taste and smell in the Qur'an, whereas the Prophet's love of perfumes was almost a leitmotif of Hadith and Sira literature, as was his love of the colour green, and of honey, especially from Wadi Du'an in the Hadramaut.

The comparison to hidden pearls, applied both to virginal girls, houris, and to young wine servers, ghilman, allows us to interpret more closely the non-figural mosaics of the Damascus mosque which are the most important surviving depictions of landscape – probably paradisiac – from the early imperial phase of Islamic civilisation.

In the year 70, the Umayyad Caliph al-Walid, son of the Caliph 'Abd al-Malik, had the Great Mosque at Damascus, formerly a temple and a church, rebuilt and redecorated with mosaics. The decoration was carried out by mosaicists sent by the Byzantine Emperor from Constantinople, and they worked under the norms of Islam: no human or animal figures were shown. According to al-Maqdisi, in his geographical work *Ahsan al-taqasim fi Ma'rifat al-aqalim* in the chapter Iqlim al-Sham, describing Syria and its capital Damascus, specialised craftsmen were summoned from Fars, India, the Maghreb as well as Rum (Byzantine Anatolia) for the building campaign and the expenditure on the Great Mosque was equivalent to seven years' taxation revenue of the whole of Syria, not counting the eighteen shiploads of gold and silver from Cyprus, and the Byzantine Emperor's gift of mosaic tesserae. This extraordinary expense was justified as propaganda in a land whose extant Christian monuments still aroused the wonder of all travellers: but after the building of the Great Mosque, Muslims too could boast of possessing one of the wonders of the world. Among the gateways leading into the great courtyard was one significantly called Bab al-Faradis the gate of paradise; the portico surrounding the courtyard had its walls covered with a dado of marble and above that with mosaics up to the roof; the mihrab was adorned with encrustations of carnelian and turquoise, and was surmounted by a great dome. The extensive fragments of mosaic surviving today on the west wall of the portico show, in a cool palette of blues, greens and gold, landscapes of large trees and streams flowing beneath them, and pavilions with pearls hanging in the doorways: a visual allusion perhaps to the beautiful girls and boys of paradise who are like hidden pearls, in attendance to gratify the blessed departed – the Islamic prohibition of figural representation, inherited from Judaism, encourages a poetic and metaphorical reading of the landscape buildings and of the pearls in their door-frames. The types of building shown could be said to correspond to the open pavilions, tower houses, palaces (khiyam, ghuraf, qusur) mentioned repeatedly in the Qur'anic descriptions of paradise. In a Hadith from the collection of Bukhari (chapter 81, section 53, number 6), the Prophet is quoted as saying 'As I was walking in paradise, I came across a river, which had along each of its banks, domed pavilions qubba made of huge hollowed out pearls. I asked the Angel Gabriel, who said "This is the River of Plenty Kauthar".'

There is nothing in the passages quoted above, to justify anachronistic back-projection onto the Qur'an text of geometrically formal garden designs of avenues and parterres and fountains with water jets of the late medieval and early modern gardens of Islamic Iran and India and Spain. There are certain themes that do emerge from the text of the Qur'an itself – the miracle of creation and of growth, the danger of sudden natural disasters, the thirst for peace, safety, cool shade and running streams as a relief from the relentless day-time heat and night-time cold and ever-present dangers of the desert, a highlighting of certain plants and fruits: but it is all much closer to a utilitarian market garden and fruit orchard and date-palm grove than to a picturesque garden organised solely or principally for visual delight. Delight is present, the promise of sensual love, picnics, drinking parties that leave no headaches, conversation that is always stimulating, never dull or boorish, rich furnishings, couches, textiles of green silk and brocade, table-ware of silver and crystal, ever-youthful and complaisant wine servers and virginal houris – but this

Mosaic landscape, Damascus Great Mosque

delight takes place in an outdoor space that is shaped by the needs of agriculture rather than by those of strictly geometrical, architecturally planned and designed horticulture. The formality of some aspects of the social use of gardens / oasis plantations is not paralleled by formality of design until well after the period of the revelation of the Qur'an: still today, a rural host will open the wooden gate in the mud-walled orchard or palm grove, pull up a wooden bench-bed *takht* or *charpoy*, place it under the shade of fruit trees or date palms, perhaps over an irrigation channel or near a spring of cool water, and, covering the *takht* with a pile rug and bolster cushions, invite the traveller guest to rest and drink and talk.

Such themes are also present in the later literature of the Islamic world. The fourteenth century Moroccan traveller Ibn Battuta visited the Tihama coastal strip of Yemen in about 1330, and describes in his Rihla its principal city Zabid, where he admired the well-irrigated banana gardens and also went on the famous Saturday excursions to the date-palm groves Subut al-Nakhl of Wadi al-Husaib during the date harvest of unripe busr and fresh ripe rutab dates: all citizens and foreign visitors went out, with the women riding camel litters, along with musicians and traders to buy and sell the fruit and sweetmeats and enjoy the pleasures of the day's outing.

Fertility and festivity went hand in hand, as described a century earlier by the gossipy merchant Ibn Mujawir in the chapter Dhikr al-Nakhl of his *Ta'rikh al- Mustabsir*, an altogether more racy account of the same festival. He begins by giving an account of the way in which date palms came to grow in the Tihama – a caravan from the Hijaz, laden with dried dates *tamr*, reached the coastal area inhabited by Ethiopians: they ate the dates and threw the date-pits on the ground, where they took root and grew into date palms: the locals observed this and planted more, so that the date palms grew more numerous, with ten varieties of date palm each with three types of fresh dates, red, yellow and green of varying shades. During the date harvest, people came down from the mountains and from as far afield as Abyan and camped in the palm groves for up to three months, snacking on savouries and sour pickles, and drinking a fermented potion of dates and wheat, women drinking with men, which led to many marriages and many divorces! The profits from the Wadi al-Husaib sale of dates and date-products amounted in the year 1227 to 110,000 dinars after tax: the Sultan and the Bait al-Mal community treasury having increased their share under Ayyubid legislation that lightened the tax burden on hard-working farmers and increased the tax-burden on date-palm owners who merely awaited the harvest from year to year. He quotes Qur'an, sura Qaf L, aya 10, 'and tall palm trees with spathes compact'. At the end of the harvest festival, all would proceed on richly caparisoned and decorated camels, tinkling with bells, accompanied by drums and pipes, to a mosque overlooking the sea at Fazza, where the footprint of Mu'adh bin Jabal's she-camel was still to be seen, as imprinted when the emissary to Yemen was returning to the Hijaz after the Prophet's death. There men and women would go to bathe in the sea, all mixed together, with much drinking and playfulness and dancing, weekly on Mondays and Thursdays only, before returning home all together.

The geographical literature is also rich in references to the products of gardens and orchards, as in the tenth century al-Hamdani's Sifat Jazirat al-'Arab where he describes Wadi Nakhla planted with banana, sugar cane, henna and potherbs, and Wadi al-Jannat well-watered and planted with grape-vines, safflower, and in its upper reaches the plantings are mixed with all types of fruit trees, and in its lower reaches mixed with bananas, sugar cane, citrons, sorghum, various cucumbers and coriander.

In the late eighteenth century, Sayyid 'Abd al-Latif Shushtari, a Persian scholar, travelled to Lucknow in India to re-join the great mathematician and translator of Newton, Sayyid Tafazzul Husain Khan. He proceeded from Agra via the once flourishing Islamic provincial capital of Jaunpur: here he found extensive flower gardens and plantations which provided a variety of flowers for the manufacture of perfumed oils by the method of enfleurage: flowers were mixed fresh every day with sesame seeds which after forty days were milled to produce a highly perfumed oil, which was exported all over India; he also found the extreme heat of the summer cooled and perfumed in garden rooms where vetiver tatties or khuss curtains of perfumed roots were hung at every window and sprinkled with water by water-carriers or even automatically by special hose-pipes, so that the breeze passing through these curtains would be both cooled and scented. Several thousand workers were busy with ice-making for the preparation of summer cold drinks – supplies were guaranteed to all courtiers and citizens in the state of Awadh. Once he reached the Nawwab's capital at Lucknow, he found Chinese and European gardeners at work in the gardens of the 400 royal palaces and villas; not only were they designing parterres, but also introducing new plants, such as the repeat-flowering Rosa Bengalensis, introduced from China, and new techniques, such as the oriental technique of bonsai to make miniature fruiting trees. On the way, he passed under wide-spreading Ficus Bengalensis, which could shelter and cover many travellers, recalling the famous Hadith of the wide-spreading paradise-tree in Bukhari's Sahih (chapter 81, section 51, number 6).

Shushtari's account in his *Kitab Tuhfat al-'Alam* recalls the earlier account, almost a thousand years earlier, of al-Maqdisi who, in his *Ahsan al-taqasim fi Ma'rifat al-Aqalim*, describes the flower gardens of Fars perfumed with roses and jasmines, and the export of floral scents, oils of violet, water-lily, narcissus, palm-flower, lily, iris, myrtle, marjoram, cucumber, bitter orange. The importance of perfumes was a constant in Islamic culture, following accounts of the exemplary behaviour of the Prophet.

The aesthetic of the Islamic garden was based on a variety of factors: on the climate – hot and arid and therefore needing the contrast of protective shade and the cooling freshness of running water; on the techniques of agriculture and irrigation, developed initially for food production; on the

social traditions and needs of the owners and users, from town-dwellers
with courtyard gardens within their houses, to rural landowners with more
extensive date palm groves in the oases, to noble and royal patrons of large
hunting parks; the cultural norms of Islam and the symbolic associations of
the literary traditions that had grown out of the study, memorisation and
internalisation of the Holy Qur'an. It was characterised by the following:
the shade of densely-planted trees; running water with springs and
watercourses; views over the countryside or out to the mountains; privacy
within the garden, which is enclosed by walls; the perfumes of roses,
jasmine, orange blossom, stocks, queen of the night *rat-ki rani*, *pandanus
odoratissimus kadhi* or *keora*; birdsong of nightingales or canaries. These
gardens were also used for family picnics or as a setting for discreet
courtship, but also for more formal receptions of guests; also as a place of
quiet conversation and meditation for scholars and mystics and at night for
the contemplation of the infinite wonders of the starry sky; most important
was their use as economically productive orchards and herb-gardens.

The gardens were also occasionally, subsequent to their use as productive
pleasure gardens, used as tomb-gardens, which echo and anticipate the
promise of the eternal paradise garden, down to the floral sculpture on the
inner face of tombstones. This funerary use of gardens may well have been
due to the fragility of ownership of secular land-holdings, and the relative
security of funerary or religious property endowed as mortmain *waqf*. The
Prophet himself was buried in his house in Yathrib / Medina next to the
mosque of palm trunks in his courtyard, incorporated now in vast and
ever-growing modern structures, but still venerated as the Rauda, the
garden. In the later tomb gardens, of seventeenth century Islamic India,
such as the Taj Mahal, the Qur'anic evocation of bliss promised to the
faithful comes closest to actual realisations of real gardens – with the
caveat that *khulud*, long-lastingness and permanence, is not a normal
quality of earthly gardens, which need constant love and attention and hard
work to maintain their order and beauty: even God Himself is always,
every day, working to maintain and renew His garden of creation, Sura
al-Rahman LV, aya 29:

'*kullu yaumin huwa fi sha'n*'
'Every day He is upon some labour.'

FINDHORN

Hassan Mahamdallie

Introduction

The December sunlight faded away and the Scottish gloom rapidly began to take hold. Shadows thrown by the tall trees lining the stretch of the River Findhorn known locally as Randolph's Leap lengthened, and the dark spaces at their roots grew. My ears filled with the pounding of the peat-brown mountain water being forced through the narrow rocky gorge a few feet away. The only other sound was the occasional rustle of fallen leaves tossed by a breeze that intermittently raced down the muddy footpath I was wandering along.

The mysterious advice given by Niels Paulsen, one of our group's two facilitators, or 'Focaliser', as he described himself, came back to me: 'This place is where Robert Ogilvie Crombie said the veil between the human and spirit world is thin.' The Scottish bibliophile, R. Ogilvie Crombie, or Roc to his friends, was in his sixty-third year when he developed the ability to penetrate the Elemental Kingdom and see the cosmic energy forms such as fairies, gnomes and elves around about him. While strolling through Edinburgh's Royal Botanic Gardens in 1966, Roc encountered and conversed with the great god Pan himself: 'I realised that I was not alone. A figure – taller than myself – was walking beside me. It was a faun, radiating tremendous power.' Roc had always insisted that Randolph's Leap was a sacred site; where the nature spirits might reveal themselves to human visitors who were, like him, attuned to their highest divine inner senses.

Randolph's Leap

Our group of thirteen visitors was half way through an 'Encounter Week' at the Findhorn Foundation, a New Age spiritual community in the Scottish Highlands, founded more than fifty years ago with the New mission of 'bringing heaven to earth'. Established in the unlikely setting of an unlovely caravan park next to a Royal Airforce Base on the bleak shores of Findhorn Bay, thirty miles along the Moray Firth from Inverness, the foundation is today home for the hundreds of people who live or work in its Intentional Community and its numerous offshoots and networks of like-minded 'fellow travellers'. They all strive to live by common collective principles drawn from esoteric spiritual practices associated with the community's original personalities. The foundation hosts (and is largely sustained by) a steady stream of visitors from all over the world; including the Encounter Week group of which I am one, who sign up to get a feel for what it is to step outside 'real life' for a time.

So here I am, amongst the shadowy nooks and crannies of the Morayshire river-bank, deep in the magical world of R. Ogilvie Crombie. Niels had advised us to walk alone and be aware of any tiny movement in our peripheral vision. On cue my imagination begins to do its work – faces suggest themselves in the undergrowth, my hearing tunes into every sound and I instinctively jerk my head when, for a split second, the breeze up-ends an autumn leaf on the path in front of me. But no supernatural spirits appear before me, nor any of the group, as I later find out. Although we all agree, as we are driven back to the accommodation and study centre at Cluny Hill, Forres, that at Randolph's Leap we had felt closer to a 'oneness' with the wondrous natural realm.

Origins

The potted history I had read before catching the sleeper train to Inverness had merely hinted at the founders' back story: 'The Findhorn Community was begun in 1962 by Peter and Eileen Caddy and Dorothy Maclean. All three had followed disciplined spiritual paths for many years.'

The Findhorn utopian experiment is commonly thought of as an expression of the 1960s counter-culture, the generational revolt that produced the hippies, Woodstock and Glastonbury, CND marches, anti-war protests, civil rights movements, feminism, flower-power, dropping-out, communes, free-love, LSD and so on. It is true that it came to prominence and grew rapidly during that era. However, it is better understood as a manifestation of the Christian dissenting traditions and esoteric belief systems of the wilder fringes of the late-Victorian and Edwardian middle and upper classes, as they emerged disorientated from an apocalyptic world war, to face the loss of the Empire and a Cold War.

Peter Caddy was born in 1917 into a middle-class family domiciled in the quintessentially suburban town of Ruislip, on the outskirts of West London. The family were Methodists by faith, one of the eighteenth-century nonconformist breakaways from the Church of England that emphasised personal salvation and free will. The boy Caddy was introduced through his father into the exotic drawing-room world of spiritualists, séances, mediums, clairvoyants, healers, paganists, witches, freemasons and occultists. One of his childhood memories was attending sessions by the spiritual medium Lucille Rutterby, who claimed to be able to receive messages from beyond – in the form of a Native American spirit guide named Silver Deer. (Indian spirit guides were all the rage in paranormal circles at the time). This was a time when a set of photos purportedly of fairies frolicking at the bottom of a Yorkshire garden could be widely accepted as genuine, and newspaper headlines in the 1920s could be dominated by the acrimonious end of the friendship between the illusionist Harry Houdini and the author Arthur Conan Doyle, over whether there was any such thing as the paranormal (Houdini being the arch-sceptic and Conan Doyle the unwavering believer).

The enthusiasm for conjuring up ghostly voices behind drawn curtains (window furnishings that also served to hide the sexual infidelities of bored suburbanites) was later memorably made fun of by Noel Coward in his 1941 farce *Blithe Spirit*, with the role of the eccentric medium and clairvoyant Madame Arcati memorably inhabited in the David Lean film version by Margaret Rutherford.

But spiritualism was clearly much more than a fad for Peter Caddy. In early adulthood, after attending Harrow public school, he fell heavily under the influence of George A. Sullivan, an amateur theatrical and dabbler in the occult and freemasonry, who in 1924 had founded a pagan sect he named the Rosicrucian Order Crotona Fellowship. The name harked back to the beliefs of the English Elizabethan scientist-statesman Sir

Francis Bacon, who was a follower of a mystic sect called the Rosicrucians. Their ideas can in turn be traced back to Judaic and Islamic esoteric traditions, for example the writings attributed to the eighth-century Persian alchemist, Jābir ibn Hayyān (Gerber in the Western canon). Francis Bacon's utopian tract *New Atlantis*, published in 1627, is said to have been influenced by Rosicrucian thinking. Bacon's vision influenced the New World colony of Virginia, that he had helped establish. (The actuality was less 'rosy', particularly for the indentured poor whites and then African slaves brought in to work the colony's plantations).

George Sullivan, who styled himself The Grand Magus, had also been an adherent of the Theosophical Society, founded in the 1870s in New York by Russian-German aristocrat Helena Petrovna Blavatsky. She had sought to revive the hidden 'ancient divine wisdoms' she believed underlay the great religions, including Christianity and the Eastern systems of Hinduism and Buddhism. Interest in Eastern spiritual practices had been opened up to the West once again, this time through the colonisation of India by the middle class administrative, military and missionary caste to which Peter Caddy and his occultist associates belonged.

During World War Two Caddy served as a manager in the RAF's catering corps in India and the Middle East. In 1948 he left his first wife for Sheena Govan — the charismatic daughter of rich Scottish businessman and protestant evangelist John George Govan, who in 1886 founded The Faith Mission to carry The Word to remote Scottish villages after he 'came to know the voice of God'. (The Scottish Highlands seems to have been a favoured playground for unconventional members of the bourgeoisie – in 1899 the notorious occultist Aleister Crowley moved into an old mansion on the banks of Loch Ness, where he was said to have carried out his experiments in black magic). In the 1950s Sheena Govan attracted a small group of spiritualist disciples, who gathered at her flat in fashionable Pimlico, London. Govan was influenced by Alice Bailey, a member of the Victorian British aristocracy and theosophist, who claimed a telepathic link with a mythic Tibetan guru, Djwhal Khul (known as DK or The Tibetan). Bailey's writings, in common with many of her contemporaries, is shot through with pseudo-evolutionary racial beliefs, eugenics and anti-Semitic tropes. Bailey's achievement was to popularise, through her voluminous writings, the term 'New Age' to describe the modern(ist) revival of

esoteric teachings she was a part of. Though she died in 1949, many of
Bailey's ideas resurfaced in the Findhorn belief system. For example, Bailey
claimed to have received a mantra from 'DK' (whose actual existence was
never established) called The Great Invocation – a New Age end-of-days
Lord's Prayer:

> From the point of Light within the Mind of God
> Let light stream forth into the minds of men.
> Let Light descend on Earth.
> From the point of Love within the Heart of God
> Let love stream forth into the hearts of men.
> May Christ return to Earth...
> Let Light and Love and Power restore the Plan on Earth...

In times of great crisis, such as war, a mass global chanting of verses
would act as a kind of distress signal, producing a Network of Light
directed at the 'spiritual Beings'. (The Christ referred to by Bailey is not
Jesus, but the figure in Buddhist prophecy, Maitreya, who is predicted to
appear on Earth at a future time when humanity has abandoned Dharma
– the 'correct way of living'). From its inception up to the present day,
Findhorn regards itself as being central to this network.

Sheena Govan, like Alice Bailey, believed she could channel divine
guidance, but located from within (instead of through telepathy with an
Ancient). This wisdom was then passed on to her Pimlico circle as
commands or instructions they were expected to discharge. Govan
exhorted her followers to connect with their own 'Christ within' and truly
submit to her instructions 'with love'. This was her take on the creed of
Love In Action articulated by Bailey: 'Being motivated by goodwill, one
expresses real love, love in service, love in action. This demonstrates as a
life of service to the one humanity'. However, Govan's followers began to
resent what they saw as her increasingly authoritarian tendencies and
divine instructions that spanned from scrubbing her flat spotlessly clean to
dictating whom they could sleep with.

Caddy introduced a new disciple into Govan's set and her flat.
Alexandria-born Eileen Combe (née Jessop) had enjoyed a privileged
colonial upbringing; her wealthy father was a director of Barclays Bank's
overseas operation. In 1939 she married RAF officer Andrew Combe, a

hardcore member of the controversial Moral Re-Armament (MRA) cult, led by former Lutheran minister Frank Buchman. Buchman recruited amongst the professional and officer class, hoping this elite would steer humanity away from both dissolute capitalism and godless communism. He preached that individuals must 'start with themselves to bring the changes they want to see around them'. His followers, including the Combes, were organised into cells set apart from society. He told them to seek divine instruction through meditation. They were to sit quietly each morning and 'wait upon God with paper and pencil in hand in this relaxed and inert condition, and to write down whatever guidance they get'. Individual members would then report to the group and seek consensus on what action to take.

Peter Caddy had been invited to visit the Combes and their five children at the RAF Habbaniyah base in Iraq where he had been stationed after the end of the war. The guest had apparently impressed Eileen with his spiritual knowledge and expertise on UFOs. It had been her husband's intention to recruit Caddy to the MRA. The reverse took place. In 1951, after hearing a voice telling him that she was to be his future 'other half', Caddy pursued Eileen, precipitating the breakdown of her marriage and loss of access to her children. In the difficult period that followed, Eileen discovered her own inner voice during a pilgrimage to the New Age destination of choice, Glastonbury. The voice told her 'Be still and know I AM God' and assured her 'all would be well' – for she and Peter had been brought together for 'a very special purpose'.

Eileen become the third Mrs Caddy, and in 1957 the couple moved to Forres, a small town near Inverness, after Peter got a job managing a run-down former spa destination perched on the hill overlooking the town – Cluny Hill Hotel. Govan also re-located to Scotland.

At Cluny Hill Peter Caddy found himself increasingly dependent on his wife's inner voice to guide him on a daily basis, given that he had never run a hotel before:

> Every single question about the running of the hotel was submitted to Eileen, who received the answers in guidance. No matter what time of day, no matter what the circumstance, Eileen had to drop everything, sit quietly, meditate, and hear The Voice. She could be up to her ears in dirty nappies, and Peter would burst in demanding immediate attention.

Cluny Hill – the 'Heavenly Hotel'

Caddy hired in some of the ex-Pimlico group as staff and turned the establishment around, but the owners got tired of mocking press coverage of the Heavenly Hotel, as they dubbed it, and Caddy's connection to Sheena Govan. The Scottish papers had run a series of lurid features on Govan, presenting her as a deranged cult leader with a Messiah complex. There were also episodes, such as in 1961, during the Bay of Pigs USA/USSR nuclear standoff, when Caddy felled the trees in the hotel grounds without permission to clear a landing site for a spaceship he was convinced was on its way from Venus to rescue the group from imminent nuclear Armageddon. He was sacked, and in November 1962 the Caddys and their three young boys ended up on social security, living in a tiny caravan parked next to a rubbish dump in Findhorn Caravan Park, with only their old friend Dorothy Maclean for company. Govan, estranged from Peter and her group, and having spent her inheritance, fell into a lonely impoverished existence, dying of a cerebral haemorrhage in 1967.

Canadian-born Maclean came from a similar social milieu as the Caddys – she had also worked in British Intelligence during the war, before being introduced by her husband to the western-orientated Universal Worship teachings of Indian Sufi mystic Inayat Khan. She had then fallen under the influence of Govan, moving to London to join the Pimlico set. Maclean demonstrated her obedience by immediately splitting from her husband on the direction of Govan's inner voice.

As Steven J. Sutcliffe observed in his book *Children of the New Age,* the three Findhorn founders were:

> white middle-class British Commonwealth citizens aged in their mid-thirties or early forties, from privileged professional backgrounds and with extensive international travel and residence. This partly reflected standard expatriate lifestyles, but the restless movement between countries and partners also suggested a wider trend in the displacement of individuals in the wake of another world war.

Harmless Eccentrics

Our group hopped on the daily 8.15 am minibus that ran the short distance from Cluny Hill Hotel where we were staying to the foundation's utopian community in-action at Findhorn Caravan Park. Our focalisers had arranged for us to have a guided tour of The Park, as it is referred to, by long-term resident Ian Cook. We trailed in Ian's wake, an energetic man in perhaps his seventies, as he led us from one iconic landmark to another, his anecdotal commentary gradually layering up the history of the place. He started at the main road into the caravan park, known as 'The Runway', in recognition of the area's former occupants – the now closed RAF Kinloss airbase. Our guide explained that in the 1960s the base and its environs were top secret, with the Caddys' group referred to in Home Office documents as *H.E.–* short for Harmless Eccentrics. Ian pointed to a whitewashed brick hut right next to The Runway. Today it is a visitor's centre, but in the early days was the caravan site's toilet block. It became the solitary refuge where Eileen Caddy could escape the noisy caravan and sit 'night after night, until the early hours of the morning', communing with her inner voice. Next we gathered outside the mothership – the preserved remains of the original Caddy caravan, a blue wood and tin structure which, as Ian pointed out, is exceedingly small. He recounted Eileen Caddy's early prophecy that the caravan would 'one day be a place of pilgrimage, and people will come here from all over the world'.

The Caddy family caravan

Eileen Caddy's sanctuary

In the first spring following their move, Peter Caddy had, in desperation, cleared the waste tip next to the caravan to grow vegetables to help feed his family. Ian explained that this is the point at which Dorothy Maclean made her entrance into the origins story. After Caddy had seeded the vegetable plot, Maclean revealed to him her ability to communicate with the Elemental *devas* connected to each plant, who would tell her upon asking what each plant specifically needed to thrive. Belief in the existence of *devas* (Sanscrit for 'of brilliant light') came straight out of Alice Bailey's playbook. Bailey had mapped a hierarchy of *devas*, from woodland spirits, elves, nymphs and fairies all the way up to the most powerful *devas,* including Roc's Edinburgh companion – the great god Pan. Only a few humans had the ability to 'attune' themselves to the devic world – and Maclean told Caddy that she was one of them:

> I shared the first message with Peter, and he immediately gave me a list of questions to ask different vegetable *devas*. Thereafter, I would take his questions to the *deva* involved and get straightforward, practical advice as well as inspiring ideas.

Pointing to the site of the original vegetable patch, Ian told of how Dorothy 'would ask questions and get an answer back – such as how often do you

Gateway to the miraculous garden

want to be watered, or how much compost do you need to grow?' The divinely pampered vegetables subsequently grew to gigantic proportions, the result, according to Findhorn folklore, of Dorothy Maclean's devic version of *Gardener's Question Time* and Caddy's spadework.

Over time, news of the miraculous garden, with its forty-pound cabbages, began to draw visits from influential individuals including Peter Caddy's old friend R Ogilvie Crombie who, delighted by this turn of events, connected Caddy with the upper-class strata of British spiritualism, crucially Sir George Lowthian Trevelyan 4th Baronet, who had embraced New Age beliefs upon hearing a lecture given by a disciple of the influential Austrian thinker Rudolph Steiner. Trevelyan introduced Caddy to his network of powerful establishment friends. As he later wrote:

> I first visited Findhorn, the community in the north of Scotland, in 1968. I suspected that Peter Caddy's garden of magnificent flowers and glorious vegetables grown on arid sand dunes was the result of co-operation with the nature spirits. He confessed that this was the truth, so I wrote a memorandum to Lady Eve Balfour which brought up the Soil Association experts to see for themselves. I was never a member of the [Findhorn] community, but for ten years was a trustee and felt closely linked.

Lady Eve Balfour was niece of Tory prime minister Arthur Balfour. When she was twenty-one years old she used her inheritance to buy a farm which she then ran on organic lines. (Her father was into the paranormal, and served a term as president of The Society for Psychical Research, as did Uncle Arthur). Caddy could present Findhorn to this rich, leisured elite as the existing example of the New Age future they were dreaming of, deserving of their support and financial backing.

Caddy was finally moving into the esoteric mainstream. Within a couple of years, and as Ian Cook puts it, 'without anybody really intending it', the Findhorn experiment was on the road to permanency.

Both the caravan park and the rambling Cluny Hill centre along with its extensive grounds are now owned by the Findhorn Foundation. Cluny Hill serves as the foundation's organisational hub, college and residential visitors centre, run by a live-in team of modestly-paid staff, each business department headed by its own focaliser. Around 500 residents live in The Park, in an eco-village comprising an eclectic mix of housing: customised caravans, Tolkien-esque circular dwellings adapted from disused giant wooden whisky barrels and new build state-of-the-art eco-homes (for those that can afford it). Ian pointed out his house, one of a number built on land purchased from a local farmer that boasts the official postal service address: 'The Field of Dreams, The Park, Findhorn'. Today property on The Field goes for £200,000–£400,000 on the open market. To buy a two-bedroom eco-house built by the Foundation's housing social enterprise on a plot of land not far from the Caddy Caravan's resting place, will set you back £200,000.

As we take it all in, a very old lady in a bright red overcoat, aided by a young female companion, appears walking slowly along a nearby path, before sitting on a bench to rest. We realise we are in the presence of the last surviving founder, Dorothy Maclean, her ninety-seventh birthday just weeks away.

Dorothy has outlived both Caddys. Peter died in a car crash in Germany in 1994, having walked out on both Eileen and Findhorn in the late 70s after falling for a younger woman. (He was into his fifth marriage when he was killed). Eileen passed away at Findhorn in 2006 at the age of 89, having attained the status of revered international figurehead in her later years. (In 2004 she was awarded an MBE for 'services to spiritual inquiry'). Her daily constitutional at an end, the fragile figure of Dorothy disappears from view, and we are off again to meet with one of the community Elders, Steiner educationalist and poet, Auriol de Smidt. A few of us subsequently arrange a longer conversation with the academically-minded octogenarian at her residence in The Park's whisky-barrel house community.

Eileen Caddy's Inner Listening, Peter Caddy's practical ethos of Love In Action and Dorothy Maclean's magical Co-Creation with the Intelligence of Nature, are the three pillars upon which Findhorn rests. However, they have undergone a gradual process of renovation and re-pointing: Inner Listening has become associated with trendy New Age meditative practices, Love-In-Action is the rationale for volunteering time and labour to keep the community afloat, and Co-Creation with Nature has been aligned with modern ecological methods – recycling, energy conservation and sustainable farming.

The old streams of Christian dissenters, Rosecrucians, occultists and theosophists now flow into the broader river of New Age eclecticism and alternative life-style consumerism. Pagan signs, little keepsakes pinned on clothing or placed in plant-pots, autumn leaves arranged as love-hearts around the base of trees, magic number systems and astrological charts, complementary medicines and potions, angels, fairies, *devas* and unseen kingdoms, folklore, belief in UFOs, ley-lines, centres of magical power swirl around Findhorn like orbiting rings of space dust around a caravan-shaped celestial object.

Inner Listening

We are back up at Cluny Hill. The thirteen of us sat on a circle of chairs arranged by our focalisers Niels Paulsen and Alison Grant. Both are longstanding members of the Findhorn community. Their different personalities complement each other and make them a good team. Niels is an introspective, softly-spoken older man, originally from Denmark, but part of the Findhorn community for decades. He is on Cluny Hill's 120-strong staff team, lives on site and takes his meals in the communal dining room. (Staff members receive £200 in wages per month plus bed and board.) Alison is a local woman, born and bred in Forres. Her Scottish verve is overlaid by a deep knowledge of all things Findhorn. Alison is a member of the New Findhorn Association, a loose outer circle of 500 individuals and 30 odd businesses in the locality who identify with the Findhorn ethos but live outside of the core community. Alison has volunteered her week to be our co-focaliser.

Our group, eleven women and two men, hail from the UK, Europe, South America, Australia and Asia. My male compatriot and room share is a young Dutch man who works in the culture sector. The majority are a mix of middle-aged and younger women: an organic agriculturalist from Tasmania; a home counties enthusiast in alternative lifestyles; two young cousins from the US whose parents had been early Findhorn devotees; a Brighton-based visual artist; a UK university drama lecturer and voice tutor; two Brazilians – one a pattern-cutter for the top international fashion houses and the other a journalist; a hospice nurse from London, an academic from Japan presently researching in Finland and a global traveller originally from Israel. Each of us has paid a fee of £500-£800 to attend the week, and each has their own reason for taking part. As you might expect we have a basic commonality – anti-consumerist, angry at the world's injustices, keyed into green and ethical concerns. (And aghast at the emergence of President Trump). A nice, interesting bunch of progressive global citizens to spend a week with. What had drawn us to Findhorn? Some wanted to find out if joining the community was a viable prospect. Others were more focused on whether they could learn alternative ways of thinking to help them live more in concert with themselves and nature. Some were maybe at a personal crossroads – searching for direction, clarity of purpose or a higher meaning in life. One or two were also there for a break, a bit of peace and quiet and a battery recharge.

Each day we would gather for a two or three hour contemplative session, variously described in our timetable as group time, nature sharing, personal and planetary transformation sharing and inner life sharing. We were also taught 'sacred circle dances' – peasant folk dances from Middle Europe – introduced to Findhorn in the 1970s by German dance master Bernhard Wosien. He maintained, in keeping with his theosophical beliefs, that 'in dancing these old forms it is as though we are entering another... you have connected with the ancient stream of knowledge which flows on through you'. Not that any of us were particularly aware of this at the time, absorbed as we were on leading with the right foot and not bumping into the person next to us.

In the Angel card session we briefly meditated before picking a card from a pack of various angelic qualities, such as Joy, Surrender, Spontaneity, Obedience. According to an online supplier:

> Less scary than tarot cards, the angel cards need no special training and can be used within minutes of opening the pack...Your cards may have affirmations, inspirations or straightforward words of guidance. Messages on angel packs are always positive and uplifting. They are suitable for people of all ages and experiences and are completely safe for children to use.

We were invited to reflect on the significance of the card we had each drawn. I got the Angel of Balance, the inner significance of which I should think about as the week progressed.

Love In Action and Co-Creation With Nature

Fate, luck or a higher force decided that three of us would be practising our 'love in action' by working three mornings in Cullerne Gardens, a piece of cultivated land bordering The Park. I searched the Findhorn site to find out what this might entail:

> In Cullerne Gardens, we grow flowers and food for the community, co-creating with nature to bring beauty and nourishment to all beings. We invite you to share our love and passion for the garden. Together, we will do

lots of sowing, preparing, mulching and planting out in our fields and polytunnels.

Although 'in the real world' I avoid any kind of gardening, I considered this a good deal compared to the fellow group members destined to action their love in the kitchens or through scrubbing the baths and toilets at Cluny Hill. Cleanliness is next to Godliness for occultists too.

'Clean from top to bottom', advised Peter Caddy, channelling Sheena Govan. 'That clears out all the darkness and puts in vibrations of love and light. Clean and polish it. There is an occult reason for this, because the forces of darkness can always find a niche, find an anchor where there is dirt and disorder.'

In the morning three of us would clamber out of the minibus at The Park, resist the temptation to grab a cup of tea and instead make our way to the purpose-built Sanctuary for some meditation. As soon as everyone was settled, the focaliser pinged her brass Buddhist bell and delivered a quick blessing – asking the divine to help us align our beloved goodness inside with the goodness around us. Twenty minutes of silence followed, during which, for my part, vague thoughts periodically emerged out of my sleepy subconscious and fell back again. Another ping and the three of us tramped off to Cullerne Gardens.

In the outbuilding we found waterproof clothes to guard against the Scottish winter, gathered in a circle and held hands for a brief 'attunement' before we started work. Every group task at Findhorn, from washing up to planting seedlings or making strategic decisions, is book-ended by tuning in and tuning out. Attunement draws on the esoteric belief that 'universal life energy is divine in nature and that the core reality of all people is divine'. The aim is to harness cosmic energy and channel it though the group. As the Findhorn literature explains:

Before group activities commence, we stop, attune to the wisdom within, attune to each other and to the task, and then move forward...Tasks are often achieved with ease, peace, joy and beauty, and sometimes with new and unexpected solutions to problems.

But as with the other ritual practices at Findhorn, attunement can be taken on a number of levels. Thankfully, no-one asks you whether attunement has merely focused you on your task, made you feel part of an

Cullerne Gardens

in-synch collective, or elevated you to an 'angelic level of consciousness' on par with Eileen Caddy or R Ogilvie Crombie.

For my part I was content to pitch in and do whatever – weeding in the garden polytunnels, collecting organic waste from the community kitchens, spreading compost on the wintering rhubarb, rolling bales of straw. It was all taken at a steady pace, giving me plenty of time to chat with one of the garden's full time staff – a very pleasant guy from Holland named Evert. He had ended up at Findhorn after becoming disillusioned with his post-graduate career in the Dutch agribusiness sector. He was clearly at one with Findhorn's green credentials and commitment to sustainable eco-friendly farming methods, even if he made no mention of *devas* or miraculous super-sized brassica. The other focaliser at Cullerne Gardens was a cheery hardworking Liverpudlian named Jules, who I judged was possibly closer to the Elemental world of Maclean and Roc than Evert.

Heaven *or* Earth?

My time in Cullherne Gardens revealed that the community could have meaning for those not aware of the esoterics of Findhorn's founders. If you were a green activist, someone who didn't like organised religion but had a spiritual belief, a stockbroker sick of the rat race with enough cash to buy one of The Park's new eco-houses, a New Age lifestyle follower or a drop-out from city life (or life in general), you could theoretically fit into Findhorn. As Carol Riddell, 'offical' Findhorn chronicler says:

> The Findhorn community is not an ideal, a vision, a high-sounding theory, or even a blueprint for transformation. There is no pretence to have a recipe for instant perfection, nor are we a community of recluses, living in retreat from the day-to-day world. The community is an ongoing, practical, working example of how a degree of transformation can occur in relatively ordinary individuals within a short period of time.

But what of Findhorn's divine millenarian vision? Of literally bringing Heaven down to Earth? Steven J. Sutcliffe argues that a decisive shift in the nature and purpose of Findhorn took place in the 1970s under the influence of the radicalised younger generation of New Age gurus who had emerged, particularly in the United States:

> Spectacular growth occurred...when Findhorn was discovered by the hippy counterculture, who brought demographic stability (swelling colony numbers sixfold to around 120) and encouraged a hermeneutical shift in New Age away from a post-apocalyptic Utopia and towards this-wordly goals of healing, self-realisation and egalitarian co-operation.

Gordon Melton, in *Whither The New Age* makes a similar observation, but emphasises the synthesis between the divine and the earthly:

> Within the New Age Movement, the language of peace, healing and environmental restoration merged with New Age language of spiritual transformation, and the images of one issue borrowed as metaphors by the other. People began to speak of healing the earth, and transforming the way in which governments relate...Occultists and metaphysicians no longer offered just a programme of occult training and a home for cultural dissent, but presented a complete alternative life-style.

This ideological flexibility and pragmatism is the reason why Findhorn has continued to exist, unlike the myriad of utopian living experiments that had disappeared by the end of the 1970s. One of the Caddys' old catchphrases had been 'adapt, adjust, accommodate'. Having said this, the ex-RAF officer wasn't particularly enamoured of all aspects of the hippy lifestyle:

They…had to learn that dirty, torn and slovenly clothes and being unwashed and unshaven was not acceptable in Findhorn… Some of us were particularly concerned because we were expecting a retired naval captain and his wife to join us for a while.

He largely reconciled himself to the influx, given the possibilities of rapid growth that the young helpers represented.

The immediate prospect, it seems to me, is not that the Findhorn community dwindles away through loss of purpose or tears itself apart around some obscure theosophical debate (although either scenario cannot be ruled out) but rather that the community finds it increasingly difficult to sustain and renew itself.

The Findhorn population is incredibly stable, but success always carries with it the seeds of reversal. Findhorn's economic model relies upon a consistently productive population, with each person putting in more than they get out. In the 1960s the average stay in Findhorn was maybe six months. It attracted a constant flow of idealistic single young people, who threw themselves into building a 'heaven on earth' and then moved on. If someone fell ill and couldn't work, they would usually leave. This dynamic gradually changed over time. In the mid-1970s the average length of stay at Findhorn was ten months and the average age was twenty-six. By 1984 the average stay had risen to two and a half years and the average age was thirty-three. In 1994 it was reckoned that the average length of stay for members of staff was four years and their average age was forty.

As with 'the world outside' Findhorn has an ageing community. Some residents have lived there for thirty or more years, most of their adult lives. Recently thirty elders instituted their own weekly meditation session. It was estimated they had a combined age of around 2,000 years (average sixty-six years old). What happens when individuals become infirm or wish to 'retire' like their counterparts in the 'real world'? Can they still be part of the community and have their basic needs met?

An afternoon with Auriol

Four of us are squeezed onto the sofa in Auriol De Smidt's unique customised whisky barrel house, one of a cluster on the edge of The Park close by the sand dunes of the Moray Firth, the Bag End eco-homes and giant wind turbines. The barrel houses were the inspired invention of veteran Findhornian Roger Douda who, back in the 1980s saw the possibilities in recycling huge discarded whisky distillery vats by turning them into small dwellings. The first one cost Douda £10,000 to build. Auriol's rests on a circular stone wall, thereby creating an extra level.

If Auriol De Smidt is representative of the Findhorn elders, one would have to conclude that they are worth their weight in gold. As she lights up the little wood burner to ward off the December chill, Auriol sketches out her life story. She was born in 1932 into a settler family in what was then Southern Rhodesia. At the age of eight she was sent away to boarding school. She felt abandoned, and resolved she would never make her own children suffer in such a way. It also sparked in her an interest in different models of child-centred schooling. Thus, when in time, she became a mother, she sent her five children to a Steiner School in Cape Town, where she was then living. She became a teacher at the school, and raised her family. In the early 1980s she came to the UK, and through a series of changing circumstances, to Findhorn community. One of her early contributions was to help set up a local Steiner school, which is still going.

A whisky barrel house

Auriol's bookshelves are heaving with Rudolph Steiner-related material, signalling her ongoing study of both his educational theories and spiritual beliefs. In 1907 Steiner broke away from the theosophist movement, whose leadership he considered to be drifting off into obscurantism. Five years later, he launched his Anthroposophical Society which became extremely influential. The name was derived from the Greek for 'human wisdom', as opposed to Theosophy ('divine wisdom'); indicating Steiner's conviction that the spiritual world must have a scientific basis, and therefore could be attained through mastering rational methods.

Auriol is a great conversationalist, and we are rewarded with her knowledge, openness and sharp analytical approach to our questioning. Although she is one of the community's handful of revered 'Elders', she retains an outsider's eye on internal developments, partly informed by the minority status that her Steiner beliefs have in Findhorn.

We tell her that we are having trouble working out what is the greater purpose behind Findhorn – what is its goal? She laughs. 'I'm not sure I've worked out what the goal is either.' She then begins to reflect on what she thinks drives it forward. 'At Findhorn we have a coming together of a large collection of different faiths. But there is a shared sense of growth. That sense of taking responsibility for our own lives, our own challenges, is quite deep in Findhorn.' 'Almost intentionally,' she continues, 'we have not said "this is our faith". We're trying to see what a meeting of faiths could look like.'

'These days we don't want to use the word "God", but what can we say about this higher wisdom that belongs to all life, that we have to connect to?' she asks. For Auriol, Experience Week is about getting participants to find 'what is calling you inside?' One of us replies that it could be interpreted as self-indulgent – sorting yourself out without regard to those around you. 'Yes, we do have to be careful. Being at Findhorn is not about having a holiday – we have to balance this sense of self with a sense of community.'

Auriol intimates that life can be tough at Findhorn. Don't you think that perhaps the experiment has run its course? I ask. 'That's a good question,' she says. 'Hmm. My take is that a lot of people have taken part in this experiment, it's worth persisting in. That's what most people are saying.' She pauses. 'I think our experiment is still very much alive. I feel that.'

BY ONESELF, TOGETHER

Marco Lauri

'I want to do it myself together.'
Giorgio, child of my friend Caterina, to his mother.

My student Marina sat in the office I share with colleagues at my small Italian university. She had just told me she wanted to write her BA dissertation about Egyptian Science Fiction. I could perceive her enthusiasm and motivation. The topic interests me deeply, as she knew, since I had written a PhD dissertation on the closely related Arabic tradition of utopian writing. She smiled shyly. I noticed the spark of curiosity in her eyes.

Now Marina has graduated with distinction. She is attending my MA course on Arabic utopian writing and Science Fiction, where I am using research by my friend and colleague Ada Barbaro and my own. In class, we discuss selected texts and how they relate to their social, cultural and political background, not unlike Marina has strived to do in her dissertation. It is on that course that we discussed some of the ideas sketched here.

'Utopia' is a 'western' word, coined by Sir Thomas More in 1516, from Greek roots in a Latin book. The concept it underlies has been long regarded as a matter of the West, and modernity. This increasingly outmoded view implies that pre-modern societies, stuck in tradition, are seldom able to question the extant social order and challenge it organically; trapped in the assumption that hierarchies and rules are divinely ordained or otherwise grounded in a transcendent dimension.

Such an approach overlooks, at the very least, the fact that transcendence itself may be the stuff of utopia, and it does indeed pervade two foundational texts of the 'western' utopian tradition: Plato's *Republic* and Sir Thomas More's *Utopia* itself, the namesake of the whole genre. Many scholars have also held that modern utopian writing takes inspiration in Hellenic philosophical reflection and the Judeo-Christian vision of a Kingdom of God – Hellenic and Biblical traditions are the twin primary sources of 'western' literate culture at large, after all, the refrain goes. However, these are also the wellsprings from where much Islamicate literary culture and thought has emerged, alongside the Iranian tradition, itself partly Hellenised since long before Islam.

It is undoubtedly the case that Muslim thought in its 'classical' period (roughly corresponding to what is called 'Middle Ages' in most Western historiography) normally upheld hierarchy and regarded it as divine. But actual social reality was often negatively contrasted to the assumed ideal. Conversely, while literary narratives and poetry routinely praised and boasted violation of social norms (especially regarding drinking and extramarital love), mocked them and denounced outward piety and conformity as hypocrisy, they usually avoided direct challenge to those norms or advocating changing them. However, this outline would also aptly describe the worldview of many cultivated Christians and Jews in the same general time-frame. The oft-heard narrative describes Islamic traditions quickly crystallising into a near-immutable fixed textual and normative corpus, stifling creativity and re-interpretation after a few remarkable centuries. A narrative of 'captive' philosophy in Muslim lands, brilliantly argued by some followers of political philosopher Leo Strauss, fits this pattern. Long before Strauss, the great French Orientalist Ernest Renan also suggested that Hellenic philosophy was a stranded stranger in Medieval Islam, unable to flourish among 'Semitic' minds narrowed by adherence to a legalistic transcendent monotheism.

These sorts of views can hardly be taken seriously anymore by specialists. Recent scholarship has done much to highlight the vibrant intellectual culture of Medieval Islam and the importance of Hellenic philosophy within it, although older dismissive outlooks still have some currency among sections of the wider public. Western non-specialist discourse still sometimes presents Greco-Arabic philosophy in a narrative of exile and return, where the role of thinkers and translators who wrote in Arabic was to keep the memory of Aristotle until such time comes that his work could return to where it really belonged – Paris, Oxford, and Padua. However, in historical terms, claims of exclusive heritage of Plato's *Republic* (or

Ezekiel's prophecies) by the 'West' are about as questionable as the corresponding claims made by the Abbasid court of the ninth century – when it regarded itself the worthy inheritor of Hellenic philosophy in contrast to the fanatical, irrational, Christian Eastern Romans. The 'Franks' of Western Europe, at the time, did not even deserve consideration as intellectual contenders in the eyes of Baghdad.

Subjects of the Abbasid Empire of different faiths and native languages eagerly translated, read, commented and elaborated Plato, Aristotle, Galen, and many others in Arabic from Greek, Middle Persian or Syriac; they copied manuscripts, taught and learned in circles and discussed and picked what suited them. Muslims among them, such as al-Kindi and al-Farabi, saw value in the wisdom of long past Pagan strangers in the search for truth and happiness. They apparently regarded these ancient wisdoms as essentially the same as Islam itself taught, or at least in general accord with it. The likes of al-Farabi also felt, however, the tension that existed between the rational mode of thought of philosophy, with its emphasis on the individual grasping of the truth by rigorous thinking, and that of the Prophetic truth passed down through transmitted words of divine origin. Most Muslim philosophers considered this difference as a matter of different expression of the same underlying transcendent reality – the philosophical expression may be more accurate, but not suited for the masses, who need religious imagery to understand a glimpse of it. Conversely, religious scholars often saw the value of Aristotelian logic, but were horrified at other philosophical notions that emphasised the self-sufficiency of human (individual) reason.

This tension played in the field of epistemology, but there was also a social epistemology at stake, that had political resonance. We see the 'autonomous knower' of the Platonic-Aristotelian tradition sparring with the 'political animal' needing to accommodate with others – in a context dominated by religious discourse. Is social, political life compatible with happiness and truth? How can we live together in true happiness? Is the order of this world truly aligned with what it should be (a transcendent reality according to Plato and Muslim thinkers alike), and how are we supposed to know that anyway? These are 'modern' questions. Questions utopian thinking usually faces. We find them, too, in medieval discussions, written in Arabic by people who had confronted, among others, Plato and Aristotle.

Ibn Tufayl's *Risalat Hayy Ibn Yaqzan* is widely recognised as one of the masterpieces of Classical Arabic prose. Despite belonging to the well-established genre of the epistolary treatise (*risala*), one of the cornerstones of pre-modern Arabic literary output, it displays remarkable originality. Its narrative form itself is peculiar – though not unique – and the use of a fictional story to offer philosophical direction and illustrate philosophical insight is possibly rarer still. Furthermore, the historical trajectory of its reception represents a significant moment of cross-cultural exchange, as scholarship has shown in recent times.

Ibn Tufayl was an important physician and philosopher who lived in twelfth century Andalus and Morocco, under the patronage of the Muwahhid court. *Risalat Hayy Ibn Yaqzan* is his main extant work. It begins with an introduction in the form of a letter, where the author describes his purpose and mentions some preceding thinkers who include al-Farabi, al-Ghazali, Ibn Sina (Avicenna) as well as Ibn Bajja, an earlier fellow Iberian Muslim who had written a small incomplete treatise on solitary life. Then, the tale starts. It traces the life-story of a single main character, called Hayy Ibn Yaqzan (meaning 'Living, son of the Wakeful') who spends most of his life in solitude on a desert island near the Equator.

The author offers two contrasting explanations of Hayy's solitary and parentless presence on the island. In the first, the child is spontaneously generated through a series of rare natural phenomena, fully accounted for by the author's understanding of Aristotelian physics and physiology; while in the second, he is abandoned to the waves by his fearful mother in an ark, a story clearly reminiscent of Moses and other comparable narratives. Hints appear later in the text suggesting that the second account is to be taken as the true one. Once on the island, the child Hayy is fostered by a female gazelle and grows up to understand the world around him, asks himself questions about it, notices the difference between himself and other animals, and ascends to ever-higher levels of comprehension. This is framed in seven-year long cycles, and at the end of each, in general, he makes a new breakthrough in his self-made research. His reflection, practical at first, moves towards the Necessary Being, the One who, he realises, must exist to account for everything else, although He is impossible for him to perceive through senses since He must be immaterial and transcendent. Hayy however concludes that he possesses a faculty, the intellect, capable of conjunction with this Necessary Being, and he manages to attain, through meticulous effort, this blessed state, the ultimate understanding and happiness – a glimpse of the eternal joy to come, after his body ceases to be.

At this point, another character comes to the island. He is a man called Asal from a nearby inhabited island, who is seeking isolation from society in order to attain the mystical union with the Divine himself. Asal's starting point is not his experience or reason, but knowledge of a divinely revealed Book (clearly the Qur'an, though the text is not explicit on this) that had been known to the society of his homeland. He desires to penetrate the deeper meanings of the Scripture to realise his own apprehension of the ultimate, divine reality.

The encounter of Hayy and Asal is surprising for both, but they come to a mutual understanding of respective experiences – although Hayy struggles to see why God saw fit to fill His Scripture, whose validity he comes to accept, with legal injunctions he considers entirely unnecessary for well-reasoning people. Asal on his part sees the bliss Hayy had attained as his own purpose and choses to follow Hayy's example and teaching. Hayy insists he visit Asal's home island so that he could teach his own knowledge to the people there and unveil the true meaning of their faith. The attempt is unsuccessful, as people are unwilling to accept that their ultimate happiness can only be reached by personal rational effort – they prefer to cling to accepted, transmitted views and habits and the outward appearance of the revealed Law. Hayy and Asal then return to the desert island to live in blissful contemplation until their souls leave the corporeal being.

Any summary such as I have given cannot hope to do full justice to the story; its richness, complexity and philosophical depths. Anglophone readers can savour it in full in the recently revised translation by Lenn Evan Goodman, which is however only the last of a long trail of renditions in English since the late seventeenth century.

There has been much discussion on *Risalat Hayy Ibn Yaqzan*'s main meaning and purpose through the centuries since its composition. Edward Pococke titled his Latin rendition *Philosophus Autodidactus* (The Self-Taught Philosopher) and Simon Ockley gave his early eighteenth-century English version the title *The Improvement of Human Reason*. Both took, with different nuances, the story of rational self-elevation to be the core of the tale. The tale has also been read as a 'mystical' text, a kind of a guide to the highest illumination of individual soul.

Other readers prefer interpretations that are more 'political'. In the early twentieth century, its French translator and editor Léon Gauthier considered the harmony between religious and rational truth to be the focus of the *Risalat Hayy Ibn Yaqzan*, a reading by Leo Strauss' followers would turn that on its head, arguing that disharmony between them is what really needs to be engaged with.

To put it as simply as possible, is the story about apprehending God by oneself, or about (not) being able to communicate the Truth to others? Does it look back more to Aristotle's *On the Soul* or Plato's *Republic*? It is clear to me that, to a point, the only correct answer can be 'both'; but this, of course, is not good enough.

I think that we would get closer to an understanding of this fascinating book if we assume that its epistemic concern relates very closely to the social-political: 'can people share the truth?' or 'can they live together in happiness?'. When seen in the context of these longstanding discussions, that were already a tradition in Islamic philosophical thinking, the tale takes its place very close to that which another time and place would call 'utopia' as a critical engagement of social order (although the result is seemingly dystopian here), with society being presented as incompatible with happiness.

Ibn Tufayl's tale had some diffusion in Arabic – it is preserved in a number of manuscript sources, and even provoked a response in the late thirteenth century from a more religious-minded scholar, the great Syro-Egyptian physician Ibn al-Nafis. His short treatise, also available in English translation, is a startling exercise in theodicy and philosophy of history – using the same premise of an individual living in a desert island and meeting society, but taking it to the opposing direction of a defence of social order.

Risalat Hayy Ibn Yaqzan was first translated in mid-fourteenth century into Hebrew, and then twice into Latin – the first time by Pico della Mirandola, (from Hebrew) in manuscript form; then, from Arabic, in 1671 as a printed work by Edward Pococke the Younger in Oxford, titled *Philosophus Autodidactus*. This edition sparked interest in wider European philosophical circles. A wave of European translations followed – Dutch, English,

German, and then many others in the twentieth century. The themes of the book resonated with European discussions of the Early Enlightenment era, and may have contributed to shape them, if it is true, for example, that John Locke shifted his interests to epistemology around the time the book appeared in Latin. (There is good circumstantial evidence for this, although not absolute proof).

In recent decades, this cross-cultural history of circulation has seen renewed and well-deserved scholarly interest, showing the far-reaching impact of an Arabic philosophical text into Medieval Jewish and Modern 'Western' thought, long after the usual time-frame generally recognised for major Muslim influence on Western intellectual trends (that is, in the Middle Ages). Notably, the English rendition of *Risalat Hayy Ibn Yaqzan* from Arabic appeared in the same period the *One Thousand and One Nights* did in French. The historical importance of an Arab Muslim source in Enlightenment intellectual milieus is particularly attractive to some contemporary critics (often of Arabic ancestry). They rightly employ this story to criticise the 'Western' pretences to exclusive universal rationality, but they also have made some excessive claims regarding the importance of the tale in Europe. The vague similarities with Defoe's *Robinson Crusoe*, published only a few years after the English translation, have attracted considerable attention, but there is no consensus; the case for direct influence remains, in my opinion, inconclusive.

The manuscript used by Edward Pococke for his Latin translation – one his father had brought to Oxford from the Ottoman Empire at request of Archbishop Laud – contains a strange interpolation by a later copyist, in the description of the desert island where most action of the tale takes place. The passage, clearly not from the pen of Ibn Tufayl's, refers to the legend of Waq-Waq, the Equatorial island where trees bear human fruit in the form of lascivious women who attract luckless sailors and, in some accounts, devour them. This theme appears in various forms in several travel and marvel narratives from Islamic Middle Ages, also finding its way into the *Arabian Nights* and getting a passing mention in a famous short story by J.L. Borges. It has evidently little to do with Ibn Tufayl, except the Equatorial island setting and the remarkably unconventional way human beings come into existence, which must have misled the copyist's hand. If we expunge this spurious passage, Hayy's life is entirely devoid of partnership with the opposite sex, to the point that Fedwa Malti-Douglas has described the tale as a 'male utopia'. While I have challenged some aspects of her reading, I do agree that Hayy's lack of any interest whatsoever in sexual partnership is indeed remarkable. I see it as an element of a deeper utopian issue – the problem of society, to which sexual reproduction is an obvious necessity. Hayy is able to fulfil all his material and, in time, spiritual needs by himself – except for sex and, at first reading at least, meaningful communication.

In 1818, Mary Shelley's *Frankenstein* appeared in print, ushering the beginning of a new literary genre in Western literary tradition, that later times would call Science Fiction. Frankenstein's Creature is also, in a sense, a 'self-taught philosopher' like Hayy: parentless and partnerless, coming to being in unconventional ways, without a mother, shorn and rejected from society and condemned to isolation – its mind a ready blank that grows through impressions. Shelley's conclusions, however, are epistemically and politically at the opposite of what Ibn Tufayl suggests – isolation leads not to individual perfection, but nightmarish folly. The rational male utopia Victor Frankenstein dreams of cannot sustain itself without the tenderness of the maternal womb; the same tenderness we may experience, as social beings, in fruitful communication.

We cannot know if Shelley read Ibn Tufayl. The text existed in English at the time, but I have not found, so far, evidence she ever came across it. It is not mentioned in her father William Godwin's impressive list of readings, whereas another Andalusian philosopher, Averroes (Ibn Rushd), does appear, as do the *Arabian Nights*. Reference to the Orient does appear across the novel – it is through eavesdropping on the lessons given to Safie, an Arabian woman, in a German isolated cottage, that the Creature learns most things it knows about humanity – and the *Arabian Nights* are referenced directly. Nevertheless, this does not prove that Shelley may have had Ibn Tufayl in mind. Whatever the case, the problems of individual and society, the nexus between epistemology and politics, resonated in Enlightenment and Romantic Britain as they did in Medieval Muslim Spain.

Ibn Tufayl, the author of *Risalat Hayy Ibn Yaqzan*, presented at Muwahhid court his younger colleague Ibn Rushd, the man who would come to fame in the West under the name of Averroes. It is not clear that Ibn Tufayl had been his teacher, but the two certainly knew each other and likely discussed philosophical matters on occasion. It is not possible to reduce the vast philosophical work of Ibn Rushd into any short summary; he commented on most of the vast Aristotelian corpus, and authored several important autonomous works, particularly in response to Abu Hamid al-Ghazali's criticism of philosophy. The harmony between religious and rational truth, both in its epistemic and social aspects, is a deep concern for him as it was for his older colleague. For both, Plato's *Republic* was a starting point – Ibn Rushd chose to write a commentary on it alongside his main work of explaining Aristotle, admittedly because he could not find an Arabic text of Aristotle's *Politics* instead. Ibn Rushd's commentary on Plato was written in Arabic, but only its Hebrew translation has come down to us via a Jewish Renaissance philosopher known as Mantinus who then rendered it into Latin, and two modern English versions now exist.

Ibn Tufayl wrote fiction. Ibn Rushd reproached Plato for using fiction and largely refused to comment on these works, limiting his analysis to the rational elements of the dialogue. Ibn Rushd held that it is ideally possible for talented individuals to reach the highest truth and take responsibility in the human community at the same time, as Plato suggested, and that the philosopher may, in the right circumstances, engage the real social order critically. He startlingly does so on the 'peculiar' topic of women, whose seclusion and lack of education he lashes out against – deepening Plato's collectivistic arguments on the same lines. He goes as far as saying that the usual treatment of women in his Andalusi society is downright dangerous – because society is utilising only half of its potential. This is a utopian critique of society – not far in its method from what we see in expanded form in the first book of Thomas More's *Utopia*, more than three centuries later. We find philosophical commitment to society here – a stark difference from the isolation Ibn Tufayl presents as his 'utopian' ideal.

Medieval 'utopian' thinkers who wrote in Arabic, within the framework of Islamic revelation, such as Ibn Tufayl, gave a specific flavour to universal problems of knowledge and social life. The question they developed from Hellenic forefathers then crossed faith and cultural boundaries and are still with us. Ibn al-Nafis would have maybe agreed with Mary Shelley that we can't be alone, that worthy knowledge is social and steeped in interpersonal feelings and obligations. Others would have preferred a higher, solitary path. In the end, Hayy's political adventure is a failure. We may see a cautionary tale against returning to the Cave after having seen the naked Truth. Alternatively, perhaps, without a political dimension, Hayy's bliss is incomplete. Aristotle was clear that we all need society in order to be human, and society needs the individual soul and its universal rationality. We are, each, by ourselves, together.

ESCAPE TO ANDALUSIA

Medina Tenour Whiteman

On a sweltering hot day in August 1982, in an apartment in the heart of the Albaicín, the Moorish quarter of Granada, with my mum looking up at the Alhambra with ice cubes in her mouth – as she tells me every year on the same date – I was born.

What were my parents doing there? This wasn't the classic scenario of *A Year in Provence*: they didn't have inheritances to live off, and there was little work even for locals, let alone foreigners who didn't speak the language and hadn't the first clue about olive farming. They were recent converts to Islam, members of a nascent Sufi group that was gaining followers there. They arrived penniless, lived on a wing and a prayer, and left penniless a year and a half later.

So I grew up in various parts of the English countryside, largely detached from Muslim groups – we sometimes travelled hours to go to *dhikr* gatherings – in the shadow of my family's previous Sufi adventures. From holidays in Spain, Granada acquired a kind of mythos for us: achingly blue skies, the smell of paella cooking over burning almond kernels, tiny apricots so flavourful they put peach melba sweets to shame, wild swimming in abandoned reservoirs full of fish and water snakes. This was an ancient landscape where the echoes of the Moors mingled with the harsh cries of goatherds, and the magnificent palaces of another era stood almost side by side with the concrete condos of the Costa del Sol.

After the advent of the internet allowed my dad to work remotely with much greater ease, my parents finally moved back to Spain from the UK in 2003, almost twenty years after their first attempt. Two expeditions, bridging (technically) two millennia: what were they in search of? Or, perhaps more to the point, what were they escaping? I interviewed them to find out.

Medina Whiteman: Could you describe the backdrop to the first time you moved to Spain, in 1982?

Tahira Whiteman: There was stagnation in the Norwich community [where they were living]. And he was offered a job in Spain.

Abdal-Lateef Whiteman: Our friends in Granada wanted to experiment with electronic music and Andalusi singing, and that appealed to me. In Norwich there was almost no economy. Collecting benefits was embargoed, pretty much. We were living outside the system.

TW: It was very exciting in Spain because all these young people were becoming Muslim. For me, the thought of bringing up children in a difficult situation, where I'd already spent one summer – which was more like a winter – I thought, get me out of here.

ALW: Andalusia had a great appeal to us… a beautiful piece of Paradise where Muslims had once lived in a very civilised way.

TW: And [the fascist dictator] Franco had just died – it was a really dynamic time for Spain.

ALW: But it was still pretty primitive. You had to queue for an hour at the Post Office to make a phone call.

TW: There were donkeys going up and down the Albaicín carrying building materials.

ALW: We were there when the first punks came to Spain. People used to tease them and chase them down the road – until they became punks themselves. (Laughter) Something happened to the Spanish, they went completely to the opposite [of the fascist repression].

TW: Women over the age of thirty-five were still wearing rusty black, and then suddenly there were women walking around with their shoulders showing. You cannot imagine the social change.

ALW: Malaga at that time still had [gender] segregated beaches.

TW: Zak [my half-brother] was living in Spain, and me being a spoiled American I was so desperate for a bit of sun that we made the trek often to see him.

ALW: And we knew quite a few people. When we arrived we had virtually nothing and we were put up very generously for weeks. We helped with publishing, whatever was going. I used to give a class of Andalusi singing.

MW: You had initially been drawn to Islam through Andalusi singing, right?

ALW: Yes. I didn't understand anything much intellectually as regards Islam. I was playing with a band called Mighty Baby. We were interested in occult things like Gurdjieff and the I Ching, partly because a musician called Martin Stone had joined who brought with him all these books of Eastern wisdom, and that interested the whole band. In fact he became Muslim in secret, with [the 100-year-old] Sheikh Muhammad Ibn al-Habib in Meknes. We were touring Germany and I thought he was looking under the bed...he was actually praying. On the same trip these books fell on my head in our tour bus. Two heavy volumes of the Qur'an. [Stone] went down to Morocco later and came back and (laughs) he was in a *jellabah* and turban, with kohl in his eyes, playing a Gibson Les Paul very loudly on stage. We noticed his playing had changed for the better, it was inspired.

MW: So the music improved?

ALW: The music improved. [The rest of us] weren't Muslim by then. But Ian Dallas [who later became Shaykh Abdal-Qadir and founded the Murabitun movement] had recorded some singing in Morocco. I listened to that for a long time. I was so impressed by it musically. We had been looking for musical clues and inspirations, like all bands were [in the 1970s]. We were searching. Some bands were secret Hindus, some

Scientologists, some Celtic Christians, some secular Jews. People had tried drugs, but they hadn't really got anywhere. Music was the drug.

MW: But also sacred music ties you into a wider, deeper thing.

ALW: We knew about the whirling dervishes and their music, Ali Akbar Khan, Ravi Shankar…but it was quite remote. When I heard Andalusi music it was nearer home. It's the granddaddy of flamenco. When I heard it I thought, I want this music, and I don't care what I have to do to get it. At that time, there were only one or two mosques in England. People didn't know what Islam was, which made it easier in some ways, because you had to find out about it person to person.

MW: There wasn't so much prejudice to have to overcome, maybe?

ALW: I think there's a deep prejudice in the British about Islam. It goes back centuries. But there were also glimmers of people being interested…I don't like to use the word 'converting', as in a way Islam embraced us, we didn't embrace it. I was basically kidnapped. Early on it was extremely difficult, and I probably would've given it up if I hadn't known that it was actually very good for me. Living in London for eight years had made me cynical and a bit arrogant – playing with a music group made you very isolated and eccentric. Although it might seem that Islam was eccentric, in fact it was going back into mainstream life. I was well aware that inside me there was something quite toxic which needed treatment. So every Thursday we had *dhikr* gatherings, there were the prayers…it was a purification process that lasted a long time – it's still going on. I'd dabbled in Buddhism before, I was hanging out with friends who were mescaline tabbing Buddhists. We'd sit down to meditate with a big Buddha in front of us…and I thought, this is just like a Quaker meeting, but with idols. (Laughs)

TW: I went to a seven day silent Buddhist retreat in New York State, and it was absolutely amazing. Then they would give talks about karma and reincarnation, but I was too much of an ex-Methodist, and an ex-social worker, to deal with that. I thought, I can't blame these poor children, all the terrible things [they deal with], for their past lives. That's when I went searching elsewhere, although I have great respect for the Buddhists.

MW: What was it about the environment you were in that was too suffocating, or didn't nourish you spiritually, which made you move to Spain in the first place?

TW: Have you ever been unemployed in Norwich in March? (Laughs.) Anyway the man in charge of the Muslim community we were involved in [Abdal-Qadir] had tried to break up our marriage – he'd already busted up one of [ALW's] marriages...it was a time of great social experimentation which was disastrous for family life.

ALW: Norwich was a trap. The men had been eviscerated economically...

MW: How?

ALW: The community somehow accepted that having a job was verboten and that you had to be self-employed. Better to be poor and outside the system, even though it was hard.

TW: He had a degree in architecture...

MW: But you weren't allowed to use it?

ALW: In truth I didn't want the kind of work that was available. But I was asked to design things for the community like letterheads and the mythical Muslim Village in England...I did organise the planning permission for the [Ihsan] mosque there, which needed a new plan and drawings. But there was in general an atmosphere that you had to go back to learning arts and crafts and avoid the outside world if possible. It was a complex situation. Often people's inheritances got swallowed up by the group.

TW: Some of the group were very poor.

ALW: There were always big plans for the future of the community, with fancy brochures selling its wares, but once Norwich got going, reality dawned. The late 70s and 80s were not prosperous times in the UK and Norwich was a backwater. Other people were starting their careers and mortgages around then and we went off on a complete tangent.

TW: We were still carrying counter-cultural ideas around with us but we had to go back into the world. We were anti-materialist but not managing too well at it. We weren't exactly highly skilled organic farmers, were we. (Laughs.)

ALW: It wasn't entirely bad as there were virtues in breaking this norm, but I think the norms were broken so much that there wasn't any realistic foundation left. Despite the great plans the Norwich community had there was quite a painful split [around then].

MW: So what did Spain promise? A better lifestyle, better health all round...?

ALW: We knew that it was a more beautiful place to live...but we had little clue of what it was like to actually live there. Norwich had become stale.

TW: We were invited to go down. It was an exciting prospect.

MW: You were pregnant with me then, and you drove down with Mo [my eldest brother] in the back seat, you had to sell his Casio keyboard...

ALW:...to buy enough petrol to get to Granada...

TW: ...He even sold his watch! Once we got to Spain we had to sleep in the car, in the pouring rain, and then we woke up in bright sunshine and looked out over a Valencia beach...It was like heaven. It was an adventure.

ALW: But I accept that to be driven to do that you have to be pretty desperate. I'd been given a car and in Granada we would be among people we knew.

MW: So then you arrived in Granada, you were staying with friends for...a couple of weeks?

ALW: The Spanish had a kind of generosity, when people are poor they tend to help each other more than when they're rich. And southern Spain knew a lot about poverty.

TW: Everything had to be shared.

ALW: Granada has this kind of melancholy quality to it. It was quite a difficult time. Abdal-Samad Romero [of Los Rosales retreat centre], bless his heart, rented a brand new apartment for us, with views of the Alhambra, where you were born.

ALW: There was bit of design work. I did some nice work for Miguel Hagerty [a well known Spanish Arabist] –

TW: – which he never paid you for! Boy I was cross.

ALW: He said, I'm sorry, I haven't got any money to pay you, but take anything you want off the walls of my house. So I took a beautiful and valuable *firman* from Ottoman times as payment.

TW: Yeah, well it didn't feed us, I can tell you.

ALW: We just coped. It was hand to mouth. Until finally a thunderbolt hit us – Abdal-Qadir had suddenly abandoned Sufism, and told us to stop the singing. He wanted a kind of political Islam, with Emirates and Emirs, based on the Amal [early Muslim community] of Medina. It was all very odd and had the effect of splitting the community as it had done in Norwich. This is when Dr Umar Faruq Abdallah arrived [an American convert to Islam who in 2000 established the Nawawi Foundation, a

Chicago-based organisation devoted to preaching and teaching of Islam], and we got on very well with him. Dr Umar started giving Arabic classes, which were very good. Many of us benefited from them.

TW: And Samira [his wife] was teaching the women the *Ajurumiyyah* [the famous text on Arabic grammar].

ALW: Dr Umar was extraordinary. We'd walk around the Albaicín talking about history...he had this dream about Islam returning to this city. Most of all he got people interested in Arabic. But there was unfortunately a big disagreement between him and Abdal Qadir and his emirs. Overnight Dr Abdallah was persona non grata. He wasn't allowed into the mosque, and the men in trench coats, who were Abdal Qadir's politburo, told him he had to leave town, which he did.

TW: And Samira was sent to Coventry too. Such wicked stuff went on. It was amazing that nobody got stabbed. People were locking the mosque doors and not letting in the rebels.

ALW: But then a group of us decided to go [to Morocco] and visit Muhammad Bin Kurshi [a saintly man from the original Habibiyya *fuqara*] in the Sahara. It was a remarkable trip, it changed everything...

When we arrived at his *zawiyya*, which was a traditional beaten earth *qsar*, we waited for him in the entrance, not knowing what to do, when suddenly these cats came in like outriders, followed by Muhammad Bin Kurshi, who quickly went around kissing everyone's hands before they could get up out of their seats. Then we all went upstairs to a long *minzah*. It was a real eye opener because we were reciting *Ya Sin* [chapter 36 of the Qur'an] while eating barbecued sheep's stomach - a desert delicacy. The room was full of smoke. That wouldn't have been allowed in Granada! It was so relaxed, it was wonderful. Barbecued sheep's stomach is like bits of rubber but we found that you could hold out a morsel over your shoulder and a cat would go *foom* and grab it. It was just *dhikr*, food, more *dhikr* for twenty-four hours...not much talk. It was hard work but also very relaxed. We'd walked into an ancient world full of men of knowledge, hidden in the desert.

That night [the man] lying next to me started snoring the minute he went to sleep. I was lying there thinking I'd be awake all night…and then I suddenly realised I must've slept. I blinked and the electric wall lights had turned to candles. No-one else was awake. Muhammad Bin Kurshi was standing alone in the room looking at me. I thought this was some kind of special moment, I'm going to be initiated into something…but he was just getting us up for *Fajr* [morning prayer].

(Laughter.)

I walked towards him. As I got near, he went (points to the left), so I had to walk downstairs to the toilet, and someone was standing there with a ewer of hot water and soap, with a towel. And then it all started all over again, the *wird*, Qur'an, breakfast, more *dhikr*, then more breakfast…we didn't move from that room until [we left] after lunch. When we went to say goodbye to Sidi Muhammad, we kissed his hand, then he went, poom! (whacks heel of palm) onto each person's [fore]head. I thought this must be a desert thing, but Hamza [Yusuf] told me later this was a kind of transmission. Who knows.

[When] we got back to Granada, everything fell apart. Something had happened in us. Suddenly there was this light, and our whole illusion of Granada collapsed like a pack of cards. That visit to the desert was absolutely crucial. It was real. Granada was a fantasy.

TW: I think all through time, people - very idealistic people especially – have been interested in belonging to, and creating, a group, and this is why people get involved in these various spiritual, quasi-religious groups. Sometimes they'll even stay long after they should have left.

MW: Why do you think people go in for these idealistic groups?

TW: I think there's a basic loneliness in people…since the 1950s, we've been taught individualism, to rebel, that there is such a thing as teenagers, so therefore you have to go off on your own. But then again, from Plato's

Republic to Henry Thoreau's *Walden* – which is a very important book for Americans, people are starting to re-read it - people have been looking for different ways of living. The Sixties was an explosion of this idealism. And the 1970s.

ALW: People have a very strong need for family, that's a well-established reason why groups exist. Even people who've been in really bad cults have said that they'd rather be in it than be alone.

TW: And people will get out of Scientology and be like, I miss it.

ALW: When I went on a Quaker work camp in my teens, in Denmark, there was this German girl who'd run away from home, because she came home late one night and her father refused to let her back in the house.

TW: It's an old need, but in the 1960s everything changed and that's when there were all these made up groups, sects, cults and things, and they were addressing a need. People had taken drugs and cut [themselves] off from their parents, psychologically or physically or both.

MW: Tell me about why you left England again to return to Spain in 2003.

TW: By then we were renting an enormous house in England, at enormous cost, Hanna [my sister] had said she was going off to Spain to go to art school and get married, Mo [my eldest brother] was in Berlin, you were in Zanzibar, Zak was in Granada, and we had friends who for years had begged us to go down and were going to give us land to build a house. So once again we're back to economics. And once again we thought we were coming to a kind of utopia, didn't we? We did.

MW: There's this playoff between hope and illusion, which ironically in Spanish is the same word, they use 'ilusión' to mean hope.

ALW: I'd come to a dead end in England, because I was working for myself, and with the cost of everything going [up]…I read the writing on my bank statement. Living under the Stansted flight path wasn't a healthy place to be either. I had some good clients and the internet was just getting off the ground. It made sense to relocate to a place with a much cheaper cost of living and a more benign environment. And sun.

TW: And where the birds weren't being annihilated by pesticides.

ALW: Agribusiness in East Anglia...

TW: That was a big thing for you. By then he was fifty-eight.

ALW: Going to the Puebla [de Don Fadrique, site of Los Rosales] was a gamble...an inspired gamble.

TW: He was hopeful. I was petrified.

ALW: For two years we lived with this idea that there was going to be something really great happening out there. It was a bit like Dar al-Islam [Sufi community in New Mexico, founded in the 1980s].

TW: We were going to be part of this wonderful centre with Muslims coming from all over the world all the time, and we'd have jobs and land and a house...

ALW: We didn't have the same vision as the hosts. It's a centre that comes to life three months out of the year, but the rest of the time it's a family farm. Which is fine, that's what they wanted, but it wasn't what we'd anticipated and we ended up moving. That was when we came to the Alpujarras [mountains south of Granada], which was the best thing we ever did. It was a great blessing because that was when we realised it was all false hope. It was a 'departure of illusion' [a *Habibiyya qasida*]...and the minute you depart from illusion about something, the doors open. Moving to Orgiva was an incredible kind of healing.

TW: We must've been nuts, all this moving! (Laughs.) *Alhamdulillah* Allah made all of that happen.

ALW: It was all to the good. [Although] the transition was difficult.

TW: All moving is difficult.

MW: I'm also interested in this tension between the desire for community and the need for sovereignty.

ALW: Behind these things there's the issue of provision, that someone else was going to provide for us. This is the sort of thing that was going on all the time with Abdal-Qadir.

MW: But you had to sacrifice something.

TW: Yes.

ALW: It was hidden, but we did think that [the group was] going to get money, and there's going to be a village, and somehow, if we pledge our fealty, we're all going to be provided for. It makes you less responsible for yourself. There wasn't much room for independence, to say the least.

TW: You've got to be so careful with spirituality, you've got to be with good people and good teachers continuously because you could get swerved into a cul-de-sac, and that could be it for life. When I first came to Islam [a man] said to me, Don't you understand? The spiritual path is not Route 66, it's got dead ends, wrong turns, giant boulders in the way… that's stuck with me for forty years. Some people said things [that struck me]…*Allahu 'Alim* [God knows] maybe they don't take their own advice, but they're mouthpieces for something.

ALW: If you take the path of knowledge it's perilous. Deceptions are everywhere, you can fall into vanity so easily. The whole thing was a learning process because when people are trapped in a hall of mirrors, it very difficult to know where to turn, because you've been brainwashed into doing things without realising you've been brainwashed. It's like anyone who's tried to expose Scientology…the cult becomes like a sea animal that puts out barbs.

TW: But the truth is it has probably helped some people, Scientology. We think it's completely mad, but I bet there's some people who could [otherwise] have been taking crack cocaine in Delmar [her home town in the USA].

ALW: It's a case of whether it's the truth. If you purport to teach the truth...

TW: How many people really want the truth?

ALW: – if you take people on a spiritual journey which leaves them ignorant, what kind of journey is that?...People often have an enormous anxiety about provision, and that's what holds them in the group. The group wants you to be dependent on the group.

TW: But they also provide for very exciting things to happen. I came to Islam with this group, and within the first few years I was in Norwich, Spain, San Antonio (Texas), Tucson (Arizona), Atlanta (Georgia), and Granada, with no money, no job. These weird cults, like The Family, and the Moonies, were in China, Chile, Austria...so although there are horrible things going on, you can convince yourself that it's wonderful, you're learning so much, nobody has an exciting life like us. It's like a movie.

ALW: Also in every group there is a certain percentage of people who are sincere, intelligent, educated, talented...

TW: It's like Moulay Arabi ad-Darqawi said, 'Beware of the goodness in people, because it can be a trap.' I think a person can come in with a good heart, and still advance on the spiritual path even though the teacher is not so good. But they've got to have the wisdom to get out when they reach a certain point.

MW: What is that point?

TW: I don't know, *Allahu 'Alim*. People can get stuck in situations – look at Asya, she's one of the most highly praised women in the Qur'an and she was married to the Pharaoh, who thought he was God! [In other cases] people might think that they want Allah, and actually what they want is a high position in the hierarchy. In every spiritual group they say the same thing, that people can be working on themselves and that the last thing to go is the desire for power.

MW: In what way are things different now?

ALW: It's just happier. We're connected to the people we want to be connected to — we're not trapped. I'm very grateful for that. We've prospered here in every way.

MW: But essentially you've regained your spiritual independence?

ALW: Yes. Because of the people we've been connected to for the last twenty-five years — people like Abdal-Hakim [Murad], and Hamza Yusuf — we've been able to relearn our Islam. We were stunted, kind of like bonsais. My philosophy in life is that it doesn't really matter where you start, it's where you end up that matters — we're down here, and we're up there (points upwards). We're from God, and we return to God.

ISLAMIC UTOPIANISM

Nazry Bahrawi

Truth needs evidence, or some recourse to reality. Nowhere is this more evident than in the struggle to come to terms with incredible successes of the Trump presidential bid and the Brexit campaign. For this is a struggle with post-truth politics, where rhetoric matters more than proof. To many, post-truth is a venture reserved for the far-right. This is not quite the case if we consider Islamic utopianism. Impounded by imagination, and harping on hope, Islamic utopianism is nowhere near empirical. Yet it is its very post-truth feature that empowers.

We must first establish that utopia is a dirty word today. When a suggestion, an idea or a person is described as utopian, this is often a denigration that means unrealistic, unachievable or naive. Yet this has not always been the case. Thinkers of yore used utopia as a thought experiment to imagine not just a different reality, but more importantly, the good life. To them, imagining utopia was serious business. This was the practice of societies in the Western hemisphere, but it is also prevalent in Islamicate cultures. Think of the positive reception to Thomas More's novel *Utopia* (1516) or Al-Farabi's classical work, *Al-Madina al-Fadila (The Virtuous City)*.

What has caused the degeneration? One way of understanding this is to re-visit the arguments put forth by the sociologist Karl Mannheim, credited as one of the founders of the sociology of knowledge. For Mannheim, utopian thought is antithetical to ideology. Invoking the spectre of Marxist class struggle, Mannheim argues in his seminal book *Ideology and Utopia* (1936) that the ruling class is given to perpetuating ideology as a means of tightening their grip on their privilege, while oppressed groups resist that hegemony by conceptualising utopian thoughts. Mannheim outlines a crucial distinction that is only gaining traction among scholars of utopian studies in recent times – the idea that utopia is not just a place but also a mode of thinking, a hermeneutical lens, a ubiquitous impulse.

For now, it must be qualified that Mannheim was not the only scholar who was critical of the practicality and value of utopian thought. His treatise has had a strong influence on the tracts of a particular group of postcolonial scholars from the Malay Archipelago. Chief among them are Shaharuddin Maaruf and Syed Farid Alatas, both of whom were former heads of the National University of Singapore's Department of Malay Studies. Both had extended Mannheim's treatise that utopian thought is incongruent with reality. Shaharuddin argues that utopian thinking has the ability to express itself as 'millenarian, populist, eschatological and orthodox' if one considers the case of Southeast Asian Muslims vying to establish Islamic states within the region. For him, these propagators of the 'Islamic state' have mistakenly diagnosed the ills of their societies, preferring an unrealistic political venture over realities on the ground. Agreeing with Shaharuddin, Alatas delineates as utopian the impracticable elements of the reformist ideas of Syed Shaykh Al-Hadi in his study of this early twentieth-century Islamic modernist from Malaya. Yet, Alatas had also made the nuanced observation that while utopian thinking is not anchored in reality, it 'breaks the bonds of the existing order'. While he does not make it explicit, Alatas, unwittingly perhaps, gestures to a less popular but nascent interpretation of utopian thinking. This is the idea that it is pregnant with revolutionary instigations – a school of thought that has ardent champions within Islamic circles.

To go about it systematically, Islamic utopianism can be categorised into three strands: namely, mystical, eschatological and reformist. Each corresponds to an overarching feature. Briefly, the mystical strand is based on the promise of individual perfectibility, the eschatological strand is fuelled by millennialism and the reformist strand embraces social progress. Let us consider each in turn.

The mystical aspect of Islamic utopianism is most compellingly embedded in the doctrine of *al-insan al-kamil*, or *The Perfect Man*. Conceptualised by the Islamic philosopher and mystic ibn 'Arabi of thirteenth century Andalusia, this doctrine holds that Muslims possess the potential to actualise divine attributes. In Islamic theology, these are canonised as *asma' allah al-husna* (The 99 Names of Allah) and include attributes such as Mercy (*Rahmah*), Justice (*'Adl*), Beauty (*Jamal*) and Majesty (*Jalal*), among others. According to Ibn 'Arabi's doctrine of *The Perfect Man*, humans must seek to emulate these attributes if they wish to attain a pristine state of being. For him, humans and God are not mutually exclusive entities but are in fact interwoven. This conforms to another of ibn 'Arabi's doctrine known as *wahdat al-wujud* (the Unity of Being), which supposes that God is both Creator and creation. In *The Ringstones of Wisdom* (*Fusus al-Hikam*), ibn 'Arabi writes: 'If you wish you can say that the world is God, or you can say that it is a creation; if you would rather, you can say that it is God on the one hand and a creation on the other, or you can plead stupefaction because of the lack of difference between the two'. This quotation posits that God is defined by a dualistic nature. On the one hand, He is the Lord of the universe (*rububiyah*), thereby making Him a worthy object of worship. On the other, He is hidden within His creation according to the doctrine of *ahadiyah*, or Divine Unity, which posits that God's essence is indivisible and spread throughout the world, thereby enhancing the central Islamic tenet of His Oneness (*tawhid*) rather than contradicting it. Here, *ahadiyah* should be interpreted to mean that 'things are re-absorbed into God' rather than the idea that God has been demoted to 'the level of things'. Ibn 'Arabi is also careful not to claim divinity in all things to steer clear of the charge of pantheism that could be levelled against him from conservative theologians. He does, however, accord humanity a privileged status in the grand scheme of things. As in-between creatures that are both corporeal (*zahir*) and spiritual (*batin*), humans are able to comprehend the dual realities of God as an essence and as the 'manifestation' of this essence in the real world, while angels can only know God as a 'transcendent or spiritual reality' because of their ephemeral nature. For ibn 'Arabi, it is this unique capability that has led God to appoint humans as His *khalifah* (vicegerents) on earth as mentioned in the Qu'ran (2:30). Ibn 'Arabi may argue that prophets are best suited to embody the *al-insan al-kamil* ideal, but he has also not ruled out ordinary humans from doing the same as they vie to become optimal versions of themselves. In this sense, his doctrine is anthropocentric, placing humans at the top of the spiritual hierarchy of living things.

With human flourishing as its end goal, this mystical version of Islamic utopianism continues to appear in the tracts of subsequent Islamic thinkers, particularly those with a Sufi disposition. Take, for instance, the renowned thirteenth century Turkic poet and mystic, Jalal ad-Din Rumi who died some three decades after ibn 'Arabi. While there is a lack of evidence that the two had crossed paths, a mythical Sufi tale recounts how the latter encountered a young Rumi walking behind his father one day in Damascus, leading him to exclaim: 'Praise be to God, an ocean is following a lake!' What is certain though is that ibn 'Arabi's doctrine of *The Perfect Man* 'recurs throughout Rumi's poetry'. The Rumi scholar Afzal Iqbal points to several verses in the poet's famous collection of poems, *Mathnawi* (*Spiritual Couplets*) that are congruent with ibn 'Arabi's doctrine:

Man is the substance, and the celestial sphere is his accident; all things are (like) a branch or the step of a ladder: he is the object.

...this (bodily part) is within Time, while that (spiritual part) is beyond Time.

This which is in Time endures till death, while the other is the associate of everlastingness and the peer of eternity.

Thou art the sea of knowledge hidden in a dewdrop; thou art the universe hidden in a body three Ells long.

The first two excerpts capture humanity's nature as in-between beings, while the last espouses God's hidden essence. Appealing to different aspects of *al-insan al-kamil*, all three qualify as poetic expressions of ibn 'Arabi's doctrine. This doctrine is also recurrent in the writings of the early twentieth century Islamic thinker-poet Muhammad Iqbal from India. Adapting ibn 'Arabi's doctrine, Iqbal widens the applicability of its scope beyond the prophets, arguing that The Perfect Man can also be personified in the figure of the *mujtahid* (or renewer), a learned individual who will rejuvenate the teachings of Islam according to the needs of his or her time. This idea of the *mujtahid* is derived from a famous *hadith* (sayings of the Prophet) prophesising the appearance of a 'renewer' in every century. Elsewhere, Iqbal's mystical poem *Javidname* describes a mystic's ascension to heaven, latching on to an episode of Islamic history known as the *Mi'raj* where the prophet Muhammad is described as having ascended to heaven. The significance of ibn 'Arabi's *al-insan al-kamil* doctrine on Iqbal's poetry has been described by the renown German scholar of Islam Annemarie Schimmel with these words:

...according to Iqbal, poetry is a surer approach to reality than philosophy, his most important ideas are expressed by the medium of poetry; and in the *Javidname*, almost each personality we meet with, teaches the central conception of Iqbal's philosophy: the development of the Ego, the inner Self of man. And even more: the ascension of the poet is the apotheosis of the Perfect

Man, for 'if man realises the significance and power of his self, he can transcend time and space, and can shatter the Universe'. This is the leitmotif of the book.

It is worth noting the connection that Schimmel makes between Islam's utopian impulse and literature, specifically to poetry. Indeed, we can posit further that the popularity of ibn 'Arabi's *al-insan al-kamil* doctrine among Muslim poets across the ages suggests that religious utopianism is only accessible through activities that engage the human senses in the way that only poetic (or literary) products can; it is not attainable by way of sheer logical reasoning. Unlike his Andalusian predecessors like al-Farabi and ibn Sina, ibn 'Arabi does not believe that philosophers are best placed to comprehend God's essence. Rather, this task is reserved for the Sufi mystic brimming with imagination (*khayl*). Ibn 'Arabi pens poetry too. For the Sufi, literariness is highly prized. One may intimate that the literary act of composing poetry and prose is a means through which the Sufi can amplify his or her imagination to gain access to the divine attributes in pursuit of the *al-insan al-kamil* ideal.

Meanwhile, the eschatological aspects of Islam's utopian impulses are expressed through millennialism, or the belief in the coming of a Messiah and the subsequent establishment of a holy kingdom. Millennialism is as much a utopian imagining in Islam as it is in Christianity in the former's notion of the Mahdi (which is the Islamic equivalent of the Christian messiah). Its strongest trace can be found in the doctrines of the Twelver (Imami) Shi'ism. Although less systematic, the doctrines of Sunni Islam are also tinged with a Mahdi imaginary, which gives rise to similar millennial tendencies. Two examples from the twentieth century can be discussed here, namely, the Al-Arqam movement in Malaysia and the fiery preacher Imam Nazar Hosein of Trinidad and Tobago. Al-Arqam's founder Ashaari Muhammad has consistently in his books and speeches spoken of the coming of the Mahdi as a figure 'who would lead Muslims to victory'. At its apex, the Al-Arqam group ran some 28 communes with over 10,000 members in a bid to create a self-reliant ideal society couched in Islamic principles. The Malaysian government, fearing sectarianism, detained the Al-Arqam's top leaders and banned its communes even though its business arm exists subliminally in the twenty-first century under the name of Rufaqa Corporation Ltd. In his writings, Nazar Hosein argues for Muslims to embrace a self-imposed exile to 'disconnect from the godless cities of the modern age and strive to establish Islam in the remote countryside'. These 'Muslim villages' for Hosein will be the new centres of utopia that will replace the modern cities of USA, UK, Canada, Europe, Australia, Singapore which are 'portrayed and marketed as heaven-on-earth'.

If the mystical strain of Islamic utopianism can be said to empower the individual, its eschatological strain is oftentimes socially divisive. Common to the Mahdi prophecy, Al-Arqam's commune and Hosein's 'Muslim villages' are premised on the elevation of one community over others. If this form of Islamic utopianism can be said to be empowering at all, this can be gleaned from the idea that the favoured communities in such eschatological narratives are marginalised groups. The Shi'ites are minorities in the wider Muslim world while the Al-Arqam group is considered a sect in Malaysia. Meanwhile, frustrated Muslims of the post-9/11 world who may have suffered Islamophobic discrimination can find solace in Hosein's discourse. Unlike its mystical strain, Islamic utopianism that is expressed in eschatological narratives selectively empowers, thus going against the grain of a cosmopolitan worldview. If a better world is at all possible, it is not for everyone. Some will literally go to hell. At the turn of the twenty-first century, this exclusivism took a sinister turn with the proliferation of *jihadi* groups such as the Al-Qaeda in the Middle East and Southeast Asia's Jemaah Islamiyah whose discourses, when stripped of their theological language, are fuelled by the eschatological notion that an ideal world is possible for a select few. Given its exclusivist leanings, the eschatological strain of Islamic utopianism in Islam can also be described as dystopic.

Similar to the eschatological strain of Islamic utopianism, its reformist strain is also predicated on the idea of social progress though this is premised on the inclusion rather than exclusion of peoples. In the Middle Ages, traces of Islamic reformism can be found in the philosophical ideas of al-Farabi in *al-Madina al-Fadila* (*The Virtuous City*), a text exploring the notion of the ideal city along similar lines to that imagined by Plato in *The Republic* published circa 380 BC. Both accord intellectuals the primary role of guiding society. However, al-Farabi's perfect society is to be led by a 'ruler-prophet' who places reason and revelation on equal standing, as opposed to Plato's 'philosopher-king' which upholds reason above all else. Its reformist slant can be seen in the way al-Farabi envisions a 'new' form of governance to be led by intellectuals. This is different from the governmental norms of his time where political power is in the hands of courtly figures like sultans and kings. Yet it was not until the twentieth century that al-Farabi's discourse could be said to have revolutionised governance for real. This is in the form of the Iranian theocracy. According to the historian of Islamic thought Roy Jackson, al-Farabi's theory 'had practical implications in... al-Khomeini's effort to produce such a "virtuous state" in Iran in the late twentieth century'. Jackson is referring to the Iranian Revolution in 1979, which saw Islamist dissidents overthrow Iran's monarch Shah Mohammad Reza Pahlavi and appoint Ayatollah Ruhollah Khomeini as the nation's new leader. In this new Islamist order, al-Farabi's idea of the 'ruler-prophet' was translated into Khomeini's doctrine of the '*vilayat i–faqih*', or 'rule by the jurist', which can be seen as a synthesis between al-Farabi's political philosophy and ibn 'Arabi's *al-insan al-kamil* doctrine. The logic was such: Islamic jurists are the modern-day embodiment of the Perfect Man. If Iran were to be the 'virtuous society' envisaged by al-Farabi, the nation needs to be governed by Islamic jurists. It must therefore no longer support the rule of the monarch. Through the Iranian revolution, Islam's utopianism is transformed into a full-blown reformist movement. Reformism, however, is not limited to the Shi'ites.

In Sunni circles, Islam's reformist impulse began to pick up speed in the transition period between the nineteenth and twentieth centuries as the Muslim world, which spans from the Middle East to the Malay Archipelago, saw the emergence of a variety of Islamic reformists who were disillusioned with what they perceived to be stagnation facing the *ummah* in the wake of Western modernity. This reformist strand was couched in the spirit of utopianism through its common vision of creating an ideal *ummah* that 'addresses the challenges posed by modernity while remaining faithful to the basics tenets of religion'. The founding fathers of Islamic modernism can be traced to three figures, al-Afghani (1838-92), Muhammad 'Abduh (1849-1905) and Rashid Rida (1865-1935). While al-Afghani and Rida have explicitly condemned Europe's colonisation of the Muslim world as opposed to 'Abduh, all three share the assumption that modern knowledge, particularly science and technology, are the means through which Muslims can better their lot. All three believe that contemporary Islamic scholars must abandon the practice of *taqlid*, or a blind adherence to tradition, and instead embrace *ijtihad*, or independent reasoning, while interpreting Islamic doctrines. 'Abduh, for instance, describes Islam's affinity to alternate between reason and revelation in his book *Risalat al-Tauhid (The Theology of Unity)* in the following way: 'Some espouse this very notion arguing that faith is founded on pure submission and is quite discontinuous with rational investigation of the contents of religion, whether it be doctrines affirmed or directives enjoined. We reply: if that claim were to be allowed, religion would not be a means whereby man could be guided.' He emboldens this claim in his interpretation of pre-Islamic Arabia, a society divided by religious decrees premised on the idea that 'reason and religion had nothing in common, but that rather religion was the inveterate enemy of science.' It was not until the advent of Islam that Arabia's religious war is resolved, argues 'Abduh. In effect, 'Abduh is tapping into an established scholarly tradition from the likes of Islamic philosophers such as al-Kindi and Ibn Rushd who had argued that both philosophy and theology are means of attaining divine truths. The idea that Islamic communities must embrace scientific knowledge is made even more pronounced in the personage of 'Abduh's counterpart from India, Sayyid Ahmad Khan (1817-98). In interpreting the Qur'an, Khan distances himself from a literalist hermeneutic of its verses. For instance, he interprets 'demons' (*jinn*) as a personification of evil desires. Concerned with educational reform among Muslims, Khan wishes to create a group of Muslim elites who can take over leadership from the British colonisers. To this end, he founded a school in 1875 that offers modules in traditional Islamic sciences alongside European arts and sciences.

So we come full circle. We began with an undesirable view of utopia. Indeed, Trump's utopian state is a dystopia for so many of us. Yet, our brief survey of Islamic thinkers suggests that utopian thought is just as replete with the pursuit of human flourishing. If there is anything at all to be salvaged from the rise of post-truth politics, it is the idea that the manufacture of hope begets hope.

SEARCHING FOR KHILAFATOPIA

Sadek Hamid

In a speech on 5 September 2006, US President George Bush warned that al-Qaeda wanted to establish a 'violent political utopia across the Middle East, which they call caliphate, where all would be ruled according to their hateful ideology.' For some observers, that predication partly came true in July 2014 when ISIS seized large chunks of territory in Iraq and Syria. Its self-proclaimed Caliph Abu Baker al-Baghdadi declared that they had re-established a religious institution formally terminated in 1924. Most Muslims worldwide rejected ISIS's claim and even supporters of the concept of a caliphate have been horrified by the barbarity of ISIS over the last two and half years.

For Western political elites, the idea of a twenty-first century, pan-Islamic polity that unites postcolonial Muslim nation states inspires fear and loathing. Nonetheless for many believers, despite the barbarity of ISIS, the idea evokes a mix of hope and nostalgia. This is because the concept of caliphate or *khilafah* is infused with memories of the unified community governed by the pious *al-khilafah al-rashida* – the rightly-guided four successors to the Prophet between 632–61. Populist Muslim discourse paints the *khilafah* in an idealised way – a sort of Islamised 'Garden of Eden', where all was well until Muslims were colonised, oppressed by Western foreign policy and persecuted by corrupt rulers. It is an image of a lost utopian, universal Muslim *ummah* that transcended borders, where faith superseded ethnic, linguistic, cultural and political differences. History, however, records a far more complex story, one in which the concept of *khilafah* held multiple meanings and whose reality was manifested simultaneously in many great achievements as well as dark episodes.

In Arabic, the term *khilafah* denotes successor, proxy, or deputy. In the Qur'an, it is referenced to the idea of human vice-regency, or trusteeship, on earth. Historically it refers to the landmass of smaller states that made up the Muslim empires that spanned the seventh to early twentieth century. This includes the periods ruled by the Umayyads (661–750), Abbasids (750 –1258), Fatimid dynasties (909–1171) and Ottoman Empire (1517–1924). Despite different interpretations and realisations, the idea of khilafah was in its essence about leadership and the just ordering of Muslim society according to the will of God – as the Historian Hugh Kennedy points out in his recent book *The Caliphate*. Modern debates on the khilafah began in the mid-1920s after the abolition of the Ottoman khilafah and conversion of Islam into a stateless religion for the first time in its history. At the time the sense of loss and resulting turmoil triggered unsuccessful attempts to address this absence through international conferences – in Cairo organised by King Fuad of Egypt and in Makkah, hosted by King Abd al-Aziz ibn Saud. Enthusiasm for a restored khilafah waned between the interwar years and remained dormant during the post-colonial, independence period as nationalist sentiment and politics dominated the newly created Muslim states.

While some Muslims yearned for a rejuvenated khilafah, until the rise of ISIS very few were actually working to establish it. However, the quest to recreate a contemporary khilafah has been most notably associated with the political project of the Hizb ut-Tahrir movement. Hizb ut-Tahrir (HT), or party of liberation, was founded in Jerusalem in 1953 by the Palestinian scholar Taqiuddin al-Nabhani (1909–77). After becoming disillusioned with pan-Arabism, al-Nabhani switched to Islamism and became the first contemporary Muslim thinker to theorise a neo-Caliphate for the twentieth century. The urgency of the task was based upon al-Nabhani's particular rationalist reading of Islam. Through his voluminous writings, al-Nabhani contended that only Islam was both in harmony with human nature and based on reason. For al-Nabhani, a correct understanding that led to solving earthly problems was only possible through a process of exact thinking altered through Divine revelation. His political theories attempted a systematic reinterpretation of the canonical textual sources of Islam; reconstructing them into a distinct ideological worldview with a coherent, detailed series of systems that were supposed to be superior to modern 'man-made' ideologies of secularism, nationalism, socialism, communism and capitalism. To his mind, communism contradicted human nature and appealed to the animal instincts of fear, misery and hunger, while capitalism separated religion from everyday life. For him, establishing the *khilafah* was not at all a moral commitment but a compulsory religious obligation decreed by God and which incurred punishment for its neglect.

For the true believers of HT a revitalised *khilafah* represents an alternative Islamic heterotopia to the West's dystopia. Its establishment would eliminate all remnants of colonialism and 'implement Islam' immediately by reactivating the shariah in its totality. This singular utopic order would then solve all the political, economic, social problems of Muslims globally, challenge Western hegemony and carry the message of Islam to the rest of the world. To apply this panacea, it was first necessary to acquire power in a strategically positioned Muslim country. Once an appropriate state was selected, HT missionaries would implement an action plan entailing the development of dedicated cadres who could make public opinion favourable to their ideas and then infiltrate all significant sectors of society. Special emphasis was placed on persuading the senior leadership of the military to help them peacefully capture power. This was a radically different approach to religious reform in comparison to other Islamist movements such as the Muslim Brotherhood who pursued a gradualist, bottom-up approach. For HT, the *khilafah* became *the* instrument of Islamic revival rather than the consequence of it.

In the mid-1950s, HT was initially able to recruit members from Palestine, Jordan, Syria and Iraq but then found itself rapidly faced with significant challenges. The rise of Nasserism scuppered its efforts to gain popular support during the 1960s and in the late 1960s and early 1970s its advance was further hindered by failed attempted coups in Damascus, Amman, Baghdad and Cairo. This resulted in the movement being banned in most Middle Eastern states, forcing many of its leaders to leave the MENA region and try and seek new opportunities in the West. Their remaining presence in places like Palestine was marginalised further by the more successful forces of Hamas and Islamic Jihad in the 1980s. In the mid to late 1990s, movement activists travelled to Central Asia to set up branches in Uzbekistan, Tajikistan and Kazakhstan and in the last fifteen years British HT members have set up cells in Pakistan, Bangladesh, Malaysia, Indonesia and developed a modest following in Tanzania and Turkey. During the last decade, Britain has developed into a critical hub in

HT's international operations and helped spread its message through English language media.

The British branch of HT started to develop a profile in the early 1990s and has transitioned through four distinct stages: the foundation (1986 –96), retreat (1996–2001), post-9/11 (2001–5) and post-7/7 (2005–present). Welsh-Yemeni Abdul Kareem Hassan and Palestinian Fuad Hussain are believed to have established the first UK branch in 1986. Initially activities were limited to small study circles that tried to recruit international students and professionals who could carry HT's ideas when they returned home. There was no need to develop a coherent strategy for Britain. Though its membership reflected the predominantly South Asian demographic of the UK Muslim population, Syrian-born Omar Bakri was chosen to lead the British branch around the time of the first Gulf War in 1991.

But this orientation changed as British-born Muslims slowly started to show interest and eventually join the organisation, allowing HT to expand its work to different cities. British Muslims searching for satisfying religious identities were drawn to HT and its ideology as they saw it offering meaning, purpose and incentives. It was a message of empowerment that simultaneously tackled three dimensions of their British life experiences; it addressed their desire for a strong internal identity, spoke to their external social circumstances and provided a connection to an idealised past and the promise of future glory. Recruits were offered compelling explanations for the socio-political problems facing Muslim societies, as well as convincing reasons to point the blame at Western powers.

For some it was the first Islamic group that provided a persuasive explanation for their marginalised condition in British society; for others, it offered an interpretation of Islam that appeared more rigorous than what they were taught at home or in the mosque. For some young people the group appeared to offer an attractive ideological alternative to the stifling inward-looking politics of their parents' generation and in some cases provided them with a surrogate family. The group's emotional sloganeering appealed to youthful angst and a desire to be given a clear direction in life with pre-packaged answers to difficult questions. Membership provided a comforting balm to those bruised by racism, Islamophobia and other forms of rejection, with the *khilafah* envisioned as an imaginary homeland that was just around the corner.

During Omar Bakri's leadership, HT managed to cause alarm within Muslim communities due to its rising popularity amongst young people and its confrontational tactics. The overriding appeal of HT in the early 1990s lay in its total ideological packaging and the inability of other Islamic trends to offer more compelling alternatives. To some observers they appeared to be Muslim Trotskyites, pioneering what was dubbed 'pamphlet Islam', producing large numbers of leaflets on different topics. Other Islamic activists resented the attention-grabbing tactics developed by Omar Bakri and hated HT for turning up at their events, hijacking question and answer sessions, distributing their literature and their generally obnoxious behaviour. HT members often also created problems for other Islamic activists operating on college and university campuses, which occasionally resulted in the closure of designated prayer rooms at some universities and difficulties for mainstream student associations.

Towards the mid-1990s, the central leadership of HT in the Middle East blamed Bakri for the fall-out from a series of controversial stunts aimed at generating maximum publicity for the group. They grew unhappy with his aggressive strategies and media exposure, which they felt detracted focus away from the party message. The international leadership was frustrated that Bakri and not the party's ideas had become the foci of public interest and forced him to resign in February 1996. Current leaders insist that Bakri's period as leader was an 'aberration'. Bakri himself later argued that HT had violated Islamic law by constricting the demands of the shariah by separating law from belief and not accepting jihad as an individual duty.

During the Bakri era, HT had become well established in Britain with a presence in over fifty universities across the UK. Following his departure, members of HT in Britain went through a confusing and difficult time, compounded by a faction that set about creating a second HT in Britain. This group claimed to be the most authentic and accused the first of straying away from the founders' original message and methods. However, by 1997 the second group had conceded its failure in the UK and instead reverted to focusing its efforts to establishing the *khilafah* in countries such as Pakistan.

Omar Bakri went on to lead the Al-Muhajiroun group (AM), a shortened version of Jamaat al-Muhajiroun, a front name for HT which he created in 1983 while exiled in Saudi Arabia. The AM group retained many of HT's aims and methods and Bakri was able to take a significant number of HT members with him to the new organisation. To distinguish themselves from their former colleagues Bakri claimed to have adopted a Salafi *aqeeda* (creed). There were also three critical differences of strategy separating his new group from HT, centred around what were to be considered priorities. First, even though they both believed in re-establishing the *khilafah* by coup, HT limited this project to the Muslim world while AM argued that it included Britain. Second, HT disassociated itself from the *takfiri* jihadism of al-Qaeda, which AM supported. Third, AM adopted a high profile style of moral correction, which led to an increasingly confrontational attitude to other Muslim groups and the British government. During this period, Bakri made tactical alliances with other extremist preachers who were starting to develop their public profiles in the UK such as Abu Hamza and Abu Qatada.

From 1996 to 2001, HT in Britain struggled to reorganise after Omar Bakri's departure and a markedly low public profile concealed the strategic reappraisal that was quietly taking place. In the days after 9/11, the HT central leadership issued a communiqué to the British national executive to adopt a strategy to 'rhetorically streamline localised international incidents – specifically the Middle East peace process, the Balkans conflict and continued US presence in the Gulf – into a narrative of the West's "oppression" of Muslims and a "War on Islam."' At the same time, HT attempted to rebrand itself as a moderate Islamist movement and made efforts to tone down its anti-Western rhetoric and to distance itself from allegations associating it with violent extremism.

These efforts notwithstanding, HT was further marginalised by the increased profile and mobilising capacity of the Muslim Association of Britain (MAB). While in the past HT could organise demonstrations to protest various Western interventionist policies in the Muslim world, in the early 2000s they were displaced by the alliance-building strategies of the MAB and its work with large numbers of Muslim and non-Muslim organisations. This was most evident when the MAB worked with the Stop the War Coalition and various civil society organisations to mobilise millions of people during the anti-war marches of 2003. HT's reputation was further undermined when the National Union of Students passed a 'No Platform' motion in 2004 against their activities on university campuses.

Following the 7/7 bombings in London, HT found itself once again thrust into the media spotlight for alleged links with violent extremism. Several neoconservative think-tanks, analysts and politicians exaggerated HT's potential threat by reproducing alarmist judgments that relied on speculation and guilt by association. Despite its record of non-violence, the movement was accused of being an intellectual precursor for more violent subversive groups because of its fierce anti-Western rhetoric and support for Muslim liberation groups in occupied territories such as Palestine, Kashmir and Iraq. This assessment located HT in the violent company of al-Qaeda and ISIS, with the organisation periodically accused of having links to terrorism. Despite the British leadership of HT distancing itself from Omar Bakri and Abu Hamza and denying any connection between their work and the activities of Al-Muhajiroun and other Jihadists, HT was threatened with proscription after 7/7 and after individuals arrested for terrorist offences were alleged to have attended HT events. Conversely, the Association of Chief Police Officers, the Intelligence services and elements within the Home Office have opposed the banning of HT on the grounds of insufficient evidence, whilst others believe that HT is useful in drawing young Muslims away from violent forms of radicalisation.

Two main problems have hindered HT's ambitions throughout the party's history: one theoretical, the other methodological. The first has been its mythological and blissful conceptionalisation of the *khilafah*. Its literature presents the *khilafah* in ahistorical, idealised terms that do not bear serious scrutiny. For all its rhetoric about presenting Islam as an intellectual alternative with ideas that are 'meticulously thought out and published in many detailed books', a close reading of its texts and examination of the ideas of its leaders reveal a striking absence of intellectual depth and political realism. This vacuity is clear in oft-repeated slogans and phrases that saturate its material with anachronistic positions on, for example, the implementation of shariah law, the social position of women, religious minorities, economics and international relations. More fundamental questions arise such as: Would a contemporary *khilafah* be modelled on the seventh century Prophetic mini city-state of Medina or Umayyad, Abbasid or Ottoman empires? How would a *khilafah* be chosen?

Is the state theocratic or democratic in its orientation? How would it be different from self-described Islamic States such as Iran or Saudi Arabia which allege to rule by the shariah?

On these questions, HT, like most other Islamist movements, offer nothing more than vague notions to increase the 'Islamic content' of state legal codes and the law-making process and implement the 'Systems of Islam' in other policy areas such as the economy, environment, science and technology and politics. Simply grafting Islamic teachings onto the features of a contemporary paradigm developed in post-Enlightenment Europe is problematic to say the least.

Its second weakness is exposed in its naïve programme for social change and capturing power. This has been demonstrated in its various unsuccessful coups, tendency to become proscribed, and history as an underground movement with marginal influence in Muslim societies. Given that HT is a fringe current among Islamic revivalist movements, how would they convince disparate Muslim theological trends to support them, let alone create practical consensus among the diverse ethnic and political interests present in the various Muslim nation states? Even if one state was established, what are the political and economic incentives that would convince more than fifty separate nations from Morocco to Malaysia to undo the post-war territorial settlements of the twentieth century? How would such a putative entity deal with the resistance it would inevitably face?

Despite these obvious pragmatic challenges, the core of HT ideology and methodology has essentially remained unchanged over the last sixty years. Constantly recalling the glory days of the *khilafah* and campaigning for its restoration has proved to be a great distraction from the challenging realities of being a Muslim in the twenty-first century. The organisation's biggest struggle remains one of relevancy. It lost its ability to shape the popular agenda in Muslim communities long ago. British Muslims, for example, are far less receptive to HT's efforts compared to twenty years ago as its radical message has grown tiresome, with most people interested in Islamic activism finding it unpersuasive. It also struggles to compete with the increasingly crowded alternatives in a rapidly changing Islamic landscape. Furthermore, Hizb ut-Tahrir has not been helped by the emergence of ISIS even though it has made efforts to distinguish its vision for a *khilafah* from that of ISIS by declaring that a rebooted Caliphate should not be secured by bloodshed and bombs.

The appeal to recreate a 'true' *khilafah* will remain a powerful symbol for Muslims. It resonates in many enclaves of the Muslim *ummah*. But like all utopias the *khilafah* is an impractical, romanticised scheme that has no counterpart in the real world.

UNRAVELLING UTOPIA

Yasmin Khan

There has always been a thin line between utopia and dystopia; If utopia is an imagined perfect place or ideal state of affairs in the social, legal and political sphere, dystopia would be its counterpart. Neither exists in pure form; in reality societies may simultaneously feature characteristics from either extremes of the spectrum or oscillate in-between. In theory, the most desirable utopias would ideally share a common ethos of peace, social justice and environmental conscientiousness, but such values are not definitive. Since there is no indisputable formula for creating a utopia, this presents a paradox – your dream might be someone else's worst nightmare. Utopian ideals tend to be underpinned by utilitarianism in order to come to fruition but this doesn't necessarily equip those ideals to be universally appealing. For instance, depending on your moral perspective, it might be tricky to square the fact that a person's Shangri-La might feature a fair dose of decadence and debauchery. Even some purported utopias exhibit aspects of bigotry, ultra-Nationalism or warfare in order to stabilise the status quo. Dystopias are drawn from our discontent about the present, stretched onto the worst imaginable scenario. In the same way as Thomas More's *Utopia* was a response to inequality he witnessed, living as he did at the epochal fault-line between medievalism and nascent merchant capitalism, contemporary utopias and dystopias are very much commentaries of the present.

The Arabic term for utopia is a*l-Madinah al-Fadilah*, meaning 'virtuous city'. In recent times though, this phrase has been somewhat subverted by Ahmed Khaled Towfik, a master of the contemporary Arabic dystopia genre. Towfik has authored and translated a plethora of popular science fiction literature while serving as a medical professor at Egypt's Tanta University. His best-selling novella is also called *Utopia*. It has been described as: 'far more convincing a depiction of a nightmarish future even than *A Clockwork Orange*'. The novella is set in 2023 on a US Marine-protected colony on the Egyptian coast, in which an elitist minority of overindulgent youth live in superficially ordered enclaves devoid of compassion towards a swarm of bitterly impoverished 'Others' living in chaotic slums outside their gated colony. Alaa, the bored rich protagonist of the novel, describes his morning routine: 'I wake up. I take a leak. Smoke a cigarette. Drink coffee. Shave. ...Have sex with the African maid. Have breakfast.' The 'Others' become voyeuristic kill-targets for sport simply to quench the boredom of the rich, culminating in a violent revolution; eerily prescient of the uprisings that subsequently emerged in Tahrir Square.

Unlike Thomas More's projection, Towfik's *Utopia* is not some far off, imagined place; it is present-day Egypt with all the dials turned up. The world of Tawfik's *Utopia*, the novelist Sofia Samatar writes:

> is an only slightly exaggerated twenty-first century Egypt, recognisable in the gap between rich and poor, the crumbling of government services, the priva-tisation of space and resources, the anger at the links between the Egyptian, American, and Israeli governments, and the yearning for revolution. The strongest aspect of the book is its depiction of the frustration of young men, both rich and poor, who have run out of options.

Today it is the Israel/Palestine conflict that provides artists with perhaps the most extreme convergence of parallel worlds. The work of artist Larissa Sansour, who was born in 1973 in Jerusalem of Palestinian parentage, focuses upon the tug-and-pull between fiction and reality: her projects, which she describes as immersed in the current political dialogue, juxtapose Middle Eastern politics against the realm of science fiction, in an attempt to find a new formula through which we can address the reality on the ground. Whilst many of us have inadvertently become desensitised by the dystopian deadlock between Palestine and Israel, Sansour's thought-experiments awaken us from our zombie states of paralysis by prompting a thorough re-examination of the status-quo from alternative parallel dimensions. In *Nation Estate* (2012), the second instalment of her sci-fi trilogy, filmmaker Sansour postulates a vertical solution to Palestine's diminishing claim to land: future citizens reside in a single colossal skyscraper, each floor embodying a Palestinian city; a contemporary equivalent to the modernist ideal of the high-rise building as a model for a future utopian society. No need for apartheid walls here, instead people can simply hop vertically between cities via an elevator which ascends through the various cities dispersed across forty-four levels, passing Jerusalem on the thirteenth floor and Ramallah on the next level, whilst a pulsating arabesque electronica soundtrack amplifies the sense of rising adrenaline. As the elevator continues to climb, the soundscape becomes increasingly ominous, reaching a crescendo as Sansour approaches Bethlehem on the twenty-first floor. Whilst the glossy hyper-technical mega-infrastructure of the building seemingly allows Palestinians to freely transgress borders using automated biometric security checks, assisted by audio broadcasts and electronic passes, the system effectively operates as a sort of glorified self-service prison. This superficial emancipation cuts right to the core of the live issue at hand: whilst the polemic scenario which Sansour constructs is deliberately absurd, it is rooted in a genuinely bizarre political situation that compels an equally subversive visual commentary, forcing us to reconsider the reality of what is going on. Sansour's fictional invention of Nation Estate offers a satirical antidote to the most controversial living dystopia on the globe, and conveys a scathing message: the creation of a mock utopia for one exclusive group of people inevitably inflicts a living nightmare on other omnipresent stakeholders, posing widespread repercussions for us all in terms of our understanding and acceptance of what makes a 'normal' lifestyle.

In her 2015 project *In the Future, They Ate From the Finest Porcelain* Sansour uses film, accompanied by a photographic and object-based installation, to explore 'the role of myth for history, fact and national identity'. In the film:

> a narrative resistance group makes underground deposits of elaborate porcelain – suggested to belong to an entirely fictional civilisation. Their aim is to influence history and support future claims to their vanishing lands. Once unearthed, this tableware will prove the existence of this counterfeit people. By implementing a myth of its own, their work becomes a historical intervention – de facto creating a nation.

As one commentary points out:

the film subtly alludes to the tactics of some Israeli groups, such the Elad Association, who make it their mission to strengthen their connection to Jerusalem through archaeological digs and excavations and to assert the longevity of their people on the land.

However, *In the Future, They Ate From the Finest Porcelain* makes no explicit mention of Israel. Sansour is pointing to a universal – that pretence, myth-making and 'the invention of tradition' is an integral part of all nation-building, including Palestinian.

Utopia lingers somewhere in the intangible liminal space between fact and fiction. Good things can emerge despite quasi-dystopian conditions. Hardship can either make you or break you. Counter-intuitively, a seemingly hostile place or set of circumstances can somehow become an incubator for creativity and productivity. Confinement can become a Citadel. For instance, forced house-arrest inflicted by Caliph Al-Hakim became the space for ibn Al-Haytham to develop his ground-breaking theories of optics in tenth century Cairo. Likewise, in the fictional realm, harsh imprisonment spurs Edmond Dantès in *The Count of Monte Cristo* to plot his subsequent 'rags to riches' revenge after making his ingenious and morbid escape.

The devastation of war can be an impetus for creativity. For instance, Iraqi writer, poet and documentary filmmaker Ahmed Saadawi constructively levered his raw insights working as journalist in Iraq to concoct an award-winning first novel. In *Frankenstein in Baghdad*, published in 2014, Saadawi transports the gothic horror of Mary Shelley's Frankenstein into the present day Iraqi capital. A destitute rag-and-bone man named Hadi Al-Attag stalks the city, collecting the human body parts scattered from different car bomb blasts which he stitches together to form a patchwork human corpse referred to as the 'what's-its-name' (*shesma*). Once the man-made monster gains sentience it embarks on a campaign to avenge each of the various bomb victims from which it/he is made. For Saadawi, raised in the Sadr City area of Baghdad, war zones have made the monstrous an everyday reality:

> fantasy is not an escape or alienation from reality. It is rather a way to reach greater depth in this reality, which is packed with fantasy as a daily behavioural and rhetorical practice, no matter how organised and logical it looks.

Or as he put it more bluntly, his Frankenstein is 'the fictional representation of the process of everyone killing everyone.' Saadawi's haunting novel is more than just a metaphor to the endless cycle of violence currently plaguing his home country. During a Sindbad Sci-Fi salon I produced at the Science Museum in 2014, the UK-based Iraqi playwright Hassan Abdulrazzak offered this compelling analysis:

> The 'what's-its-name' embodies a twisted kind of hope as its body parts consist of people from different religious backgrounds: Shia, Sunni and Christian. Such a united body of Iraqis is a utopian dream in the midst of an on-going dystopian nightmare.

Whilst the basic survival of their present remains an ongoing struggle for much of the population in the Levant region, the manifestation of technological futures is penetrating the zeitgeist in much of the Gulf, perhaps even more obsessively than in the West. What was once the pinnacle of aspirational science fiction literally seems to be blurring into a state of science fictional-fact in the Emirates' ever increasing skylines, man-made islands and cutting-edge blueprints for technological innovation.

> One of the most ancient ways of living came head-on against extreme wealth and capitalism – glass and steel against wool and camels. There's been a quantum leap and there's a temporal gap. The two things have been stitched together and there's a missing piece of history.

observes the Qatari-American artist Sophia Al-Maria, who famously coined the term 'Gulf Futurism' to encapsulate the notion of living in an existing future; a place where the highest technological advancements coexist with deeply rooted religious traditions. In her 2008 essay 'Gaze of Sci-Fi Wahabi', Al-Maria posited that the Gulf was on an 'exodus from reality', that could be fruitfully interrogated through the language of Science Fiction 'in order to "rearrive" at the place of critical engagement unrecognised and uninhibited':

> built on the retreating sands of reality and increasingly submerged in the unreal, the Gulf has become a place where individuals are forced to fracture their lives into multi-dimensional zones of illusion and reality. Squeezed by the intense hyper-pressurized conditions of life in the Gulf, by puberty young girls

have stepped into their black abayas already diamond-cut: multifaceted and many-faced. Worn veterans of poly-existence, they effortlessly navigate the complicated culturally specific binary code of public and private, truth and lies, me and you.

From Brutalism to Zaha Hadid, attempts to visually translate utopian ideals through urban landscapes and architectural design is nothing new. But the manufacture of such idealised landscapes is overshadowed by a darker side of 'progress', as social planners devise extravagant schemes while neglecting practical needs of people. Slave labour, exploitation of immigrant workforces, outer-city worker slums, punishing dissenters and the marginalisation of minority groups are all part and parcel of the incongruous reality that bulges beneath the glossy veneer.

In the 1905 utopian fable *Sultana's Dream* the tables are turned; and it is women who have the upper hand. Written by Rokeya Sakhawat Hossain, and originally published in Madras in an Indian ladies magazine, the novel is considered a classic work of feminist science fiction. Hossain was born in 1880 during the British rule in a part of the Bengal now known as Bangladesh. She was raised in an upper-class landowning Muslim family but was denied a school education as, like many women at that time, she was under strict *purdah*. She learned Arabic alongside Qur'anic studies through home tuition and was conditioned with literature on the 'proper' conduct for women. Her sympathetic brother secretly taught her Bengali and English though she primarily spoke in Urdu. She married a magistrate who proved to be a strategic supportive ally to her creative endeavours.

Deeply troubled by the social injustice inflicted on women around her, Hossain became compelled to write *Sultana's Dream* in English when she was just twenty-five years of age. The novel envisions a nation referred to as Ladyland, a technologically advanced matriarchy where the women operate in complete freedom, whilst the men who were previously busy increasing their military power are now secluded to the *madana* – a play on the Urdu word *zenana* (women's quarters) resulting in a harmonious crime free society. Scientific research underpins the system; while the men cook, clean and care for children, technological advancements are driven by the women which include air travel, an instrument to collect heat from the sun for mass distribution, and a university enterprise that draws water directly from the atmosphere using a network of suspended pipes, that are also used to control the weather and prevent storms.

Hossain went on to be a staunch advocate for social reform, setting up her own girls school to drive change which still survives today, along with other educational establishments named after her in honour of her legacy. Hossain's erudite ability to subvert dominant discourses through fiction and then extrapolate her vision into real action beyond the margins is a testimony to the power of her ideas that had liberty and equality at its heart. *Sultana's Dream* was published a decade before American writer Charlotte Perkins Gilman produced the novella *Herland*, about an isolated society made up only of women who reproduce via pathogenesis. Unlike *Herland*, Hossain's fictional vision does not eliminate the existence of men, and yet the notion that any group of people must become downtrodden in order to vindicate another group is inherently troubling. There is no disguising the fact that the aspirational feminist utopia is also an unapologetic dystopian vision for the men in her story. Hossain's husband, upon reading it, affectionately concluded the tale was a 'terrible revenge'. Arguably it was this inherent imbalance, amongst the other salient points, that Hossain sought to expose through her written parody.

Alas, the patriarchy Hossain subverted in *Sultana's Dream* has yet to abate. A feminist rhetoric in Saudi Arabia has recently emerged through a viral music video featuring women on skateboards singing 'God rid us of men' – a derisory dialectic that is symptomatic of the continuing battle for gender equality. Meanwhile, dreary predictions now begin to percolate in the West of an automated future for humanity: sex robots, robot-human marriages and robot nurses for the elderly. A perfect dream or sentimental nightmare?

Should we conclude that utopian pathways are a divergence from these real problems we face? After all, the flip-side – fictional dystopias – have proved to have influenced the direction of contemporary counter-cultures and the subsequent morphing of societal norms to a far greater extent than existing traditions of utopian thinking. For instance, robots, Big Brother and the cybersphere are amongst many of the dystopian sci-fi artefacts that have become embedded into our contemporary lexicon. The rise of the surveillance-state in and of itself is a disconcerting parody of a dystopia. Perhaps it was easier to imagine or hope for a better place when the world was unmapped and we knew less. The notion of 'euchronia' – imagining better futures – emerged later in the eighteenth century as utopias moved from No Place to a possible future time and place. These utopian visions had far greater expectations of a better life – it was about liberating us from oppression.

In comparison, the current trajectories for the future seem rather feeble and lacklustre. We have scaled back on what we think utopias should be. Now we self-construct miniaturised microcosms to revolve around ourselves. We seem to have given up on ideological utopianism and outsourced it onto technological ideas of progress. Now freedom is creating your own online avatar and accessing any choice of content with the click of a finger. Yet deep down we know this ability to self-curate virtual utopias merely offers us a temporary escape from the hyper-realism of our current predicament.

Perhaps we need to simultaneously combine the spirit of utopia and dystopia through striving to establish optimal conditions that enables us to be the best we can be, whilst accepting we might not always succeed. The two must co-exist side by side. Without failure how can we appreciate perfection when we see it? Fragments of utopian visions can eventually bear fruit, others may prove futile, but if we can continue to flex our imagination we stand a better chance to succeed in cultivating a better world.

THE NEVER-ENDING JOURNEY

Colin Tudge

We can never reach Utopia – the name means 'no place' – but it's a fine ideal to keep in sight. Life perhaps should be seen as one long pilgrimage with perfection – 'Utopia' – as its goal. Progress towards Utopia ought to be what 'progress' really means.

But although all governments talk of progress, Utopia seems to recede. Wealth is increasing and technologies grow smarter but the wealth and the know-how seem largely or mainly to reinforce the status quo, with the rich growing richer while the poor grow poorer and the Earth as a whole runs down. We need, wholesale, to change our ways – what we do, how we organise our affairs, what we think, our preconceptions, and our attitudes (for attitude in the end is all, or at least is the *sine qua non*). We need in short a transformation; metamorphosis; nothing less than a Renaissance.

This sounds like a very tall order and so it is. But the agenda, the things we need most urgently to think about and act upon, can be summarised in a simple diagram.

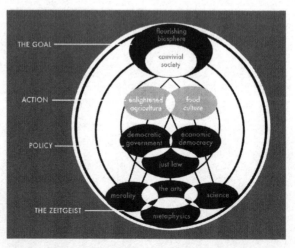

The subjects in most need of attention are shown here as balloons – eleven of them, all interlinked, and arranged in four tiers. The top tier shows what I suggest should be our Goals if Utopia is to mean anything worthwhile: convivial societies within a flourishing biosphere. The next tier down, labelled Actions, should include everything that we do, day to day: health care, building, transport, education, and all the rest. Here I am focusing on food and farming – enlightened agriculture a.k.a. real farming, complemented by true food culture – because they above all are the things we really need to get right (and in practice are getting most wrong). Tier 3, Infrastructure, includes the way we organise our affairs – through governance, the economy, and law. Tier 4, supporting all the rest, here labelled Zeitgeist, 'the spirit of the age', includes all those grand ideas that shape the way we think, and indeed shape our attitudes to other people, to our fellow creatures, and to the Earth itself. These I take to include morality and science, both of which are rooted firmly (did we but realise it) in metaphysics. Finally, the arts shape our worldview perhaps more than anything else. Artists of all kinds are the jokers in the pack, inviting us to look at the world afresh and to question all our presuppositions. Communities and indeed entire nations base their whole lives on mythologies which, in practice, are largely constructed by creative artists: the painters of the Italian Renaissance; Nietzsche; Wagner; Sir Walter Scott; George Orwell; Bob Dylan and John Lennon.

It's important to re-think the contents of all of those balloons but equally important are the lines that connect each balloon to every other balloon. We need to look at every topic from every point of view, which gives us a kaleidoscopic overview of reality. But then we must go one step further and look at every point of view from every other point of view. Seeing every point of view from every other point of view brings us as nearly as we can to a holistic view of reality.

So let's look at some of the ideas within the balloons.

The Goal

We begin by spelling out what we are trying to achieve – 'convivial societies within a flourishing biosphere'. These days the world's most powerful governments don't seem to think this is necessary – unless we count Trump's vague but chilling promise to 'make America great again'. Britain's last seven governments (starting with Thatcher), drawn from all the major parties, have simply focused above all on 'economic growth', meaning year-by-year increase in the weird and fanciful notion of 'Gross Domestic Product' or GDP: the sum total of all the wealth that has been created (or deemed to have been created) by us all for doing whatever we do – building hospitals, making bombs, cutting hair, or digging holes and filling them in again. GDP is supposed to be increased by 'competing' on the neoliberal 'global market'. The market is supposed to be open to everybody but in the absence of regulation (for 'deregulation' is equated with freedom and seen therefore as the greatest good) it is dominated by corporates and wildly distorted by the machinations of bankers. No account is taken of the means by which wealth is produced, or what it is used for, or whose hands it finishes up in. Materialism rules, of course. Wealth is the sole measure of success. Prime ministers may pay lip service to other values – David Cameron even spoke of 'compassion' while he and his chancellor railed against people on income benefit – which, outside the House of Commons, would properly be acknowledged as incitement to hatred, among the vilest of crimes. Cameron promised too to be 'green' although his government resisted all serious green measures unless forced by the EU. New PM Theresa May makes no claims to greenness, which again is chilling, but at least is honest.

But if our new Renaissance is to get anywhere then we must spell out, upfront, what we want to achieve. 'Convivial' means literally 'living together' and implies those qualities that seem to have gone missing: harmony; justice; equality – akin to the French revolutionary 'liberty, equality, fraternity'. Conviviality requires the best possible balance between the need for personal fulfilment (fulfilment is a far better concept than mere 'happiness') and the equal need to respect and serve the whole community and all humankind. Concern for the community is an exercise both in altruism and in self-interest. For most people, a harmonious and just society is their most valuable asset. Taxes, well spent on the public good and the good of the biosphere, should be our best investment.

'Flourishing biosphere' implies a world in which a maximal variety of other creatures live according to their individual lights, evolving in their own sweet ways. Note 'biosphere' meaning 'living world' – our fellow creatures and their habitats – not 'environment', which literally means 'surroundings': stage scenery; real estate. The biosphere must be valued as God's creation (even if you don't believe in God), of which we are a part. Other creatures should be seen as family. The fabric of the world must be seen to be sacred, even though it may be necessary at times to dig into it. The fashionable concept of 'ecosystem services' might sometimes be useful but as a general guide to attitude and action it is seriously inadequate.

Action

'Action' should include every practical thing that we do: health and social care; education; building, including architecture; engineering of all kinds. We ought to focus on food and farming first because agriculture above all is the *sine qua non*. A shut-down of farming even for a few weeks would kill almost all of us. Agriculture occupies a third of all the land on Earth including the bulk of the most fertile land. The world's national parks, ostensibly dedicated to wildlife, are mostly in uplands and other such places where farming is difficult or impossible (and most wild animals find them difficult too). Farming is by far the world's biggest employer. And so on.

But modern agriculture comes in two contrasting guises which, despite claims from the ruling oligarchs, are largely incompatible. The kind that is now beginning to prevail, with the full backing of the oligarchs and helped by taxpayers' money, is anomalously called 'conventional'. In line with the dictats of the neoliberal, 'free'-market economy farming is seen as 'a business like any other' while business has been reconceived as the means to maximise wealth. While oil is still available and affordable and so long as workers require to be paid it is cheapest – most profitable – to replace farm labour and the skill that goes with it with machines and industrial chemistry, and to call this 'progress'. The collateral damage is enormous – to societies, to all Earth's habitats, to wildlife, and indeed to the climate – but the damage, including the social damage, is largely left uncosted, and so the illusion is maintained that what can properly be called 'neoliberal-industrial' (NI) agriculture is 'efficient' and truly of economic benefit (though in truth it benefits only a few). Big machines need big spaces to work in and agrochemicals are best bought in bulk to achieve economies of scale; so NI farms are encouraged to be bigger and bigger, employing fewer and fewer people. Farming that relies on big machines with minimum or zero labour must be kept simple, so NI agriculture tends to be monocultural – wheat and maize as far as the eye can see, pigs in units a million-strong. The dispossessed farmers and their dependents retreat to urban slums – which, worldwide, are now providing shelter of a kind for a billion people, or so the UN estimates.

The alternative kind we call 'Enlightened Agriculture', aka 'Real Farming', and is designed expressly to provide everyone who is ever likely to be born with food of the highest standards, without cruelty or injustice and without wrecking the rest of the world. Centuries of experience and a growing dossier of modern science tell us that farming that is truly 'sustainable' and resilient should be as diverse as possible (mixed in species and genetically), and low-input – as far as possible, organic. Mixed organic farms are complex and so must be skills-intensive. Enterprises that are complex and skills-intensive benefit little from scale-up, so enlightened farms should generally be small to medium-sized. All in all, the kind of farms the world really needs are the complete opposite of the kind the oligarchs are now seeking to make the norm.

Critics of the enlightened approach say that small mixed farms could not possibly feed the world – but in truth, though they receive no support (and indeed are actively done down), they still feed 70 per cent of the world's people. More and more studies are showing, too, that small mixed organic farms can be more productive per unit area than the industrial kind, at least on average over a decade or so. We are told too that food produced from small farms would be too dear – but this is yet another alternative fact. For instance, 80 per cent of what we spend on industrial food in supermarkets goes to the supermarket and the rest of the food chain. The system looks economically 'efficient' only because the economy is designed to favour it. All in all nothing justifies the switch from traditional mixed farms to high-tech monocultures except the desire and the perceived need to maximise wealth – and to concentrate that wealth in fewer and fewer hands.

Food culture is the necessary complement to enlightened farming. People who truly appreciate good food demand good farming!

The infrastructure

To underpin good action of whatever kind we need sympathetic governance – people in charge who know good things when they see them and help good things happen; an appropriate economy; and just law. All are seriously awry in the modern world, as illustrated all too clearly by Britain.

Governance must for starters be democratic. As Winston Churchill said, democracy is the worst form of government except for all the others. Yet increasingly we are dominated by oligarchies that are anything but democratic – compounded of (partly elected) government, the corporates, the banks, and more and more of the once-independent academe that now, by government decree, depends more and more on corporate funding. Democracy implies among other things that the government is on our side. But the oligarchies largely come across as self-serving, self-perpetuating power groups narrowly focused on the concentration of wealth and power, as the growth of industrial agriculture very well illustrates.

Economics really does need re-thinking from first principles. It is conceived, and taught, as a game of money, as if its sole purpose was to increase and deploy wealth. In truth, the economy forms the matrix of our lives, the mechanisms by which we may translate our aspirations into action. Economists must have moral awareness, or they cannot know what they should be trying to achieve. They must be ecologically aware for if we simply focus on short-term wealth then we will wreck the world, as indeed is happening before our eyes. It is possible to devise economic models that do strike the right balance between individual aspiration and the needs of society – notably that of 'green economic democracy', designed to deploy fairly 'conventional' financial mechanisms for social ends (as in social enterprise, ethical investment, and so on), and also serve the biosphere. Again, the present, neoliberal economy, geared exclusively to material wealth come what may, leads us towards the complete opposite of what we really need, and what most people want. Coupled with uncritical technophilia, it threatens to kill us all.

We need good law. It should provide what Thomas Hobbes called 'the Leviathan' – the irresistible force that is greater than any one person or any one community and ensures that villains do not get out of hand. Good law and law enforcers save us from the need to carry swords or cudgels (depending on social class) and to wreak personal vengeance when we are wronged, and so start endless vendettas. But as all serious thinkers have been saying for thousands of years, the law must be impartial, dealing fairly with everyone, and right now, especially as corporates claim more and more 'rights', it doesn't look that way. Law that truly dispenses justice is vital but, like democracy (and utopia), it remains elusive.

The Zeitgeist

Science is wonderful and necessary – but again has been horribly misconstrued and seriously corrupted. It is not, as the modern myth has it, and as so many scientists apparently believe, the royal road to omniscience. The high technologies to which it gives rise are not the road to omnipotence. We must support good science but also recognise its limitations. The whole society, too, must recognise that scientists are human and corruptible. To force them to accept corporate funding (because, increasingly, there is no other) is intrinsically corrupting and, very demonstrably in many contexts (not least in farming) has indeed led to corruption.

In short, scientists and those who control it, need to understand the philosophy of science and have true concern for society and be politically aware. But scientists, alas, are too often 'trained' within their own particular bubble, and brought up to believe that they are special, and party to the truth. The 'high' technologies that emerge from science are taken as symbols of progress whether or not they improve the lot of humanity or the biosphere. Science construed with due humility and with true awareness of the world at large is one of humanity's greatest assets. Science without self-awareness and the technophilia to which it gives rise is perhaps our greatest threat.

Moral philosophy should be high on all core curricula. Again it is horribly misconstrued. The Enlightenment concept of utilitarianism prevails: 'greatest happiness of the greatest number'. But it matters who is made happy and for what reasons. Bear-baiting makes some people happy while one bear is miserable – but does that make it good? Too often too, utilitarian ethics emerges simply as an exercise in cost-effectiveness. Many appeal instead to 'deontological' ethics where good is conceived as carrying out orders from on high. This isn't all bad (if the giver of orders is an all-wise, beneficent God) but all too easily it manifests simply as 'loyalty' to whoever is in charge, to the corporate boss or to some political party. Deontological ethics with no other guidelines gave rise to the infamous Nuremberg defence: 'I was only obeying orders'.

The form of morality that really stands up is that of 'virtue ethics'. Critics say that we cannot 'objectively' decide what the virtues ought to be – but here we can appeal, in an essentially democratic style, to humanity itself. The great religions, which to a significant extent encapsulate the collective wisdom of their respective societies, all agree on the three prime virtues: compassion, humility, and a sense of reverence for the biosphere. The greatest of these, as the Dalai Lama stresses, is compassion.

Virtue ethics really can carry the day. If all of us strive to be personally humble, and humanity as a whole does not put itself above the rest and treat other creatures and the Earth as 'natural resources' and as chattels and indeed regards them with reverence; and if we treat other people and all other creatures with compassion; then there is hope for the world. This is where the focus now needs to be. There is always scope for more science and of course technology is vital but we have enough already to carry us through. The urgent need now is to bring the necessary virtues to the centre-stage.

Finally, under Zeitgeist, is metaphysics. Metaphysics literally means 'beyond physics' and it addresses what many have called 'the ultimate questions'. The first of these, I suggest, is 'What is the universe really like?'; and metaphysics, unlike science, throws the net wide and acknowledges the essential concept of transcendence – that there may be more to the universe than meets the eye, or ever can meet the eye – which is the idea that lies at the heart of all religions. The second ultimate question is 'What is good?' which embraces the whole of moral philosophy but also asks what difference it makes to include a sense of transcendence. Thirdly metaphysics asks, 'How do we know what's true?' – and in contrast to conventional epistemology it focuses largely on intuition which in its extreme form leads us to mysticism.

The fourth and final question is 'How come?' Thus, scientists may finally conclude that the whole universe is compounded from superstrings and some already claim that superstrings explain everything. But still we need to ask – how come there are such things as superstrings? How did they come into being? How come they have the qualities they do? The question 'How come?' belongs exclusively to metaphysics and is of course unanswerable, but demands to be addressed nonetheless. We need in the cause of humility to be reminded of our own incognisance.

Metaphysics lives on in all religions but there it is entwined with the various theologies. Fair enough – but it also needs to be disentangled. Indeed, some suggest that the loss of metaphysics from general discourse and education is the single greatest cause of the world's ills. It implies that most of us these days never get round to discussing the biggest of all life's questions. We are, as aeroplane pilots are wont to say, flying on instruments, guided by algorithms, and most of us, including or especially those with wealth and power, have no clear idea what they are trying to achieve and why – except more wealth and power. We really do need to re-think – starting with an idea of what we really want in life. Perfection – Utopia – will always be out of reach but perhaps, as Robert Louis Stevenson suggested, it is better to travel in hope than it is to arrive.

CANCER: KEY TO UTOPIA

Naomi Foyle

Last year I had cancer. Receiving the diagnosis was the worst experience of my life, yet after the shock subsided and I accepted the necessity of treatment, the six months of my illness became a kind of utopia: both a 'no place' in which I learned to live with uncertainty, and a land of love and miracles: the weight of a decades-long depression lifted, estranged relationships healed, and physically I had 'a complete response' to chemotherapy – my tumour disappeared, and minor surgery revealed no trace of disease in my affected breast or lymph nodes. With impeccable festive timing, I was pronounced All Clear on 23 December. Now, many celebrations and a month later, even though a decade of follow-up treatment lies ahead of me, I cannot wish that I had never been ill. Motivated to eat well and exercise more, grateful for every blessing life has granted me, and closer to the universal power I call Spirit, I feel healthier and happier than I have for years. It's possible, in fact, that cancer was the best thing to ever happen to me.

Yet, in a more common post-op patient reaction, I also see the frightening shadow of the disease everywhere I look. In the tactful euphemism of Cancer Research UK, one in two people in the developed world 'will be affected by cancer'– though if half of us get the disease who will remain unaffected? And that's not the half of it. Although it's a suspect cliché, I can't help but feel that the world itself has cancer: in the systemic, destructive, lethal growth of the disease I see also the nihilistic spread of global capital and its grave threat to the biosphere. My own peculiarly positive experience, though, leads me to believe that both the alarming statistic and the controversial metaphor can be turned to advantage. In fact, if any achievable paradise on earth must incorporate the existential realities of illness, mortality and conflict, cancer could be the key to utopia.

The thesis is eminently debatable, of course. Right at the outset of 'Illness as Metaphor', her magisterial critique of cancer myths, Susan Sontag famously declares that: 'the most truthful way of regarding illness – and the healthiest way of being ill – is one most purified of, resistant to, metaphoric thinking'. And although elsewhere she qualified her stern embargo, Sontag is, in many ways, right. As a patient I too rejected the aggressive rhetoric of the 'war on cancer', with its implication that to die is to be a 'loser', having flubbed the most important battle of your life. The punitive notion of a 'cancer personality' is abhorrent, as are the historical uses of the social trope: the Nazis, Sontag points out, described Jews as a cancer requiring 'radical' treatment. The dangers, as well as the misrepresentations, are real. In the essay collection *Becoming Earth*, Alaskan marine biologist Eva Saulitis, who died of breast cancer in 2016, rejected battle imagery with the quiet statement: 'Cancer is indifferent, not malicious. It is not mean or evil, no more so than a tsunami or hurricane. It's a force of nature, unleashed from some unknown point of origin.' That's absolutely true, but still, that 'unleashed', and the negative simile with giant waves and storms, betray the imagination's craving to understand through comparisons. Cancer's very name is a metaphor – the ancient Greeks saw a resemblance between a tumour's blood vessels to the pincers of a crab (*karkinos*; or *cancer* in Latin) – while to speak of Sontag's towering intellect bolsters the argument that language is inherently figurative. Metaphor per se is not the problem, I believe, but rather the false and negative myths that grow up around disease.

Sontag herself concluded that when cancer becomes more curable 'it may then be possible to compare something to a cancer without implying either a fatalistic diagnosis or a rousing call to fight by any means whatever a lethal insidious enemy'. She predicted, however, that, stripped of such sensationalism, 'the cancer metaphor will be made obsolete', and although later, in *Aids and its Metaphors*, she concurred that 'all thinking is interpretation', she resolutely maintained that it is 'still sometimes correct to be 'against' interpretation.' But now, nearly forty years after the first publication of 'Illness as Metaphor', when 25 per cent of cancer patients survive, and incidence is 50 per cent of the population of the industrialised world, it seems that people are not 'purifying' their language of figurative devices, but instead are searching for new and improved images for the illness: metaphors that better reflect patient experience, and allow for meaningful reflections on mortality. Thus 'the war' is giving way to 'the journey' – in fact, a voyage we embark upon at birth. For cancer travels with us from the beginning, an inherent aspect of life. After her cancer returns Saulitis is haunted by a glut of dying salmon in the woods, the fish expiring naturally in a stink of rot and ammonia after spawning; her sensitive but unsentimental observations provoking Kent Meyers to note, 'Only a wildlife biologist could see in that stream the charged and lovely overflow of life that made it, and see also that the cancer inside her is of the same remarkable wildness.' So too, is the urban world: Simeon Nelson, creator of *Anarchy in the Organism*, a public art project exploring cancer from the perspective of complexity theory, created delicate drawings that 'make an explicit analogy between tumour growth and the growth of a town into the countryside' – and also between cancer treatment and ecological balance. Prime instigator of this new normative perception of the disease is oncologist and author Siddhartha Mukherjee, who, in his landmark cultural history *The Emperor of All Maladies: A Biography of Cancer*, finds an energetic, non-martial language to convey his brilliant central insight: cancer is a force of *human* nature, he contends, cancer cells 'hyperactive, survival-endowed, scrappy, fecund, inventive copies of ourselves'. Although, honouring Sontag, he insists, 'But this is not a metaphor', the Magritte allusion, calling into question any straightforward relationship between language and the world, undermines this claim; as do his adjectives, which connote both children and the 'demonic pregnancy' Sontag identified as yet another facet of the cancer myth. She cites St Jerome, but the association is inscribed in the very heavens, where in the Western zodiac the sign of the Crab represents tenacity, loyalty, motherhood and family. Are these associations truly baneful? Now that cancer no longer implies certain death, but a long, arduous treatment in which loved ones and communities participate, could this 'Queen Crab' represent the determined effort of care the disease demands?

Even allowing the use of metaphor, though, it may still be hard to see cancer as a source of human harmony. Cancer is a ravaging, still usually fatal disease. I was extremely fortunate to develop a treatable variety – 'cancer-lite', if you like – but although great medical advances have been made, no-one who is 'affected by' cancer, myself included, escapes suffering. As Mukherjee observes, cancer drives the body to 'the edge of a physiological abyss', and in its indiscriminate race to kill growing cells, chemotherapy often tips the patient over the edge. Despite doctors' best efforts to haul them out again, half of all cancer patients die within ten years of diagnosis, as most probably will I should my disease return: secondary breast cancer is still incurable. Given this dire situation, the military metaphor is in some ways justifiable: I am sure many patients experience their illness as an 'enemy within' that must be stamped out, while as Mukherjee explains, the American national research drive launched in the nineteen fifties, was called the 'War on Cancer' to encourage the type of 'direct, targeted research' performed by necessity during actual wars. Gradually, with the development of ever more toxic and expensive drugs, the disease has also become the site of an epic socio-political conflict between the medical establishment and alternative practitioners, often misconstrued as a war between reason and faith. Finally, to zoom out, curing the illness, as Ziauddin Sardar has noted, is not of huge importance to the developing world, where people are far more likely to die of diarrhoea from dirty water. Though Sontag's renowned aphorism 'everyone who is born holds dual citizenship, in the kingdom of the well and the kingdom of the sick' has the ring of great truth, to contend that cancer is a passport to global harmony might well seem sick. Even should the interrelated catastrophes of climate change, Trumputinism, Brexit, European neo-fascism, global neoliberalism, Zionism and the war in Syria represent an advanced form of the disease, perhaps it is terminal.

These objections, however, ultimately only reinforce my point. It is precisely because cancer presents such a complex, traumatic and still largely intractable challenge to human health that it demands a 'complete response' from societies affected by it. In turn, these wealthy countries could be morally transformed by their new priorities. In its psychological, biological, social, environmental, political and spiritual dimensions, cancer is a skeleton key to the future: fitted to the right locks, it has the potential to heal a great number of related ills. Let me explore this utopian vision through the prisms of the three 'miracles' wrought by my cancer experience: my psychological, physical and spiritual cures.

*****

Cancer might not be malicious, but psychologically it is generous in the time it gives people to prepare for death, or the possibility of it. In that often tragically foreshortened space profound personal decisions can be taken, states of despair transformed into gratitude and acceptance, long-standing hostilities resolved in forgiveness. All this was my experience, but far from being a result of my physical cure, my conviction that cancer can help heal the world was seeded when I did not know the stage of my own illness. In a light-filled moment, with the gentle force of an epiphany, a day after diagnosis my chronic depression and anxiety began to lift, a process that shows no sign of abating.

This change is to me, still, astonishing. Beset by night fears as a child, and enduring a turbulent adolescence scarred by three suicide attempts, over the subsequent decades I had settled into a coping relationship with unreliable mental health, seeking counselling when things got too difficult, and finding a sense of purpose through my involvement with creative, political and faith communities, including my Palestinian activism and growing interest in Islam. I worked hard and achieved success in some areas. Still, I was not as strong as I perhaps appeared to be. To relax, I drank wine; too much wine, I knew, rarely taking days off. In 2015 I went through another bad patch, convinced I would never find emotional or financial stability. Dark thoughts sometimes entered my mind. One evening I told friends that I was not expecting to outlive my mother, who died from colon cancer at fifty-two. And though I had vowed after my teenage trauma never again to try and take my own life, that year I wrote a cathartic poem, 'The Co-Pilot', in which the suicidal speaker courts 'a welcome diagnosis of cancer'. I felt ashamed of the poem, not least for its relation to a real-life tragedy, but writing it did help me identify the 'death drive' as just one aspect of my psyche. My rational and loving nature, I comforted myself, was captaining the plane, would get all the passengers home safely.

So I flew on, writing, teaching and travelling. On my return from Toronto in May 2016 I discovered a lump in my left breast. Oddly perhaps, I didn't panic. My mother had had cysts removed in her late thirties, and I assumed I had inherited that predisposition. But it wasn't a cyst. At the clinic for a biopsy I worried about whether or not to cancel my trip to Prague, where I was due to teach a summer Creative Writing course. I was told to get the results when I returned; that the worst case scenario was a lumpectomy. This wasn't exactly reassuring. I left home to realise a cherished fantasy of working in a European capital, all the while balancing on the edge of a chasm. In Prague I bought a notebook inscribed with an Einstein quote: 'Life is like riding a bicycle: To keep your balance you have to keep moving.' It became a dream journal, recording positive symbolism of open roads, glasses of water and lobsters; but in it I also wrote a poem accepting the possibility my breast was harbouring 'a death star'. Another physicist offers an image of my state of mind at the time, if you can call an invisible cat an image. Trapped in a box with a radioactive particle that would inevitably at some point decay, triggering the release of a fatal poison, until the lid was lifted Shrödinger's cat was infamously (and ridiculously in Shrödinger's mind – his *gedankenexperiment* was designed to critique a branch of quantum physics) both dead and alive. Pre-diagnosis, I remained, like that indeterminate feline, suspended in a state of impossible simultaneity: wandering the ravishing streets of Prague, in full view and undeniably alive, but feeling both in glorious health and terminally ill.

In fact I had cancer. In the end I was summoned home early for the results of my biopsies: two diseased lymph nodes and a large, fast-growing breast tumour – too large for a lumpectomy. Unless chemotherapy could shrink it, I would need a mastectomy, while my lymph nodes would have to be 'cleared' – all thirty under the arm removed – putting me at risk of lymphodema, a chronic, painful swelling of the limb. In the meantime, my liver and lungs would have to be tested as soon as possible, in case the disease had spread. My friend who attended the diagnosis with me, said I took the news calmly, but in fact I was paralytic in the midst of a slow-motion avalanche assaulting me from all directions, the news simultaneously a complete shock – I'd been expecting colon cancer – the fulfilment of a long-known prophecy, and also a verdict: a punishment for drinking too much alcohol, for writing that poem and inviting this disease, for failing, failing, failing to take proper care of myself. Although I was beautifully cushioned by friends that afternoon, once alone in my bedroom at midnight my heart imploded in my chest. I'd given myself cancer, ruined my own life, why couldn't I just stop breathing now?

I was also terrified. Fear gripped my guts all night and long into the next day. It didn't help that I had to get up at four a.m. to catch a bus to Heathrow. Exhausted, incapable of eating, my stomach cramped with dread and guilt, yet determined to finish the course I was teaching, I hauled myself back to Prague via Frankfurt, all airports still beset by storms. Finally seated on my connecting flight, I hunted in my cabin bag for the Einstein notebook – and as I opened the pages on the seatback tray table and uncapped my pen, the fear clutching my ribs suddenly dissolved. It was a radiant moment: for a few minutes I didn't know what to think.

Finally, I wrote a short entry, remarking 'So it is possible not to feel fear', noting how much water I was drinking, and expressing gratitude to the friends who'd seen me through the diagnosis. Looking back, I see how those lines planted the seeds of my eventual growth spurt in resilience. Although I'd believed intellectually for years in 'the optimism of the will', cancer taught me in the space of a day what I hadn't fully emotionally internalised after decades of counselling: that fear of the future and anguish over the past were corroding my ability to enjoy the present and shape a desirable life – and are not inevitable responses to misfortune. As to why my dread dissolved with the raising of my pen, after one cancelled and three delayed flights in two days, I am sure that making my Frankfurt connection released a certain amount of tension, but I also believe that my life-long commitment to writing has given me internal resources I can only describe as subconscious. It strikes me now that my epiphany occurred while I was on a plane: I might not have felt 'in the captain's seat', but the life-force, like an auto-pilot, over-rode the 'co-pilot' of my morbid poem.

Or perhaps Einstein was right. Returning to Prague, though a marathon, was a good idea: remarkably my mood remained buoyant and my journal describes the following day as 'perfect'. I had also come back to attend a concert of Beethoven's *Eroica* with a Czech friend, and take full advantage of my seven day ticket to visit the Jewish Quarter. Accomplishing these things gave me a sense of control over my life, and also reminded me that each day offers so much to be grateful for. Relishing the balmy weather, discovering Beethoven's tender and playful sides, seeing in the Moorish tilework of the Spanish Synagogue a symbol of co-existence between Islam and Judaism, I felt a heightened sense of the present, sheer joy at simply being alive. More soberly, visiting the Holocaust memorials and museums in the synagogues strengthened my awareness of just how fortunate I was: not a victim of centuries of persecution, remembered only in an inscription of the annihilated, but a citizen with the (then) right to travel and work in Europe, about to receive thousands of pounds worth of free medical care, and a person who, in my various writings, had already created a fulsome record of myself. Although I was experiencing panic attacks, waking up with a racing heart, in those post-diagnosis days in Prague I came to perhaps an obvious conclusion, one clear to any person of faith though I had never felt the truth of it so strongly before: no-one knows what tomorrow will bring, and the best response to uncertainty is to focus on the gifts of the present.

Eventually though, I had to return home, irrevocably altered by a life-threatening illness, and the process of strengthening my new resolve took a little more time. Uncertainty in the period leading up to the CT and MRI lung and liver scans was not always an elegant flickering shadow-cat. I had low points again, in particular dwelling on the possible side effects of my treatment – the thought of permanent heart damage, 'burning soles', tinnitus or lymphoedema frightened me terribly, as did the prospects of mastectomy and metastasis. But I also understood that my anguish at having developed cancer was a sure sign that I wanted to live. Considering my past relationship with suicide, this, I knew, was a real advance, a solid foundation on which to build a healthier state of mind that would stand me in good stead for the rest of my life, however long that might be. I was also encouraged by the enormous amount of support available to cancer patients. Partly my depression continued to lift because my vulnerability was no longer a secret I had to hide. Suddenly, I didn't have to convince anyone that I needed help: counselling and hypnotherapy, dietary advice, adventure holidays, pampering sessions, massage, holistic retreats were all being thrown me, free of charge, by the NHS and various charities. I grasped as many of these life-ropes as I could.

Counselling and hypnotherapy helped reinforce my epiphany on the plane, driving home the insight that the past is not a prison or a graveyard but a set of experiences we can choose to learn from. This sense of choice has become very real to me. I now understand anxiety and depression as negative thought patterns I might experience at times, but can decide to identify with or not. Naturally, I would not have greeted Stage Four cancer with elation, but having had time to reflect on my condition, I approached that particular oncological consultation in a far calmer frame of mind than previous appointments. Fortunately the scans confirmed that the cancer had not spread. What I knew by then, though, was that the result didn't matter. Whatever stage the disease had reached, I would have to respond in the same way: by living as well as possible. The gifts cancer had already given me, of love, friendship and a vivid sense of the day's potential, would have increased in intensity had I been terminally ill, and I believe I would have made peace with that outcome. Quite quickly, the experience of having cancer had helped me move from abject despair to a more robust sense of resilience than I had ever before thought possible to achieve.

I am, I know, atypical. Being 'cured' of depression by cancer is not a common outcome. One does not have to ascribe to the ancient Greek belief that both conditions were caused by 'black bile', to understand that, for many people a cancer diagnosis triggers depression, or worsens existing mental health problems. But studies at Columbia University have shown that about 10 per cent of people with clinical depression stop feeling depressed when diagnosed with a life-threatening illness. I was one of these. I can't claim I will never feel depressed again but so far it remains true that having cancer has vastly improved my mental health. As to why, I know the reasons are complex. I quit drinking the day of my diagnosis, and, as much as possible during chemotherapy, started exercising more, both changes proven to help lift mood. But resilience also has a social cause. According to Prof David Westley, associate professor of psychology at Middlesex University, this minority response might be because some people 'diagnosed with cancer or something of that sort...seek out and accept support from family and friends, as they did not before'. That is certainly true of me. Although having cancer revealed inner resources I didn't know I had, it also provoked me, normally reluctant to reach out when I felt low, to request help from others. Shortly after my diagnosis I emailed my social network asking for specific kinds of assistance, from mangos to country drives, a red flag to which eventually even Facebook acquaintances responded with a wealth of practical and moral support. It was an incredible, humbling and nurturing outpouring of love. I know absolutely that had I gone through treatment alone I could not have thrived in the way that I did.

****

In its binary construction, Susan Sontag's clarion (if begrudging) metaphor of the Two Kingdoms does not place illness and death at the centre of civic life. As the great advances in cancer treatment demonstrate, however, when human intelligence is focused, even in a politically circumscribed way, on public health, incredible medical advances can be made. My physical miracle, the complete disappearance of a highly aggressive form of breast cancer, was the result of a breakthrough in cancer research: the development of Herceptin, the first targeted drug for some kinds of breast, oesophageal and stomach cancer. Highly effective against tumours that contain a large amount of HER-2 (human epidermal growth factor receptor), and, unlike chemo, not a danger to healthy cells, Herceptin is expensive. Previously approved by the NHS only for secondary breast cancer, in 2006 Herceptin was made widely available after a court case brought by a woman in the early stages of the disease. Breast cancer is sometimes called a 'sexy cancer', as if topless women unfairly attract a disproportionate amount of research, but this does a grave disservice to the countless women who, as recounted in *The Emperor of All Maladies*, fought long and hard – some dying in the process – to get access to life-saving drugs. Siddhartha Mukherjee also describes Big Pharma's reluctance to invest in rare cancers unlikely to recoup costs; breast cancer in fact gets attention for being common as muck. Here in the UK cancer research and treatment is funded to a large extent by charities: naively, I was shocked to see donor plaques on many of the chairs and 'ice-cap' machines (used to help prevent hair loss) in my NHS chemo ward. Am I really a utopian dreamer to wish for the Kingdoms of the Well and the Sick to be reunified and reformed, into a Mortal Republic in which governments focus on health not war, a world where research into all illnesses will be amply funded, every sick person will get the best possible treatment, and sustainable communities will care for each other and the planet?

Clearly, yes. For the world has cancer, and a very difficult case of it. Abandoning all deference to Sontag, Mukherjee argues that cancer is the iconic disease of modernity: the rapidly multiplying abnormal cell, he claims, is a 'desperate individualist … a phenomenally successful invader and coloniser … in part because it exploits the very features that make us successful as a species or an organism'. It's a convincing image. At this stage in human history we still, as a species, largely behave as if the only successes that matter are those achieved by the aggressive domination of other people and the natural environment. Just like cancer, the neoliberal world order pursues untrammelled growth. Just like cancer, which evolves, generating drug-resistant mutant clones of itself, global capitalism outwits and co-opts resistance – every activist has a smartphone, powered by toxic rare earth metals; every foreign journalist a giant's carbon footprint. And just like cancer, consumerism is a parasite that ultimately destroys the host. The current epidemic of depression and anxiety in developed democracies, especially among the young, suggests that our current social model is robbing human life of meaning, while global capitalism's omnivorous destruction of wilderness and traditional ways of life represents a full-scale assault on the planet and all its people.

It would be easy to despair. But to me this state of emergency, like my cancer diagnosis, shines an eco-floodlight on resilience. Politically, resilience is a concept at the heart of the ever-growing resistance to neoliberalism and neo-fascism, a resistance generated by an international network of grassroots organisations committed to the vision of a future run on sustainable and egalitarian forms of power. In *Hope in the Dark* – her eloquent manifesto written in response to the second Gulf war and reissued after the Trump election – Rebecca Solnit documents the successes of this global environmental justice movement, an impressive litany of victories, from women's suffrage to the liberation of East Timor, too often ignored, underrated or forgotten. This demoralising amnesia, Solnit surmises, is partly due to the fact that many of these campaigners reject obstinate 'Leftist' narratives of binary oppositions and traditional antagonisms, working flexibly instead to find common ground against a shared foe. Thus, the astonishing shutdown of the World Trade Organisation talks achieved by activists in Seattle in 1999 was the result of 'at least some rapprochement of blue-collar workers [represented by unions] with environmentalists, anarchists, indigenous activists and farmers from Korea to France', while elsewhere in America eco-activists have worked effectively with Republican ranchers. What unites all these people, Solnit argues, is hope, by which she means active hope: 'not like a lottery ticket you can sit on the sofa and clutch, feeling lucky ... [but] an axe you can break down doors with'. Seventeen years later, it's clear that the widespread failure of the intellectual Left to understand working class fears and resentments has fed the rise of American and European neo-fascism. Yet the catastrophe of Trump's election is now being met by precisely the kind of defiant, energised co-operation Solnit champions: as I write, the Women's March on Washington is celebrating a truly global success.

All this activity might seem tangential to, or even more important than, curing cancer, but to borrow a phrase from Gloria Steinem, the struggles are 'linked, not ranked'. Solnit's advocacy of a 'peace-making practice, in contrast to ... warlike modes of intervention', finds powerful echoes in the history of cancer research. For all the 'search and destroy' aggression of the American 'war on cancer', its considerable victories, as Mukherjee compellingly documents, were won by co-operation and collaboration. In the mid-fifties a visionary director of the National Cancer Institute decided to avoid in-fighting and time-wasting by forming a national research consortium, a proposal which 'changed the field': for the first time, oncologists 'had a community'. Since then, the major breakthroughs in cancer research have been generated by networks of researchers, while huge delays have been caused by isolationism – the tendency of, say, geneticists not to speak to clinicians, even when attending the same conference or prize-giving ceremony. Patients became part of this community too, chaining themselves to gates until oncologists agreed to do research *with* them, not *on* them. A culture of dialogue built up that quietly challenged the dominant military metaphor, until, in 2001, Samuel Broder, director of the National Cancer Institute from 1989 to 1995, could publically remark:

> 'War' has truly a unique status, 'war' has a very special meaning. It means putting young men and women in situations where they might get killed or

grievously wounded … The National Institute of Health is a community of scholars focused on generating knowledge to improve public health. That's a great activity. That's not a war.

As befits a 'great activity' in service of health, post-war American cancer research was founded as well on ambitious compassion. Trailblazing chemotherapist Sidney Farber also pioneered holistic cancer treatment, a concept he called 'total care'. Working from the forties to his death in 1973, Farber personally toured the beds of sick children every evening, followed by 'medical residents, nurses, social workers, psychiatrists, nutritionists, and pharmacists. Cancer, he insisted, was a total disease . . . [that only] a multipronged, multidisciplinary attack would stand any chance of battling.' Reading this passage for the first time, I felt I had discovered Queen Crab, ancient symbol of fierce nurturing, lurking under the granite monolith of the medical establishment.

Unsurprisingly, in patriarchal and hypercapitalist America, Farber's war discourse won out; his 'total care' seemingly left as a footnote to history. Europe was a little, but not much, better. It is sadly telling that Cecily Saunders, the British founder of modern palliative medicine, 'avoided the phrase palliative care because care, she wrote, "is a soft word" that would never win respectability in the medical world'. Yet my experience in Britain, and my knowledge of Canadian cancer care organisations, demonstrates that the concept of total care is making a come-back. Slowly but surely, even in the beleaguered NHS, Farber's dream is being revived and institutionalised as the 'integrative treatment model' – itself a response to yet another cancer war.

No reader of this essay will be unaware of the conflict between the medical establishment and alternative cancer treatment practitioners. Having lost my mother, brother-in-law and a close friend to cancer, neither was I. My diagnosis changed me from a bystander to a conscript. Though psychologically I rejected 'warrior' imagery, seeing the disease as a message from my body to take better care of myself, when it came to treatment I had no choice but to put my body on a battle line. Shortly after my diagnosis two friends warned me against chemotherapy, one furiously convinced that no doctor ever prescribed it for their own family. I don't subscribe to conspiracy theories, and did not share my friends' hostility to orthodox medicine, but at the same time I don't believe science is infallible. I object to Big Pharma's track record of extreme profit making and aggressive marketing, while Mukherjee makes clear that advances in cancer treatment have come at the price of some extreme experiments – due in part to surgeons' pride, for ninety years women were subjected to unnecessary radical mastectomies, suffering the removal of muscle and even ribs in an operation that was either too large or too late. The dramatic increase in cancer rates also concerns me. 'Breast cancer is the new flu,' one nurse told me, and I was staggered to learn that one in eight British women will get breast cancer. Like many other people, I find it hard to believe that this rising incidence is simply due to the eradication of other diseases. Why would estrogen, implicated (like HER-2) in common breast cancers, kill so many young and middle-aged women? Is it not possible that synthetic estrogen in plastics, meat, dairy and the water supply overwhelms our bodies' ability to cope with the hormone? Worried about the quality of my drinking water, I had to be an activist. Contacting experts in the field, I learned that synthetic hormones, like GM crops, constitute 'emergent pollutants': toxic substances omnipresent in such trace amounts it is impossible to tell the long-term effects of daily ingestion. This was not reassuring. In the end, trusting Dr Jennifer Sass, a senior environmental advisor to Obama's White House, who told me tap water is always better than bottled, because it's regulated and not in contact with plastic, I bought a steel flask to fill from my Brita filter.

I am not a science sceptic. Rather, I would like science to seriously investigate more theories about cancer. My friends also told me of three local women who had successfully treated breast cancer with metabolic and Vitamin C therapy, and an extreme diet, including drinking one's own urine. I researched online, discovering clinical evidence for the anti-cancer effects of fasting and turmeric, and several 'refuser' bloggers, all alive and kicking on their daily vegetable juice and enema routines. In the month after my diagnosis, a waiting period when I was having no orthodox treatment, I gave up alcohol, started a green juice fast, and began investigating probiotic foods. I was therefore frustrated to hear my GP dismiss all natural remedies as 'unproven', and basically cons. My oncologist said turmeric might interfere with chemotherapy:

evidence for the root's potency, surely. And though I know there's a lot of money to be made from supplements, I doubt Vitamin C turns enough profit to conduct large-scale cancer trials. I didn't argue with my doctors though, because gradually I was rejecting an oppositional view of cancer treatment.

Vitriol against the medical establishment seemed misplaced. One prominent 'refuser' had had surgery, but rejected chemotherapy; another had had chemo, and then rejected hormone therapy. At the same time, dangerous quacks aside, 'unproven' does not mean 'disproven'. Supplements simply remain understudied. Mukherjee notes that, in the sixties, while half a billion dollars was poured into testing the viral-causation theory of cancer, America spent only one twentieth of that amount on studying the relationship between cancer and nutrition. He also states that 'there are more chemicals in plants than we know of or know how to use. As yet, there have been few unbiased trials of these medicines in cancer treatment or prevention.' Meanwhile, alternative therapies continue to work remarkably well for some people, though I decided early on not to be one of them. Such regimes are expensive and exhausting: every website suggested a different food to avoid, and the amount of supplements recommended to me by well-meaning friends and Cancer Options – an organisation that provides clinical evidence for non-conventional treatment – was dizzying. How on earth would I know what exactly to take? Then there were the small matters of death and statistics. My mother had refused chemo and gave her surgeons permission to perform only limited surgery. Adopting alternative therapies, she lived for five years, as long as 50 per cent of people with her cancer at the time. Though she might have survived longer with conventional treatment, I long ago accepted that she had the right to choose quality of life over quantity. Still, as I faced similar dilemmas, the memory of her death – and the knowledge that two writers I admire, Kathy Acker and Audre Lorde, had both refused chemo and died – highlighted the risks of the alternative route. In contrast, although chemotherapy is a rough ride, currently 99 per cent of Stage One and 90 per cent of Stage Two patients taking the conventional path survive at least five years. It was an offer I couldn't refuse.

Wanting to do everything I could to help myself, though, I adopted the integrative treatment model, a both/and approach to healing the cancer treatment wars. Although some supplements are incompatible with chemo, slowly, unevenly but increasingly, supporting patients through conventional treatment with holistic therapies is becoming the new best practice in the UK. Between the NHS and various charities I was, as I have said, offered a great range of psychological and physical support. In Brighton, a brand new cancer treatment building, the Macmillan Horizon Centre, is dedicated to complementary therapies, including a meditation room designed by Brian Eno. Urged by my oncologist to keep my weight up and eat red meat for iron during chemo, I adopted the NHS recommended diet, low in animal products, high in grains, pulses, fruit and veg. I kept juicing and when asked to 'compromise' between my clinically-supported fasting regime and the need to maintain a healthy BMI, restricted my fasting to the twenty-four hours before each treatment cycle.

Trying to feel in control of my treatment sometimes meant being pushy. When it came to surgery, while I could adjust to the idea of losing my breast, I didn't want to run a greater risk of lymphoedema than I had to. If only two of my lymph nodes were infected, I didn't see why all thirty had to be removed. The Cancer Options consultant told me America had adopted a minimalist approach, and recommended surgeons in London who might deviate from the NHS standard procedure. I got a referral to the Royal Free, and saw a surgeon who agreed instantly that only a maximum of twelve nodes needed to be removed. My oncologist then suggested I visit the local surgical team again, 'to see what they can offer', and to my surprise the Brighton surgeon now offered to remove only four nodes. When I asked about statistics he cited an American study showing no difference in survival rates. It astonishes me that the NHS is performing excessive surgery on countless women, but I assume it does so for reasons of cost: had my four lymph nodes still been infected, I would have required a clearance, so offering all women the option of a sentinel node biopsy would inevitably mean more demand for the slab. More alarming was hearing of a woman in the Northeast pressured to have a reconstruction at the same time as her mastectomy, clearly to avoid the expense of two operations. Silicone implants can inhibit the effect of hormone therapy: surely women have the right to see how they feel without reconstruction?

It's a personal decision, but as time went on, taking strength from the decisions of women like Audre Lorde and poet Clare Best, I leant toward rejecting reconstruction altogether. Rather than having painful tissue grafts to create a numb ball of flesh on my chest, I would prefer simply to adapt to a new shape.

But then the miracle announced itself: the MRI scan taken after my fourth chemotherapy session, the first to include Herceptin, revealed that my tumour had disappeared. I had to wait, in a state of suspended disbelief, for my in-the-end minor surgery to prove this was indeed a 'complete pathological response', with no trace of disease left in the cells. I had a one-in-three chance of achieving this outcome, perhaps less given my low BMI, and even my oncologist agreed that perhaps there had been a 'synergistic' effect between my orthodox and holistic treatments. That was gratifying to hear, but what struck me was how incurious she and my other oncologists are about why chemotherapy works better for some patients than others. I was told that it was impossible to isolate factors, but given that BMI is strongly correlated, it surely couldn't be impossible to tell whether simple dietary measures like teetotalism or veganism also have a significant effect.

What strikes me too, is that, however precarious my finances, I'm a white, well-educated middle-class woman. We live in an unevenly polluted world, where even in wealthy nations some people are more exposed to carcinogens or have poorer access to health care services than others, and any 'complete response' to cancer must address fundamental issues of inequality. Here in the UK, Black British women run double the risk of secondary breast cancer than white women do: there is a concern public health leaflets featuring white faces are not hitting home with this population. Perhaps genetic or cultural issues are at work too, as are the latter in Gaza, where the high incidence of late diagnosis is attributed to women's reluctance to take up breast cancer awareness training offered by the authorities. In Gaza the problem is fatally exacerbated by Israel's routine refusal of visas for treatment: campaigning on public health issues in the Strip inevitably leads back to the Occupation. But everywhere, seeking better outcomes for cancer patients intersects with environmental and political issues. Globally, international corporations all too often discount evidence of toxicity in plastics, pesticide, cigarettes, food and water. And although fighting the illness is not a top priority for countries dealing with widespread malaria, cholera and schistosomiasis, as the developing world climbs out of poverty, it too will face cancer epidemics: 42 per cent of cancer is strongly associated with indulgent lifestyles.

Cancer, an inherent possibility of our cells, even when 'non-genetic' a disease of damaged genes, is unlikely to ever be fully eradicated. Seriously seeking to reduce both incidence and death rates means, not only funding medical research, but also making connections between public health, environmentalism, corporate power and socioeconomic inequality. Politicised cancer advocates take comprehensively progressive positions: at time of writing the fiercely independent American charity Breast Cancer Action is calling on the US Senate to block Trump nominees for senior health and environmental posts. Currently though, most UK cancer charities focus on medical research and patient well-being. Much as I benefited from this work, I hope I have made the case for lifting higher the rock of conventional medicine and giving Queen Cancer freedom to roam: through tenacious co-operation and ambitious compassion, reactivating Farber's dream of 'total care', not just for individual patients, but for the entire human family and the planet we depend on.

****

And if all this – having cancer, curing cancer, curing the way we think about cancer, curing the world – still seems like an uphill battle to you, as it says in the Holy Qur'an:

> Warfare is ordained for you, though it is hateful to you; but it may happen that you hate a thing which is good for you, and it may happen that you love a thing that is bad for you. Allah knows, you know not. (2:216)

This verse resonated deeply with me during my illness. Like conflict, cancer is an inherent feature of human life, and a teacher if we let it be. Susan Sontag argued that cancer myths fundamentally serve to mask Western society's fear and denial of death: 'as death is now an offensively meaningless event,' she wrote, 'disease widely considered a synonym for death is experienced as something to hide' – or to wage war upon. Freed of these myths, then, what cancer can teach us is how to accept death. It was not surprising, then, that my cancer journey took me into the realm of religion.

For cancer is not just a psychological, physical, and political challenge, but a metaphysical one; not just the problem of oncology, but an ontological opportunity. With its volatile nature, its potential for spontaneous remission or harrowing return, cancer provokes deep consideration of the mind-body connection. As Sontag argued, homilies to 'think positive', or 'beat cancer' place a huge burden on patients – treatment can work very well on angry, bitter people, while confidence is no guarantee of survival. Preliminary trials, though, have suggested that regular hypnotherapy during and post-treatment can increase life expectancy, while Mukherjee cites evidence that brain hormones can alter the biology of cancer cells. But beyond the chance to study the mysterious relationship between mind and matter, a cancer diagnosis can also profoundly test or strengthen faith in a transcendent higher power. Brought up a Quaker, I am now a person with spiritual beliefs who belongs to no organised religion. Faith communities strengthen the individual's relationship with the divine, and without one, my belief in the essential goodness of the universe can sometimes feel shaky. Right after the diagnosis any such faith I had felt shattered. Yet when a Christian friend said that day that having cancer would be a spiritual journey, even in the depths of my despair I knew that viewing my illness in this way was the only path through it. Over the following months, remaining true to the ecumenical spirit of Quakerism, I fed my spirit through involvement with a variety of faith traditions. What I found was that the wisdom of holy texts, the beauty of sacred architecture, and the warmth of loving community helped to shrink my mental anguish almost as completely as the chemotherapy shrank my tumour.

In Prague I took heart from a Tarot reading which strongly suggested that the purpose of this experience was to enable me to take greater control of my health. Although this is an on-going process, fasting soon brought me a sense of calm, while visiting the Holocaust memorials in the city's old synagogues set my own suffering in the shade, and enabled me to see how blessed I was. Back home in Brighton, a Christian 'silent gardening' group literally put me in touch with the beauty of creation, while a pagan friend brought me a totem he had conjured up at a Druid camp – a brooch of mouse energy, helpful for putting one's house in order. Reading *Becoming Earth*, I saw how Eva Saulitis's Buddhist practice, as well as her deep respect for nature, had helped her accept imminent death. More happily, at a New Year's Eve party, I discussed the story of my name with a Jewish Naomi, celebrating the message of inclusiveness in the Biblical Naomi's return home with her Moabite daughter-in-law Ruth. And throughout my illness I grew closer to Islam, superficially through the customs of fasting and covering my bald head; more significantly by reading the Qur'an, inspired by the constant focus on good deeds and forgiveness.

I had been interested in forgiveness for some time, working through the Desmond and Mpho Tutu's Forgiveness Challenge some years ago, though without quite feeling I had got the full benefit from my efforts. During counselling, as I wrestled with the remnants of my childhood anger, a verse from the Qur'an sealed my forgiveness, not just of one person, but of the past:

> The good deed and the evil deed are not alike. Repel the evil deed with one that is better, then he between whom and you there is enmity will become as though he was a good friend.

> But no-one is granted it except those who are steadfast, and no-one is granted it except the owner of great happiness. (41: 34)

What I took from this wise verse is the sense of a virtuous circle: that a forgiving person is a patient and happy one – someone who has decided to focus on love, not anger – and that being forgiving in turn creates happiness and stability. The ability of cancer to accelerate the process was borne out when three significant but sadly long antagonistic relationships suddenly resolved in mutual forgiveness. These were profound changes, personal miracles that have infused me with a lasting sense of inner lightness. Reflecting on these breakthroughs, it seems to me that, despite Nelson Mandela's great example, forgiveness is still rare in the political arena. Partly this is because the process is so often co-opted by the powerful, who can never be trusted not to re-offend. Partly though, perhaps it is because we do not talk enough about this essentially spiritual practice.

Did prayer also help me? Prayer is sometimes conflated with hope. But for me, living with cancer involved letting go of hope, even in Rebecca Solnit's active sense of the word. The Palestinians, having resisted Zionism for over sixty years, do not hope, but practice *sumud*, 'steadfastness', simply refusing to surrender their rightful claim on their homeland. After my initial spasm of anguish, I became more steadfast, somehow believing that my cancer was an opportunity for spiritual growth. Post-diagnosis, I asked people of faith to pray for me, giving few particulars except to come through chemotherapy with no permanent damage, but still did not myself pray for survival. What would it mean to ask Spirit to save my breast or my life, and then lose them? And am I really so special I deserve to live when others do not? What I needed was the strength and grace to accept all possible futures. Still, of course, I did all within my power to regain my health, and was touched and grateful when Muslims, Christians and pagan friends all responded to my request. Gradually, as I discovered what to ask for, I began to send requests for strength and prayers of thanks up to Spirit.

It is impossible to say if 'God answered' all these prayers, but when my oncologist later acknowledged that my remission may have been due to 'synergistic factors', I included among them the power of faith. Faith, rather than hope, helped me surrender to cancer, not in a militaristic but a near-Islamic sense of the term: by submitting to the experience, I become more open to the mysteries of life and death, and more humble. I remain ecumenical in outlook, my respect for religion, already stronger in recent years, deepened enormously by the support different faith communities gave me while I was ill. In a strange way, it feels sad to be re-entering 'the Kingdom of the Well', a world where, apart from the occasional flurry of 'cancer weepies', cultural phobias and taboos around illness and mortality persist. Imagine if it was common practice to return to work after extended sick leave as one might from a research trip, or return home from hospital as one might from a long holiday, giving a slide show on one's experience. This might sound absurd, but in a society that honoured illness and death as part of life, surely such sharing would be closer to the norm.

In the world most of us inhabit, these remain intimate stories. I have tried to protect the privacy of others in this account, but self-censorship plays a part too in obscuring such narratives. It is frightening to expose one's vulnerability to others. More generally though, I wonder if a cultural shift toward viewing cancer as a spiritual journey, not a war, might help promote respect for religion, and provide opportunities for the kind of interfaith conversations we need to have at this time of rising intolerance. Some political miracles would be welcome too!

****

Cancer, I have claimed, is a master key that fits many locks, one that can open doors to the future we and the Earth need and deserve. Evoking also images of bony fingers, mortal journeys and compassionate Queen Crabs, I have scuttled back and forth over Susan Sontag's famous prohibition on using illness as metaphor, noting that she herself foresaw a time when the negative myths that have accrued to cancer will lose their relevance. Sontag also found counterexamples in history, though; acknowledging that 'if it is plausible to compare the polis to an organism then it is plausible to compare civil disorder to an illness', she cited approvingly Machiavelli, Hobbes, and Lord Shaftesbury, all of whom used metaphor to promote, respectively, foresight, a rational response and tolerance in response to social ills. What these thinkers have in common, Sontag noted, was a lack of apocalyptic melodrama: society, for them, by definition could not suffer a terminal disease. We live in more fearful times, but to return again to my cancer metaphor, the planet may not require palliative care. The times have been dark before and, as Rebecca Solnit believes, perhaps in this darkness lies our survival.

Solnit quotes Virginia Woolf's journals, an entry composed six months after the start of the First World War: 'The future is dark, which is on the whole the best thing the future can be, I think.' 'Dark,' she seems to say, Solnit comments, 'as in inscrutable, not as in terrible. We often mistake one for the other. Or we transform the future's unknowability into something certain, the fulfilment of all our dread.' Really though, darkness – like light, which can burn as well as illuminate – is ambiguous. Politically, darkness may, as Solnit points out, represent the 'backstage' of the world's theatre, overlooked places fomenting dissent; it may, like a cancer diagnosis, be a rich soil nurturing resilience. Largely avoiding the term 'utopia', she also insists that 'paradise is not the place in which you arrive but the journey toward it.'

For the utopian project is always conditional. Heaven itself has its critics: though the Abrahamic faiths all, at heart, insist that we should treat each other as we wish to be treated ourselves, religious leaders still peddle divine justice in place of the earthly variety, annoying Marxists, while irreligious self-proclaimed 'Caliphs' defile the fountains of paradise with the blood of innocents, fuelling the arguments of fundamentalist atheists. Though alternative communities like Damanhur in Italy, Findhorn in Scotland and Auroville in India all demonstrate that our species is not inevitably selfish, violent and eco-cidal, small-scale egalitarian societies have inherent limitations; most people do not want to, or simply cannot, leave their families, jobs or the wider world. That, however, is good: to protect the planet we need to change that wider world. And real utopian visions, like positive metaphors, have the power to inspire people to so.

By 'real utopia', I mean one that does not 'magic away' conflict, suffering and death. To do so is to truly create a 'no-place'. For despite the best efforts of the Californian transhumanists, no place on Earth is free from sickness and mortality. Even if cryogenics proves medically successful, frozen souls will awaken to the loss of everyone they have known and loved. And, unless we are genetically modified beyond recognition, anger and fear will always be primal emotions we have to contend with. To engage seriously with the concept of utopia is not to hope that we can make civic water supplies a fountain of eternal youth and peace, but rather to have faith that human beings can learn to get along.

My cancer journey has strengthened that faith. In our species, the fear of death all too often provokes greed and aggression, but I have experienced for myself how this fear can be transformed by loving care, into acceptance, gratitude, and even joy. In these dire times the climate catastrophe is slowly acting on the body politic as cancer can do on individuals: motivating us to overcome differences and unite in the face of a lethal threat. While honouring the spirit of Sontag's ground-breaking critique of 'illness as [negative] metaphor', I hope I have contributed in a small way to the tradition of Machiavelli, Hobbes and Shaftesbury, using positive imagery for cancer in order to encourage a 'complete response' to physical and social ills: the co-operation that effective medical research and political activism require, and the compassion called for when cures fail, or collective forgiveness is required. I look forward to taking a more active role in environmental justice campaigns as I recover. Now, though, it's time to oil my new crab-headed front door key, and clip on the pedometer that monitors my new exercise regime. I'll give the last word, then, to Eduardo Galeano, quoted in *Hope in the Dark*:

> Utopia is on the horizon. When I walk two steps, it takes two steps back. I walk ten steps and it is ten steps further away. What is utopia for? It is for this, for walking.

ARTS AND LETTERS

UTOPIAN LANDSCAPES

Noor Iskandar

Imagining a Utopia emboldens my intrigue towards the terrains we inhabit. My focus is on void and wounds. On spaces and places. The Chinese American geographer, Yi-Fu Tuan, suggests that 'place' gives you security while 'space' offers freedom. We are attached to one and long for the other. I have trouble distinguishing the two especially when it comes to emotional territories – the personal, the sacred, the spiritual. Wandering through the world and looking through a lens helps me demystify these concepts. Perhaps utopia exists in that fleeting oneness with air. When the temple of the soul is aligned with the envelope of nature. Under the *muqarnas* (with their infinite geometry) of Iran, by the valleys of Kashmir, the ruins of Anatolia, the vignette of Andalusia, the bruises of Balkans, I gather how Utopia transits across states of mind, shifting, projecting, drifting.

It is ironic how the term 'Utopia' was coined. Greek for 'No-place'. There is that dissolution of anchors and stability. Utopia: the abode of desires should shake your ground but holds you in place. Utopia feeds on your solitude and makes you food for the vultures. Utopia is a conversation you have with the universe while the universe emphasises your insignificance. Utopia is the tension between you and the Divine.

An aged lady basking under the splendid spill of colours from the reflections of the Nasir-ul-Molk Mosque in Shiraz, Iran.

A man drowned in the golden leak of the sun from the viewing point of Punthuk Setumbu, Yogyakarta

In the act of devotion, a worshipper submerged himself in the divine water body surrounding the Sri Harmandir Sahib, also known as the Golden Temple, the holiest gudhwara of Sikhism.

STANDING UP FOR PALESTINE

Shanon Shah

On 25 July 2014, at the height of the Gaza War, the Palestinian singer-composer Reem Kelani performed to a packed house at Rich Mix in East London. Towards the closing of the concert, she confessed that she had felt like cancelling the concert as Israel's military offensive intensified and the Gazan death toll escalated. But in the end, she decided that this event was cultural resistance *par excellence* and went on to rouse the audience with an encore of '*Mawtini*' ('My Homeland'), the unofficial Palestinian anthem. The atmosphere, which was already emotionally charged, became even more electric for both Palestinians and non-Palestinians alike in the audience. Those who were familiar with the song began standing up and singing along fervently.

'The reason why I chose that anthem is that it goes back as far as the 1930s,' Kelani recalls during our interview. 'So, the Zionist argument that oh, well, there was no such thing as Palestine to start with – this bunch of farmers, they didn't have a sense of national identity. No shit. So where does "*Mawtini*" come from?'

Clueless, I had to look it up. '*Mawtini*' was written in the 1930s by the Palestinian poet Ibrahim Touqan, with music by Muhammad Fuliefil, as a patriotic song which then became popular throughout the Arab world. In 2004, it was adopted as the Iraqi anthem after the US-led invasion of 2003, replacing the Saddam-Hussein-era anthem '*Ardulfurataini Watan*' ('The Land of the Two Rivers').

Kelani brims with pride at the trouble she invites by singing this anthem regularly. 'Once I was performing at some Middle East conference in Germany and there were complaints the day after. Turns out that the Israeli delegation had complained saying that – and this was one of the greatest compliments in my life, better than a five-star review in *The Guardian* – people think she's singing a simple love song about Palestine, but it's so subversive.' And it's not just the Israeli government that gets uncomfortable with this anthem. It also makes the Palestinian Authority (PA) uncomfortable because it reminds Palestinians of the colossal losses they have endured since the creation of the nation-state of Israel in 1948. The remembrance of this historical tragedy does not fit into the current politics of the PA, which Kelani scathingly likens to Vichy France.

I meet Kelani in the café of the Tabernacle, a church-turned-arts centre in Notting Hill. She is just as vivacious and gregarious in person as she is on stage. She thumbs through the latest copy of *Critical Muslim* – issue 18, 'Cities' – approvingly; it prompts her to explain the other challenge behind her Rich Mix performance. One guy on Facebook said, 'instead of singing, go cover your hair and pray more and ask God to forgive you for letting men see you, especially when Gaza is being butchered,' she says. Although chagrined by the condemnation, she could understand the logic behind it up to a point. 'Because a lot of people were being killed. We were in a state of collective mourning. So, whether I am in Gaza, London or Timbuktu, we are supposed to be mourning for the dead. And what you do not do when you're mourning for the dead is sing and dance and jump onstage. So, on the outer surface, the argument makes total sense.' But the response has to be contextualised. 'If I am in Gaza, I would not be singing and dancing while the guys are dropping bombs obviously.' But in this case, apart from her professional obligation to the organiser, Arts Canteen, the need for cultural resistance demanded that she went ahead with the show. 'It was about humanising, giving names and sounds to those who were being butchered in Gaza. It was also about bringing everyone that night into Palestine.'

Ultimately, however, Kelani felt 'bullied and terrorised' by the abusive emails she consequently received from several Palestinian and non-Palestinian Muslims. 'On top of all of that, inside me, I didn't want to sing either. I was so broken. But as soon as I got onto the stage and saw all of you – and it's not fake modesty because of course I'm onstage and there's all that prima donna spiel – there was some strength, some safety, not safety in numbers in a socio-biological way, but there was that group, collective resilience.' Palestinians have a word for this collective resilience, she says – *sumud*. 'And that's what was happening that night,' she concludes.

It is this combination of passion, artistry and conscience that initially drew me to Kelani and her work. I first met her a month before her Rich

Mix concert, when I invited her to perform at the Waterloo Festival
organised by St John's Church, known for promoting progressive causes. I
put together an evening concert with the cringeworthy but well-
intentioned title, 'A Taste of World Music', and invited Kelani to perform
after chancing upon her website. Almost immediately, I received a phone
call from Chris Somes-Charlton, Kelani's husband and manager, asking for
details about the event and the church more generally. When they were
convinced that we were legit and that our festival was about community-
building, Kelani responded with a resounding yes. And during the night,
she mesmerised the audience with her humour, intelligence and
powerhouse vocals.

Kelani was born in 1963 in England, raised in Kuwait and is now based
in London. In 1986, she qualified as a biologist at Kuwait University. She
then worked for two years as an assistant marine researcher for the Kuwait
Institute of Scientific Research and another two years in research
management at Kuwait University. During this period, she was also a
literary translator – she assisted her father Yousef in the English-Arabic
translation of Manfred Ullman's seminal book, *Islamic Medicine*, in 1980.
But her switch to a full-time career in music did not necessarily begin with
full-blown advocacy of Palestinian folk music. She says that she initially
thought Arab music was boring, but one day she went to a traditional
Palestinian wedding and was transformed. Since then she has become a
tireless researcher and performer of these musical gems from Palestine and
other parts of the Arab world.

Only later on did I appreciate what a towering figure Kelani is as a
performer, musicologist, and cultural activist. And this is what made her
appearance at St John's all the more admirable – here is an artist whose
primary motivation is social justice. This is also what drives her community
engagement across Britain and beyond. As a rebuttal to the holier-than-
thou condemnations she sometimes receives, she relates an anecdote about
her activism with Northern Women for Palestine, prefacing it by declaring,
'What I love about our comrade activists in the North of the UK is that
they all come from causes for miner's rights, women's rights, suffragettes
and trade unions, so their fight for Palestine is not mono-causal – it's part
of all of that.' Among the events that Northern Women for Palestine
organises are cooking workshops for British women to experience

Palestinian food and Palestinian embroidery sessions. Kelani was invited in early 2016 to conduct a music workshop.

'For the first time in my life, I saw Asian women with *hijab* – British Asian, from Bradford or nearby, in a workshop like this. One of them came up to me in tears afterwards – mind you the workshop was women-only – and said "My three-year old child came from kindergarten telling me, mum, music is *haram* (forbidden)." Another woman in *hijab* who was also in tears – turns out she's from Kashmir – said, "Reem, what you do is *da'wah* (inviting people to Islam)".'

I tell Kelani that this is what I feel about her work, too. Growing up in Malaysia, I say, the status of Palestine was often inextricable from a kind of angry Islamic utopianism that was anti-Jewish and anti-Western. The implication of this always made me extremely uncomfortable – defending Palestine and Islam became synonymous, which in turn entailed hating Jews and the West. Kelani bristles at this. 'That's what shocks me with younger Muslims here in Britain, too, especially of Asian background. You know, they start quoting some awful things like the Jews are the descendants of pigs and monkeys.' Kelani's defence of Palestine and her own personal Palestinian-ness are not built upon such foundations.

'I always say I'm Palestinian first, Muslim second and it annoys many Muslims. Palestinian culture is also part of Christian identity – even Palestinian Christian men are circumcised!' Apart from this historical and cultural fact, Kelani believes that turning the Palestinian struggle into an Islamic issue actually plays into the hands of the Israeli occupation. 'Because it is Zionism's interest to say, oh, they are all Muslims – it's a struggle between Muslim and Jew. No, it's not. It's a struggle between Zionist fascists and indigenous Palestinians – Muslim and Christian and Jewish. This would be wrong even if Palestinians worshipped cows.' She points out that Muslim Palestinians are beaten and banned from going to pray in Al-Aqsa, while Christian Palestinians and Christian priests get battered and beaten and are prevented from going to pray in the Church of the Holy Sepulchre; she challenges Muslim defenders of Palestine to take on the Church of the Holy Sepulchre as the symbol of their struggle. It is this ecumenical conviction that enables her to form such organic alliances with different Christian communities, from St John's Waterloo to Greenbelt, the mammoth annual Christian arts festival.

So far so good, but this is the easy part of our conversation. My own ignorance is laid bare when I ask Kelani if she has any kindred spirits on the Israeli-Jewish side. This unleashes an impassioned reply which I struggle to keep up with. 'If I listen to a Ladino song from Muslim Spain by a Jewish-Spanish Ladino, I feel very Arab, I feel very Muslim. Because it's from the same basin of cultures. But if I listen to a *klezmer* song, played by a settler on an ethnically cleansed Palestinian village, over my dead body – there is no meeting point.'

Kelani then launches into a history lesson. 'Some of the greatest musicians before the creation of the State of Israel, some of the greatest musicians in the Arab world, were Jewish – take the wonderful Egyptian Jewish singer, the late Layla Murad. Layla's father Zaki was a cantor in the synagogues of Cairo and Alexandria, yet he saw himself as Egyptian. So, when the State of Israel was created, Layla Murad and her brother refused to go, saying "We are Egyptians – there is no contradiction".' Upon learning more about this story, I wonder if Kelani has slightly downplayed the tensions between Layla Murad and her family when she later converted to Islam. Still, the point is persuasive – there has been a vibrant, indigenous Jewish presence in the Middle East that predates the creation of Israel. But that is not my question, which is about whether there are bridge-building equivalents of Kelani in the Jewish-Israeli cultural sphere. Are there, perhaps, Ladino artists who are pro-Palestinian? I try again but she does not budge. 'No, because the majority of those reclaiming Ladino culture are repackaging it as Israeli music and take part in world music festivals as Israelis and many of them have served in the Israeli army. How can I work with someone like that?'

I am floored by Kelani's relentless criticism and my curiosity only grows. We all know about conscientious objectors, or Refuseniks, who disobey or refuse to serve with the Israeli Defense Forces (IDF) on principled grounds, I continue. Are there no conscientious objectors in the cultural and artistic sphere as well? 'So now I have to feel sorry for a guilty oppressor, yeah?' she retorts. I immediately recoil and stammer, 'No, no, I'm not asking you to feel sorry for anyone.' She continues: 'Sometimes it's all about their suffering for what they did, but what about the suffering of those whom they killed? I am quite non-compromising on this, and I will not mince my words. Yes, we have a few Refuseniks in our movement, comrades, and even in the BDS (Boycott, Divestment and Sanctions) movement. But they have to prove themselves real hard before I trust them. Because when you say those who are involved in the cultural sphere, what culture? What is Israeli culture? No, please, keep your hands off my culture.'

This is where we begin to address the vexed issue of cultural appropriation and its discontents. I imagine that Kelani would probably not take kindly to the American writer Lionel Shriver's hope that the concept of cultural appropriation 'is just a passing fad'. In her now infamous speech at the Brisbane Writers Festival in 2016, Shriver implied that allegations of cultural appropriation amounted to censorship and an attack on artistic freedom. And, according to her, these criticisms were now bordering on the ridiculous: 'Seriously, we have people questioning whether it's appropriate for white people to eat pad Thai. Turnabout, then: I guess that means that as a native of North Carolina, I can ban the Thais from eating barbecue.'

I thought that Kelani would probably rankle at this trivialising of the concept. To begin with, for her as a Palestinian, even cuisine is intensely political. 'Hummus is now "Israeli food". Couscous is "Israeli food",' she says. She tells me how integral the aromatic herb mix za'atar is to her Palestinian identity. I sheepishly admit that I only became aware of za'atar through the recipes of the famed Israeli-born British Jewish chef Yotam Ottolenghi. 'I'm going to kill you,' Kelani jokes. But after we have a bit of laugh about this, she explains that she does not see Ottolenghi as the enemy. She even gives him credit for clarifying when certain dishes and ingredients – hummus and za'atar, for example – are Arab or Palestinian in origin. What she takes issue with is that Palestinian perspectives, voices and stories are constantly silenced in the mainstream media even when fun and light issues like cuisine are discussed. Type in a Google search on 'Palestinian za'atar' and the very first entry that shows up is a link to Ottolenghi's online store – that sort of thing. For Kelani, this is symptomatic of a larger ideological climate in which Palestinians are painted as a people without history, who are only capable of suicide bombings. To Kelani, this phenomenon is part and parcel of contemporary Zionist politics and inevitably involves a silent takeover of Palestinian culture. And this is cultural appropriation. Kelani can see I am hooked and launches into another lecture.

'Because how can a Brooklyn Jew and a Moroccan Jew and an Egyptian Jew have one monoculture in fewer than sixty-seven years? This fact of "Israeli culture" has to be created. I will give you an analogy I always give. You are the Other, I am the Oppressor. You have three forms of Oppressor-Other relationship – the Nazi, the fundamentalist of any faith, not just Muslim, and the Zionist. The Nazi would look at the Jewish Other and say, you exist, but you're *Untermenschen*, you are subspecies. You exist but I hate everything to do with you – your DNA, your genetics, your shape, your nose. The fundamentalist, especially the Abrahamic fundamentalist, says you are the Other and you will only be saved if you become like me. So, the first type of Oppressor says you are never me – you are under me. The second Oppressor says you will only be saved if you become like me. The Zionist wants to be the Other!'

Kelani softens when she notices that I am processing this gradually. I realise that I am now in an uncomfortable position, too – I recognise and respect her truth and her analysis but am unsure what to do next. I have always been a firm believer in building bridges but basically Kelani is telling me that some divides are simply unbridgeable. Or rather, that it is insulting and unjust to place the burden of bridge-building on the shoulders of the oppressed party. A further irony, she alleges, is that the majority of voices calling for Palestinians to reconcile with Israelis are secretly anti-Semitic anyway. She is careful not to name any names – after all, we are talking in the midst of the bitter controversy about anti-Semitism in the Labour Party. Instead, she says, 'To please the outside world, I am asked to "work with Jews". A lot of it is projection and some of it is total political naivety, like let's play Happy Families. "Come on, work with a Jew, be a friend with a Jew." *Habibi*, I have worked with Jews and befriended them, they are fellow human beings. If there is an issue about their Jewishness, it's a positive thing because we find we have a lot in common.'

In fact, Kelani counts several pro-Palestine British Jews among her best friends. 'It's going to sound like a cliché, "Some of my best friends are Jews." But some of the toughest and most productive, hardworking and long-suffering comrades for the Palestinian cause are anti-Zionist Jews, and they are to be celebrated, they are to be welcomed and embraced. And for me, Judaism should be everywhere, not just enclosed in a ghetto paid for by the American taxpayer.'

She recounts a story about the Orthodox Jewish supporters of the Palestine Solidarity Campaign. 'These are Orthodox Jews who live in Stamford Hill and walk all the way to Trafalgar Square on Saturdays because they wouldn't drive in observance of the Shabbat. So, our comrades from Palestine Solidarity Campaign had to drive to Stamford Hill to pick up the placards to take to Trafalgar Square because our Orthodox Jewish comrades had to walk – they were reconciling their Orthodoxy with a fight for justice.'

Kelani admits that she has her own internal religious issues to reconcile as well, a major one being the relationship between her faith as a Muslim and her vocation as a musician. 'Sometimes I think music is part of my faith and sometimes I think no, it's totally contradictory to my faith. And it's a journey, a *jihad*, a struggle, to understand it – also because the issue of music is nebulous in Islam.' Music is not unambiguously condemned in Islam, like the consumption of pork and alcohol or illicit sexual relations. But still, the ambiguity is not enough to put her at ease – she has to deal with people who spout dogmas like 'Muslim women should not sing'.

This conflict is accompanied by Kelani's own heritage – as her surname illustrates, she is a descendant of the twelfth century Sufi sheikh, Abdul Qadir Gilani. 'Some people say, can you please remove Kelani from your name? You can't be a singer if you're a Kelani,' she continues. She grew up in a pious household. 'We were told that you fast, you pray, you do your *zikr* (remembrance of Allah), all the main tenets – and there was also the cultural Arabic element.' Although Kelani's mother did not wear *hijab*, many of her aunts did, which is why she says she is not a 'hijabophobe'. At the same time, her father instilled a strong sense of camaraderie with Christian Palestinians, too. 'Don't forget – twenty per cent of historic Palestine is Christian,' she says. Growing up in Kuwait added to the baggage; some aspects of Kuwaiti society traumatised her, she says. 'I'm told that the national curriculum says that a woman who wears perfume and walks between men is *zaniya* (an adulteress) and they are *zani* (committing adultery),' she says in disgust. 'The same textbooks teach that anyone who is not Muslim is going to *jahannam* (Hell). In Kuwait in the 1970s, women were not even allowed to read Qur'an. So suddenly when they televised the Qur'an competition, from either Malaysia or Indonesia, we were all crying – it was so revolutionary. Women reciting the Qur'an!'

These examples give her strength, and she says she finds them even in her own family. 'I have an aunt, my father's sister, who wears the *hijab* and is very religious. This woman loves me incredibly but she never talks about my music. It's like my music is the dead sibling, the dead daughter. And then every now and then she'll say, "Reem, you know what you do is *haram*, but I'm so proud of you!" Isn't that wonderful?' Kelani beams when I roar with laughter. 'Then she flies kisses to God. She also says, because I swear a lot, "Reem, it's *haram* to swear, but it spills out of your mouth like honey". Because I say it in such a humorous way.' So, some divides can be bridged, and delightfully, too, according to Kelani. 'That's why it's also important for me to know that even those who are more sure of their version of Islam will also be at a conflict about what I'm doing, not just myself. It shows that both sides of the story need to comfort each other.'

She is unapologetic for her disdain at what she calls the 'nationalising' of Islam throughout the Muslim world. 'There's even this thing they do now in Egypt', she says. 'Ask me what my name is.' 'What's your name?' I ask, suppressing a giggle. 'Reem, *insha Allah* (God willing),' she replies, deadpan, and my face cracks with laughter again. 'But I say God has willed it, hasn't He? I was in Cairo and I wanted to book a hotel for my research project on the Egyptian composer, Sayed Darwish, who was from Alexandria. I called, "Hi, is this the Windsor Hotel?" The reply was, "*Insha Allah*". I said, "*Insha Allah* yes or *insha Allah* no?"' Kelani's discomfort, however, is not at expressions of piety necessarily but the divisive consequences of particular forms of it.

'Another thing happened to me in Egypt. I was calling an *oud* (Middle-Eastern lute) maker, because I wanted an *oud* made for me. "Hello, is this Waziri", I said. "Yes, *insha Allah*". When I finished the phone call, he wanted to say goodbye. He said, "*La ilaha illallah* (there is no God but God – the first half of the Islamic declaration of faith)". So you are forced to respond, "*Muhammadun rasulullah* (Muhammad is the messenger of God – the second half)." But what if I was a Christian? What if I was a pigmy from wherever? So, no Christian could call him to ask for an *oud* to be made. This is serious.'

We move on to talk about her music. And her music – whether in her live performances or her albums – is really something else. Her song choices, her arrangements, her band, her album artwork, her own vocals – everything pulses with passion and inspiration. Her two albums, *Sprinting Gazelle:*

Palestinian Songs from the Motherland and the Diaspora (2005) and *Live at the Tabernacle* (2015) are hard to come by but can be bought from her website.

I ask what the oldest song she has ever collected is. 'It's not so much a particular song but a song form – and a lot of these song forms are Mesopotamian. It's like some of the Palestinian embroidery – some of the stitches date back to Canaanite times. So, we have a famous song-form called *ataba*, it features on "A Baker's Dozen" (in *Sprinting Gazelle*). So, this *ataba* form, the stanza is four lines – the same word in Arabic is mentioned in the first three, but every time it's a different meaning.' And the title track, 'Sprinting Gazelle', dates back to the Ottoman era. 'This is what scares Zionists,' she says. 'Because we offer the continuum in the narrative, that indigenous Palestinians of all faiths – Muslims, Christians, Jewish Samaritans – have been there from time immemorial.'

It is not just pro-Israel or Zionist propaganda that Kelani is challenging. Growing up in Malaysia, Palestine was presented to me as a quintessentially Islamic concern. In my Islamic Studies classes in primary and secondary school, the liberation of Palestine was often part of a larger checklist for the ultimate Sunni-Islamic utopia – popular items included imposing the *tudung* (headscarf) on women, punishing Muslims who did not observe the Ramadan fast or Friday prayers and who committed *zina* (fornication), eradicating homosexuality and Shi'ism, and subjugating non-Muslim religions. One common thread that ran through these dogmas was not just a criticism of the Israeli state but an intense hatred for Jews; this is a part of the DNA of this version of Islam. Not surprisingly, people grow up with this ideology.

There is thus a part of me that wants very badly for Kelani to reach more and more Muslim audiences, speaking and performing as counter-*da'wah*. And *insha Allah*, she will. But the responsibility should not be hers alone. Kelani is already making Palestinian culture visible (and audible) to the best of her abilities, collecting ancient folk songs and political anthems and ensuring they continue to flourish. They will only live on when others listen to them carefully, understand them and are moved to act. And this act could be as simple as singing alongside Kelani and supporting Palestinian artists like her.

ALEXANDER DETAINED

Sharbari Z Ahmed

There were no stomping black boots or whistles. No lights were shone in our faces. We were not wrenched out of our beds and shoved onto cattle cars in a grey winter dawn. We were not herded into ghettos ringed with barbed wire. The killings and torture were done in secret. We knew about that but we didn't know all of it. I cannot say that we were not warned. As much as we were kept in the dark, much was revealed, either by design or callousness. All the signs were there as they have been in the past for such things and somehow we, the people, were in a state of inertia, shock, maybe some awe, but probably we were just naive. It could never happen again we said. Not to us. We are Americans, the chosen people.

When they did come for me, they came silently, gradually, graciously handing me clues along the way. There was the blue car with the dark tinted windows that idled across the street from my sixties cape every day at different times. The Christmas card that was torn and hastily taped together; the mail that never made it to its intended destination. There were of course the more obvious signs: the mother who was thrown in jail for protesting the war after her soldier son was killed, the lack of news about who was dying over there, the sudden takeover of 96.7 FM by Christian rock bands.

They came when the noon sun was high, and efficient. They were dressed plainly, suit jackets in neutral shades. Sunglasses that hid their eyes were as opaque as their car windows. They did not take them off when they informed me that my son and I were being moved to a facility 'for our own safety.' They handed me a piece of paper. It said that at this time I was to be remanded to the custody of the Department of Homeland Security and

sent to a 'secure facility'. For my security. Apparently my child and I were
in grave danger.

The television was on when they came. The wars had taken a turn for the
worse. The President's approval rating was at an all-time low. He had made
an Israeli dignitary wait in an anteroom off the Oval Office for forty-five
minutes before seeing him. His bombers had not managed to find a cell
hideout they had been aiming for and ended up killing eighteen members
of a wedding party. The cell leader was not in attendance. We had also been
assured that other enemies had a nuclear facility that they were building
with the express purpose of bombing us and destroying the world. Russia
had offered them a place to build it – just over the border – since the bone
of contention had been that our enemies not be allowed to have a nuclear
facility within their borders. But this also was not acceptable and our
enemies went ahead without consulting Washington DC.

We were sending the drones in for freedom, the President explained
patiently, and calmly but somehow the American people, who had been so
willing to give him the benefit of the doubt earlier, just weren't buying it
anymore. Too many of their sons had already died in Mesopotamia. Despite
his waning popularity the President was jovial most of the time. The news
showed him golfing and happily rolling pastel-coloured Easter eggs on the
White House lawn with his silent, statuesque wife by his side. But he was
growing more and more dismayed at how little the people understood the
danger our freedom was in. There was a newfound urgency in his voice as
he explained that our way of life was tenuous.

If they were affected by what was on the TV, which was turned up loudly
so I could hear it from the kitchen, the man and woman in the sunglasses
did not show it. I was given thirty minutes to gather what I needed.

'I need to call my husband,' I said. 'Is he coming with us?'

'No ma'am,' the woman said.

'He's Muslim too you know?' I said. 'He converted.' This time the man
spoke. 'We are aware of that ma'am.'

Of course they were. But it was my suitcase whose lock was always
broken at the airport. Not his.

'My son is still in school.'

'He has been secured,' the woman said. This is the point in a horror
movie where the kettle would whistle or the cat would knock a plant off

the windowsill – making everyone jump. Secured. He had been secured. Because at seven he was a threat to national security. He loved Darth Vader, felt a certain sympathy for his plight so I knew, on some level, he would have been amused that they thought he was as dangerous as Darth Vader.

'Is he all right? Is he hurt?' I said. I felt cold. I shivered. In the past three years words had taken on new meanings. They were used as codes. Security no longer meant what it used to, neither did freedom. It seemed that every time the Secretary of Defence or his boss uttered those words, people died.

The woman did not take her sunglasses off but her body stiffened. She looked up at her partner. He answered.

'Of course not ma'am. He is at the shelter already where he will be given a meal while he waits for you to arrive.'

For a moment I tried to grasp what he meant by shelter. I automatically thought of concrete bunkers.

'They have video games,' the woman added when I did not respond. Her partner did not like that she had volunteered this information. He cleared his throat and shifted his weight from one foot to another like a restless horse in a stall. But this information was meant to calm me and somehow it did. I pictured my son sitting on the floor of 'the secure facility' happily playing Super Mario with another little one who had a name like Abdullah or Mohammed. My son's name was Alexander after his paternal Polish great grandfather but his middle name was Salim, my maiden name, and that was all they had needed to 'secure' him.

My son had pale skin, jet-black hair and hazel eyes. His father joked that he looked like Damian, the devil-possessed kid from *The Omen*. His eyelashes were long and thick. His nose was sharp. His blood, rich with the history of three continents, made it hard to pinpoint exactly where he was from. He could have been from the Russian steppes or, when he tanned, from São Paulo. As my neighbour Mrs Dreyfus pointed out, 'He looks like a Jew.' This was said in a slightly accusatory tone like I was wilfully denying his heritage. When I looked at him I saw a little fair-skinned Bengali boy. A Bangladeshi American, Muslim, with Hindu roots, and yet part Micmac Indian from Canada and with an ancestor who fought alongside George Washington.

Six months earlier I heard the tapping noises on the phone for the first time. It was always at the same time of day – 3.30 in the afternoon.

Sometimes the phone rang and the caller ID could not identify the number. I assumed it was the ever-persistent telemarketers so I never picked up, but one day Alexander did. No one was at the other end. This happened at least three more times. Then certain files went missing on the computer. Files I did not remember deleting. My husband backed everything up, admonishing me, half kidding, 'It's only a matter of time. You have to plan for Armageddon.'

But the war I knew about was two thousand miles away, trapped in a graphic next to Rachel Maddow's head. It would never be at my front door. Then a falafel joint that we frequented run by the same Syrian family for thirty years suddenly closed down. Its windows were boarded up 'until further notice'. Kindly, moustachioed Mr Abdellah who owned the place was the one who told Alexander that he shared a name with a great leader and sparked my boy's curiosity.

'Iskander conquered the world by the time he was seventeen,' he told my son. 'You got ten years. Better get cracking.'

'Did he have to kill people?' Alexander asked.

Mr Abdellah nodded his head thoughtfully. 'Sometimes, yes. Sometimes great leaders have to do bad things for the greater good. Like our President.'

I shook my head. 'There's no justification for what the President is doing,' I said. Mr Abdellah looked at the two people in the restaurant and cleared his throat. He was uneasy. He winked at Alexander, and handed him a warm lamb falafel wrapped in tinfoil. 'Your mother doesn't agree.'

Alexander nodded his head knowingly. 'She thinks he is a – what did you say mommy?'

I shrugged, now embarrassed that I was being exposed. Alexander had a way of blurting things out to strangers. Once, he announced to a startled plumber that I waxed my upper lip twice a month.

'A war monger!' Alexander cried as he suddenly remembered a snippet of my regular diatribe against the President. 'Was Iskander a war monger?'

'The people he conquered would say so,' I said, deciding to weigh in on the conversation before Mr Abdellah could object to the President being called that.

'I am a simple man,' Mr Abdellah said, smiling at us. 'All I know is what I read in the school books back in Damascus. That will be ten dollars even.'

As I was walking out I noticed for the first time that he had an autographed picture of the President and the First Lady taped behind the cash register.

Now Mr Abdellah was gone. Americans were 'disappearing' every day, plucked off the street and detained in 'secure facilities' all over the country and in one spot in Cuba. But the war was not officially here yet. I kept reminding myself as I went through the days, writing, working out, being a class parent. I lost track of how many Betty Crocker cupcakes I made. Sometimes when the news got too bad, I took refuge in pretending to be a model mom.

My husband called on my cell phone as I was stuffing maxi pads into a duffel bag while the agents waited downstairs.

'What's doing,' he asked. I heard voices behind him. There was laughter, light heartedness. It was Friday, Memorial Day weekend, 2.30 in the afternoon. People would be leaving work early, heading to the Hamptons or some other destination. Summer was here, the days were longer, the air sweeter.

'I'm going to blow out of here early,' he said. There was a burst of laughter behind him. 'David wants me to go out for a drink and then I'll be home. No later than five.'

'There's no rush,' I said. 'I'm not going to be here.' I was shaking. My cell phone beeped before he could respond. 'Wait,' I said, thinking it might be Alexander. 'I have another call.' I switched over. 'Hello?'

'Yasmina?' The voice was fearful.

'Shakil?' I said. It was my childhood friend. The only other kid invited to my first birthday party. I knew that because there was photographic evidence. Shakil did something with derivatives, was a graduate of Wharton, a decent tennis player, a spelunker, a newlywed. He had met his wife Melissa when he was a junior at Choate but she had not given him the time of day until she saw him again at their ten-year reunion. He had driven up in an Audi. Shakil had never set foot in a mosque. He never ate rice with his fingers.

'Where are you Yasmina?' He said.

'At home. Where are you?'

'I'm at JFK.'

'Where are you going?'

'Texas.'

'Okay. For work?' I was confused. Shakil sounded distant even though I could hear him clearly.

'They are sending me to someplace near Austin. I'm trying to make sure they send my dad to the same place. Luckily, mom is in Bangladesh. I told her not to come back any time soon.'

It took me a moment to register what he was saying. I was not alone. I was not the only one they were 'securing'.

'What about Melissa?' I said.

'She's going to come out there as soon as she can.'

'They haven't detained her?'

'No. I'm not even sure why they're sending me anywhere. I mean I'm not part of the community. I haven't been to a mosque in years.'

I closed my eyes and sighed. In all the years I had known him I had accepted his self-loathing – his disdain and mistrust for all things Islamic or Bengali. I didn't even take it personally when he told me he found South Asian women unattractive as a rule, a ludicrous attitude but one that seemed to be a part of who he wanted to be. He had never treated me unkindly.

'Did Melissa convert?' I asked.

Shakil snorted into the phone. 'Of course not. And I never would have asked her to. You know that.'

'They have Alexander,' I said.

'Oh no. Where? Where is he?' My cell phone beeped insistently. Matthew had hung up and called me back. 'Wait Shakil,' I said.

'I'll call you back,' he said. 'To find out about Alexander.'

'What if they take your cell phone?'

'They can't do that,' he said. 'Jesus! This is still America, Yasmina.'

'Is it?'

'Look. I can't deal with all your conspiracy theories right now,' he said. In all the years I had known him he had never raised his voice to me. 'There is an explanation for this,' he added, more quietly. 'There is.'

His voice hurt me. The phone beeped. 'Shakil, I have to go.' 'Talk soon.' I switched over. 'Matthew?'

'Hey,' he sounded annoyed. 'So I'll be home...'

'Matthew, that was Shakil. He is being sent to Texas. They have Alexander and they are sending me to him. Everything you said was true. They have built camps and they are taking me to a camp. I just want to get to Alexander.'

'They are there now?'

'Yes. Downstairs. I have to pack.'

'Did they hurt you?'

'Not yet.'

'They have Alexander?'

'Yes.'

'What if they take your cell phone?'

'I don't know. Please stop shooting all these questions at me.'

'The moment you reach wherever they are taking you, call me.'

'Can you stall them?'

'No.'

'I'll go straight to the camp. You have to tell me where it is the moment you find out.'

'Call Ben.'

Ben Seidel was our attorney. A year earlier, Matthew had been slightly injured in a car accident that was not his fault. Ben had won him fifty thousand dollars. He was a relentless, perpetually indignant man. The thought of him comforted me. There were still laws in place...somewhere, and Ben would find one that would stop this.

'Okay. What if they send you to Texas?' Matthew said.

'Then I will go. I just want Alexander.'

'This is really happening.'

'You called it.'

'How can you be so calm?'

I looked at my face in the mirror above the dresser. My lips were white.

'Because I don't know what will happen,' I said. 'I just want my son.'

'Be careful. Don't antagonise them. Obviously they think they have something on you and right now they are holding all the cards.'

'They're holding the only card I care about. They have nothing on me. I didn't do anything.'

When Alexander was born, I began to read inspirational books on motherhood. In one I read that being a mother was like walking around with your heart outside your body. As I suspected I was one big Achilles heel. My vulnerability was repeatedly thrown into mean relief. Two years earlier I was in Washington DC to collect a small literary award I had won for a short story I had written. I had attended the awards ceremony and dinner and given a drunken speech about arts and activism but chose to skip the other activities they had planned the following day. Instead, I went to the Holocaust Museum. It was a Sunday afternoon and the museum was not crowded. I walked through it silently. Every muscle in my shoulders and jaw were tense. I stood in a cattle car that was used to transport Jews to Auschwitz. When I gazed into the empty eyes of Jewish and Gypsy children in a black and white photograph all I saw was Alexander. I read Hitler's fatwa, encased behind bulletproof glass, calling for the murder of all Polish men, women and children. Polish, like Alexander's ancestors. My son, who looked like a Jew and was of Polish blood, would have been taken to a concentration camp had he been born then and in that place. I knew that with a deep certainty as I gazed at a hill of eyeglasses removed from Jewish prisoners glinting under a spotlight. I felt: there is so very little separating my son's fate from all those children who had been killed, just a gossamer thread of luck and time. Luck was something I never trusted. I disliked games of chance and refused to play poker. Naturally, then, life made me very uneasy. There were, however, a few things I knew with certainty, and I knew holocausts were taking place at the very instant I was standing in the cattle car in the museum that still held the souls it had transported to their ends.

After I walked through the exhibitions, I vomited into the museum toilet and bought *Night* by Elie Weisel in the gift shop for Matthew, who was always complaining he had nothing to read on the commute to the city. When I lay in my hotel bed that afternoon all I could think was, 'How did I get so lucky, if there is such a thing? Why was I chosen to live in a time and a place where my child and I would be safe? What was my responsibility?' My appetite was gone and I just wanted to get home and hold my child.

'Ma'am?' The woman agent was standing in my doorway. I was still staring down at the maxi pads, at a loss for what to pack next. She had removed her sunglasses. Her eyes were blue.

'We need to get going. I'm sure you want to see your son.'

It was subtle, but the inference was clear. They would use Alexander in any way possible. Of course they would.

'Where are you taking me?' I said.

'To a secure facility in New Paltz.' That was upstate New York, almost three hours away.

'Is that where my son is?'

'Yes.'

They must have taken him before he even got to school. What must he have been thinking, having been told repeatedly of 'stranger danger'? Had they accosted him on the street in front of his school? Had they forcibly bundled him into a car? Had they put a bag over his head? What if he was drugged? How terrified he must have been! Now there was anger in me. Finally.

'How many camps do you have?'

'Ma'am?' The blue eyed agent perfectly feigned confusion.

'Concentration camps. How many concentration camps has Halliburton built?' I nearly spat the words out. This time her surprise was genuine. I had thrown her. She looked towards the stairs. She wanted to run. She waited a moment before answering, formulating her thoughts. 'These are not concentration camps, Ma'am. These are facilities that have been created for your protection.'

'Protection from what?'

'I cannot say Ma'am.'

'You are only protecting Muslims and those of Arab descent, are you not?'

'There are certain groups at this time who are more vulnerable than others,' she replied in a robotic voice. 'It is security measure that is necessary at this time.'

Security. Again. 'But the war is over there,' I said lamely.

'Things have changed. Terrorism knows no borders,' she replied. She glanced at her watch. 'Do you need assistance to finish packing?'

I shook my head. I ran into the bathroom and took Alexander's Sponge Bob toothbrush. I went into his room and grabbed his stuffed manta ray, his Game Boy with three games, his Batman pyjamas, six pairs of underwear, ten pairs of socks, and as many of his clothes I could hold in my arms. I contemplated taking his juicy cup as he called it, a cup with a no-spill top that he sucked on every night while falling asleep since he was three. His version of a security blanket – to Alexander security meant safety. We had been trying to wean him off it, telling him that nearly-seven year-olds did not need that kind of security. I decided to leave it because I did not want to believe that we would be there, wherever they were taking us, for too long.

When I walked back into my room I realised that I had taken too many warm clothes.

'How long are we going to be detained?' I said.

'I cannot say at this time,' she replied. She forgot to remind me that I was not being detained.

'Then how can I pack?' I said.

'At this time you are instructed to take as much as you can pack in two suitcases. One each for you and your son.'

'Fine.'

I dumped the clothes and toys on to my bed and walked into the hallway. Matthew had stored our suitcases in a crawl space in the hallway. I pulled out two over-sized American Touristers that I had pounced on at a sale at Marshalls ages ago. Alexander's mini suitcase with wheels sat next to our suitcases. It was colourful and grimy. Alexander had dragged this suitcase filled with essentials like crayons and toy soldiers around the world. We had been planning a trip to Vietnam for August right before school reopened. The tickets had been purchased, hotels had been booked. Shakil and Melissa were going to join us a few days into our stay. They had been invited to a wedding in Bali. I pulled out Alexander's small suitcase as well. I could say that it was like carry-on luggage. I dragged the suitcases into the bedroom and placed them on the bed. I unzipped the larger one and pulled the top back. Inside the top was taped a piece of paper with Arabic writing on it. It was an *aitul kursi*, a blessing from the Qur'an, protecting the contents of my suitcase and ostensibly the owner of it as well. My mother had taped it into all my luggage after my suitcase got sent to

Hawaii when I was on my way to Boston. She even taped one to the inside of the driver side visor in my Subaru Outback. I never thought much of it. I dismissed it as superstition but went along with it to humour my mother.

I looked at the agent who was staring at the paper. Her face was expressionless. I could only imagine what was going on in her head. Bomb detonation instructions perhaps, or a coded message to a fellow terrorist.

'Ma'am?' the agent said. 'I suggest you remove that *aitul kursi* so you don't have to repeatedly explain what it is. Your luggage will be subject to extensive inspection.'

I looked at her closely then. She was blonde, but it was not her natural colour. Her eyes, like I said, were blue. I noticed that she was darker than I had first realised, more olive than tan. She had read the piece of paper and pronounced *aitul kursi* perfectly.

'Where are you from?' I asked her.

She hesitated before answering me, looking towards the staircase, where her partner waited at the foot of it.

'Michigan,' she said after a moment.

'What ethnicity are you?'

'My father is Italian and my mother is Lebanese. '

'Muslim?' I whispered.

'Ma'am, I will not answer any more questions at this time. You must finish packing. Now.'

I obeyed her, realising it was futile and also, strangely beyond caring. What difference did it make after all? I began packing in earnest and realized all I needed was one suitcase. Better to flee with, I thought.

When I was done I had one suitcase filled with both mine and Alexander's clothes that would see us through summer and fall. I asked the agent if I could take the small duffel bag for toiletries. She nodded assent.

'I will take your things downstairs,' she said.

A new calm settled over me. I would see Alexander soon. I could hand him his game boy in person. He would crawl into my arms and I would gather my nerves for what lay ahead. Matthew would arrive with Ben, who would have contacted the ACLU by then.

I called Matthew and told him while the agent watched me. Her eyes never left my face.

'New Paltz?'

'Yes.'

'That's where Alexander is?'

'Yes. That's what they told me.'

'I called Ben. He'll come with me.'

'Call Sara,' I said. Sara was my best friend. She was a cinematographer and on a film shoot somewhere in the Ozarks. I could have called her myself but Sara would have immediately wanted me to refuse to go with the agents. She would rant and demand to speak with them. Sara was single and had no children. Sometimes she forgot I was a mommy because I was so good about not letting motherhood define me. I did not carry a picture of Alexander in my wallet. I never went on about his latest antics. Alexander had tested as a gifted child but no one, except his school, his grandparents and Matt and I knew that. If he said something really funny that I knew people would appreciate I would share it with them, like when he thought 'son of a bitch' was pronounced 'sullivan pitch' and said that every time he stubbed his toe or fell off his skateboard. In general what I had observed was that people without kids rarely knew how to talk to one and about one. Matt's buddies were all single or divorced. Shakil was good with Alexander being a big kid himself but Sara talked to him like he was a potential misogynist. Sara met Alexander's assertion that girls had cooties with a lecture on Betty Freidan. I had learned to keep my love of motherhood a secret. As far as anyone knew I was just someone who had given birth. It was a label. What that really meant, none of them knew.

I locked the door to the cape that Matthew and I had paid too much for and stood on the stoop looking out into the street. It was 3.15. Alexander's school bus pulled up at the end of the road. Children spilled out and ran into their mother's arms. Most of the children were blonde and white. One was black. I recognised a new friend Alexander had made, Sebastian Cruz. They both loved to play Star Wars on their X-boxes. The school bus pulled away having successfully discharged its precious cargo. These children did not need to be specially protected by their government. A black child could now drink from the same water fountain as his white classmates. He could sit at the front of the bus. All school notices were now printed in both Spanish and English.

Sebastian walked by with his stepfather, a cheerful man who did not speak English.

'Where's Alex?' The boy asked me as I was getting into the Ford Taurus with the tinted windows. The female agent held the door open for me.

'One minute,' I said.

'Ma'am,' her partner began.

'One minute!' I snapped. I knelt down so I was eye to eye with Sebastian. 'He'll be missing school for a while,' I said. 'I drew a picture for him,' Sebastian said as his stepfather looked at the agents waiting for me. When he looked at me his brown eyes were full of understanding. He shook his head and looked down at his scuffed shoes. Sebastian pulled out a piece of white paper from his backpack and held it up in front of him.

'This is Darth Vader,' he explained, pointing to a large black figure at the centre of the page. The figure held a long red light sabre. His head was disproportionately larger than his body.

'He just cut off Luke Skywalker's hand.'

He pointed to a brown figure lying on the ground with a bloody stump where his hand should have been.

'Alex likes Darth Vader but I want to be a jedi,' he said and handed me the drawing.

'You know Darth Vader used to be a jedi,' I said.

'Can I come over for a play date tomorrow?'

'Not tomorrow, but soon, I promise,' I said. Tears sprung to my eyes. I patted Sebastian on the head. His stepfather took my hand in both of his and said something in Spanish. He must have thought I was being deported. He was wary of the agents, but looked into my eyes and nodded. '*Dios te bendiga.*'

'I am going to get my son,' I said to him. 'I'll see him soon.'

I heard the female agent clear her throat. I nodded to Sebastian's father and got in the car.

LAST OF THE TASBURAI

Rehan Khan

Prologue

Courage. Elek invoked it. The hilt of his sword slipped in his hand. His boots slid on wet shingle, as his knees buckled. He couldn't see Father, but was certain he was close. The moonless sky cast a blanket over the shore. Thick fog rolled in from the Black Sea. He squinted through the murk.

Dark shapes leapt off longboats, swiftly moving from the edge of the water up the pebbled beach. His heart pounded as he swung his gaze right then left; he knew these were soldiers coming ashore. He could hear their boots trampling on shells. Hundreds. Heavily armoured. He wiped the sweat off his brow, as a voice inside pleaded for him to flee.

His Father was out there. Hold firm. Elek sensed they'd seen him, transfixed like a frozen bystander. A knot tightened in his stomach. There were too many of them. He turned to run, scrambling back up the bank, making for the lookout tower. He was short of breath and felt light-headed but remembered what he had to do.

Shouts behind him intensified. He sped up. His foot jammed against a rock and he fell flat. The sword clattered to the ground. He was up once more, making a clumsy grab for the hilt, but it caught on a boulder; he'd have to leave it. Sounded like a wall of metal closing in on him. Run.

Elek was through the tower door. He dropped the deadlock before rushing up the stairs. Would it hold them for a minute?

Smash. The door held, rattled violently. Again. This time the door flew off its hinges. Ironclad soldiers swarmed in, broadswords raised aloft. The spiral staircase was too narrow for the pack – they'd need to come up one at a time. He scrambled up the stairs on all fours, like a wild animal with a hunting party on its tail.

Elek released the second deadlock door; it fell from a slender murder hole in the ceiling, cruel spikes protruding from it. This door was reinforced with sheets of metal, stronger and harder to breach.

He glanced around the circular room with its dusty floor. Threadbare, but for the fire, a healthy supply of wooden logs and coal and a brass tube the size of a man set within a metal frame in the centre of the room, connected to a chimney rising up and out of the tower. Seizing a pair of tongs he lifted the red-hot poker from the hearth. It would ignite the powder left by the pyromancers in the oblong tube. His Father had told him the resulting fire would be seen for miles. Neither of them had ever set it off. Not until today. Suddenly he felt calm. He was dead already.

Elek stepped toward the brass structure. The door rattled. The soldiers were trying to get in, but they wouldn't be able to, not before he'd sent the warning to the people of the Athenian archipelago.

An image caught his eye. A bloody red silhouette formed on the outer window, before bursting through it, sending thousands of shards across the floor. He stepped back.

Shaped like a man, yet flickering like a flame, the Ifreet's eyes glowed molten red, the tips of its fingers and toes tar black. Before he could react, the demon shifted, and stood before him, the tube behind it. Elek lunged, driving the burning metal poker at the Ifreet. As it pierced the demon's body, the metal melted like wax dripping over a roaring fire. He recoiled, removing what remained of the poker. A cruel smile formed on his enemy's face.

The demon gripped his wrist: searing heat made him shriek and drop his makeshift weapon. With his left hand he reached for the hunting knife strapped to his waist. The Ifreet was upon him, ramming him to the ground. His head hit the deck as the demon grabbed his ankles, yanking him out the shattered window. It leapt, hovering in mid air, before it let Elek slip from its burning grasp. The air rushed at his face and as he hurtled head first towards the rocks, his eyes caught sight of the Ifreet, poised like a leaf caught in a breeze, floating. Courage.

1. Following Orders

It was a challenge running over rooftops in Avantolia. The vertigo was making Adan dizzy. The roof ended with only one way ahead: a narrow crossbeam to the other side. He looked down. His head was spinning, but he saw them stumble in the dark alley a hundred feet below. The three criminals kept glancing around. The rain lashed Adan's face, and the wind whipped around him.

It's just a piece of metal. Focus. A couple seconds, and it's over.

This time he gazed ahead, sliding one foot onto the crossbeam. The howling wind tugged at him, and his boots slipped on wet metal. He stretched his arms out. Nice and easy. No need to rush. Shouting came from below. They'd spotted him. He looked down and wobbled.

Adan growled and ran the remaining distance over the beam. The brickwork on the roof's edge was loose, but he moved before it crumbled. The building ended. Another roof was far below. He remembered his master's words. Never hesitate. Let your movements flow. Adan leapt, arms out wide, robes flapping, and heart pumping. His feet hit the loose gravel on the roof. He rolled, stood, and ran again. Adan used the tower's internal stairwell to reach ground level. All he needed was to keep out of sight and follow the criminals until one of the masters showed up.

Adan heard footsteps and turned sideways. The criminals hurtled out of the narrow alley, crashing into him and knocking him over. The first one was at least six feet tall with broad shoulders and a face crisscrossed with scars. The second brute was bigger with an eye patch, close-cropped hair, and stubble. The warrant for their arrest said they were seafaring men. The third man was of medium build and wore an iron mask.

'Tasburai,' said Scarface.

'Apprentice.' Eyepatch chuckled. 'Let's do him before the master shows up.'

Adan might have been sixteen, not as well built, and not as mean-looking as these fellows, but he wasn't a pushover. His master said half the battle was in the preparation. His hand closed around the hilt of his sword, Tizona. The criminals froze, watching the blade forged from pure Orlisium steel. No, Adan could take them without Tizona. Master Suri-Yi would be impressed.

Scarface came for him. Wielding a large hunting knife, he was a blur of arms and legs. It was too late for the sword anyway. Scarface was on him. Adan shifted, catching Scarface's heel and shoving him into a heap of decomposing rubbish. If he had smelt like salty deck slop before, he was even more rotten now.

Eyepatch circled with upraised fists. He moved like an experienced prizefighter. Scarface rose, but Adan slammed a boot into his stomach, sending him sprawling deeper into the refuse and knocking him out cold. On the ground was a circular bin cover. Adan bent down, swivelled it in his hand, and threw it like a discus. It caught Eyepatch in the midriff.

The iron-masked man had shifted his weight one way then another, but hadn't moved. Eyepatch pulled a long strip of rusted metal from the scaffolding. Brandishing it like a crowbar, he came for Adan. 'Come on, kid,' he shouted, swinging it wildly over his head.

Eyepatch plodded forwards with heavy steps. Adan skipped, ran at him, and shot under his opponent's legs before he whacked Eyepatch on the backside, sending him flying into the air. Adan surveyed the sailors. The warrant said they were wanted for political crimes. Looking at them now, Adan found it hard to imagine. Still, it was his role as Tasburai to arrest criminals against the Avanist Revolution, and so were enemies of the republic.

The man in the iron mask retreated. His feet dragged on the ground as though terrified of a dark wraith. He was staring behind Adan. Adan spun just as Master Naram-Sin shot past him. Naram-Sin was lean and wiry, and rammed into the masked man.

'So you thought you'd get away from me?' said Naram-Sin.

'Please, I beg you. Release me from this mask. I can't live like this!'

'Only when you're in the Oblivion.'

'No! Not that place, please! I'll pay whatever you want. Don't send me there!'

'I'm not interested in your money. Only your title.' Naram-Sin kicked the man in the head. He grabbed his ankles, tied them together, and dragged him away.

'Coming…they're coming,' the man in the iron mask mumbled.

Naram-Sin whacked him again and knocked him unconscious. As he went past Adan, he said, 'Kill these two.' Then Master Naram-Sin was gone, carrying the slumped form of the masked man over his shoulder.

Adan ran his fingers through his wet black hair and surveyed the two sailors. His instructions weren't to kill. He was just to bring them in for questioning by the Secret Police. The man in the iron mask had mumbled about someone coming, but who was coming?

Adan stared at the two for several minutes. He was still working out what to do when his master, Suri-Yi, bolted out from the alley where the criminals had emerged. As always she was dressed modestly in dark robes and a high-necked tunic. Her long, silky hair was tied in a ponytail and clipped in place by a ceremonial brooch. The emblem of a Tasburai master, a circle surrounded by four smaller ones, was etched into the skin of her right and left wrists.

'Where is the iron-masked man?' said Suri-Yi.

'Master Naram-Sin took him.'

She clenched her fists.

'He's headed for the Oblivion,' Adan continued.

Suri-Yi's eyes narrowed to small slits. He recognised that look. He gulped, knowing how her enemies must have felt in the moment before she attacked.

'What about these two?' Adan asked.

'Leave them.' Suri-Yi turned and walked away.

2. Laying a Trap

Ylva crashed through the forest, feet slipping on moist leaves and damp, soggy ground. Her heart was pounding as if it was about to come out of her chest, and her arms were scratched up by nettles. She ducked late, slammed into a low branch, and fell in a heap. She felt naked without a weapon and easy prey for the horsemen riding up.

Father said it was best she not carry weapons when they captured her. Too right, she reckoned, but it didn't make her feel any safer. She, a sprightly young'un, surrounded by men on horseback? She'd heard a nasty tale or two of what happened to girls like her. Still, her old man had a knack for knowing about things others could only guess. He wasn't headman for nothing.

The Nostvekt horsemen were all around. She could see their mounts through the trees. They were laughing at her—a timid teenage girl ripe to be put to work and too easy to catch. She knew she had the better of them, but showing off was for another time and place. Get to the castle city of Kronnoburg, her old man had said.

A soldier trudged towards her, his bright boots getting sloshed up in the mud. Net in hand, he expected to snare her like a pheasant. Shall I let him? No. Father didn't say nothing 'bout making it easy like for 'em Nostvektians. She wanted a bit of fun first.

So Ylva lunged wide, rolled through brambles, got more cuts on her shoulders, jumped up, and ran. She skidded on her knees, sliding on the ground. The net flew high and past her. She turned, gave the soldier a cheeky smirk, and sprinted away from him.

Two more riders came over the ridge with spears in hand. They weren't going to use weapons on her. She was too precious. They wanted her for selling in the market, and there was no need to damage her before some wealthy widower paid a handsome fee for her. She sped up. The soldiers exchanged glances. A boulder was ten feet ahead, dry enough to leap off. She hit it plumb, launched into the air, and took the closest rider by surprise. Yanking his neck with her porcelain-coloured hands, she shimmied herself into the saddle behind him. The soldier lost his grip and thumped to the ground like a sack of potatoes.

This is more like it! Now she was going to enjoy them chasing her. Father wouldn't mind.

'Yah!' shouted Ylva. The horse responded to her command and galloped down the ridge, leaving behind the Nostvektian soldiers.

The mare was strong. It ran well. Ylva put half a field between herself and the pack. It was like the training she'd done with Father time and time again. He was a man of method and made sure she practised regularly. There was a deep gorge ahead about fifteen feet wide. She'd moseyed around it earlier in the day. She debated whether to jump it or not. Racing downhill with the land before her opening up, she turned to look. At least a dozen Nostvektian soldiers were on her tail. Good. I have their attention.

The wind pushed back her mousy brown hair as she clutched the reins and dug her heels into the horse. The mare leapt, sailing over the gorge. Half the soldiers pulled up. Cravens, she thought. The others made the jump. They would be spitting mad when they caught her. They'd probably want to sell her first before the other slaves. She was too much bother for them. They'd find some fat, rich nobleman who could do with her as he pleased.

She steered her mare towards Castle Kronnoburg's great walls. The soldiers would want to stop her from reaching the castle and save themselves the embarrassment in front of the guards in the turrets. Those who had jumped the gorge were breathing heavily, pushing their horses, and shooting murderous glances at her, but she knew they wouldn't act on impulse. Nostvektians were too prim and proper.

Ylva was grinning. It had been a while since she'd enjoyed herself like this. The past few weeks had been filled with training, instructions, and map memorisation. The maps showed the interior of the so-called impregnable Castle Kronnoburg. Her father tested and pushed her on every detail, forced her to undergo additional physical training, and taught her to fight without her precious weapons. She felt lost without the sword hilt, bow grip, or spear handle. She longed for them like a lover, but she'd have to do without until the ruse was over.

The valley dipped, and Castle Kronnoburg disappeared over the horizon. She rode hard, urging her mare down the green hill. She loved the breeze on her neck and cheeks, and the sun upon her head. A few moments later, she looked around. The soldiers hadn't come over the ridge. She pulled up her horse, jumped off, and sent the mare on her way. Ylva took up a position on the ground and held her ankle. As the Nostvektian soldiers rode down the slope, they slowed.

'Mercy!' Ylva cried out, one hand on her ankle and the other raised in submission.

'Ha, stupid girl, what were you thinking?' shouted one of them.

Another grabbed her by the elbow and pulled her up. Ylva cried out, mimicking a searing pain, and she collapsed into the soldier's arms.

'No better than an animal,' said the soldier. The others burst out laughing.

A soldier tied her arms and feet and hauled her stomach first onto his horse. She'd ride into Kronnoburg in this sorry state, but she kept reminding herself it was only a role. Ylva looked carefully at the soldiers' faces. She didn't want to forget. When she was reunited with her trusty weapons, she'd pay a visit to these men and see who laughed last.

3. Oblivion Prison

Adan despised this place. The stone walls were cold, and the air was lifeless. Mostly he hated the smell—damp as though soaked in fetid water. The familiar pain ran up his neck as he entered the Oblivion Prison. It gripped him every time like a clamp upon his spine, and it wouldn't let go until he left this infernal place. Adan glided along the labyrinth of corridors leading to the lower cells. Master Suri-Yi was by his side, and they followed Master Naram-Sin.

The tunnels were charcoal grey and poorly illuminated. The walls were bereft of windows. Suri-Yi had accompanied hundreds of men and women down these corridors. That's what happened to opponents of the Avanist Revolution. They disappeared into the Oblivion Prison, or the Pit as it was better known. They were condemned by the republic, captured, and incarcerated by the Tasburai Order. Looking at Suri-Yi now, Adan couldn't see an ounce of remorse. Why should she be remorseful, though? She was Tasburai, and they were above the law.

The Revolutionary Guard, the Copper-Tops, accompanied them. Dressed in black, their helmets glinted like newly minted coins. Their soft leather combat boots squeaked on the shiny surface as they marched in unison. None paid him any attention, but they never did. Maybe it was better that way. No one wanted to be reminded of this grisly business. Each visit to the Oblivion Prison left Adan feeling guilty, as though an infection had crawled into his mind.

Deeper and deeper their little party went, wheeling a sealed casket through unidentifiable passageways. The thumping from within the casket had almost petered out. They reached the vault door. Adan held his breath. The door was a circular armoured-steel structure with vicious spikes. Two Copper-Tops stood on either side. Batons in hand, their faces were half hidden by masks. They were protectors of the entrance to the Pit.

'Tasburai confirmed,' barked one of the guards.

The vault door swung open. As always the clerk was there. He sat behind a small desk in the centre of the enormous hall. He was a thin man with round spectacles and a fluffy moustache. He was immaculate in his high-collared crisp grey uniform. The accusing look came first. Then he recognised Naram-Sin and Suri-Yi, and his facial expression softened a touch. Armed Copper-Tops stood every ten paces around the hall, gazing straight ahead like statues.

The clerk was shuffling paper. He was always flicking through sheets and rolls of it, files and records of citizens who had disappeared to protect the republic.

'Master Naram-Sin and Master Suri-Yi, a pleasure,' said the clerk. The first time Adan had heard those words, he'd actually believed them. He knew now pleasure didn't register with these servants of the republic—these keepers of the Oblivion Prison.

Suri-Yi merely nodded to the clerk. She had told Adan early in his apprenticeship that the less he said before other servants of the republic the better. She had warned that any idle statement could be used against him in the future. 'Guilty until proven innocent' was the republic's mantra, and it was indoctrinated into its loyal subjects.

'Sealed casket?' the clerk asked.

'Yes,' Naram-Sin replied.

The clerk rose, and his chair screeched over the marble floor. Smacking his lips, he approached the casket. Like an officious head teacher, the clerk wanted to ensure standards were maintained, so an inspection of the prisoner was a must. He'd never turned anyone away, though.

'Slide open the casket viewer,' he instructed the guard.

The metal section of the viewer was pulled away and revealed a glass interior. The man in the iron mask stared back. He began thumping the glass. His words were lost behind the seal.

'An iron mask? My, you have gone to some lengths with this one,' said the clerk.

'I want him in the Pit. Not a cell. Lower him in the casket. We'll throw in the key afterwards. Maybe one of the other prisoners will unlock it. If not, he'll rot inside,' said Naram-Sin.

'His crime?' asked the clerk.

'Member of the subversive movement the Shining Fist. Wanted for political crimes against the republic,' he replied.

'Approved,' said the clerk.

'I want to question him first,' said Suri-Yi.

'No,' Naram-Sin replied.

'I believe he has information about merchant ships disappearing in the Black Sea. It could be a sign. They might be returning.'

'Ha!' Naram-Sin snarled. 'We killed all the Magrog. You oversaw it. They will not be returning. Enough of this nonsense.'

'And if you are wrong?'

Naram-Sin laughed. 'The world has moved on, Suri-Yi. You should too. There are now more important priorities.'

'Such as?'

'Spreading the Avanist Revolution,' said Naram-Sin, turning to look at the clerk.

'I still want to question him.'

'No!'

The clerk and Adan looked from one to the other. The clerk clapped his hands. The enormous wooden door behind them swung open and revealed a chamber. The Copper-Tops wheeled the casket through.

'Naram-Sin, you do not have the authority,' said Suri-Yi.

'I act upon the directives of Chancellor Sargon. You would defy the chancellor?'

Immediately the Copper-Tops turned to face Suri-Yi. Their hands were on their weapons. Adan's breath quickened. He'd been here dozens of times to deliver prisoners to the clerk. What was going on? Suri-Yi swung her gaze around the chamber.

'Do it your way,' said Suri-Yi.

'I wasn't asking for your approval,' said Naram-Sin.

The Copper-Tops lifted the casket and placed it into a wire cage tied to a pulley. They hauled it over the lip of the Pit, which was a circular opening in the ground shaped like a well. It spanned the distance a horse would run in three strides. As the cage began its descent, the thumping from within the casket grew louder. From within the belly of the Pit, Adan could hear faint voices crying out.

Adan stood at the edge of the Pit and looked down at its smooth circular walls. It was a self-run prison. The inmates decided who lived and who was not useful. No guards patrolled it. No one had ever escaped. It was said to be the size of two cornfields chiselled from the rock face below. Adan didn't want to know and had no intention of visiting the infernal place.

Naram-Sin removed the key to the casket from his robes. He looked across at Suri-Yi, smiled, and threw the key into the Pit. Adan never heard it reach the bottom. The rope lowering the wire cage was still running along the pulley. They waited in silence. Eventually the rope stopped moving.

'Your heart is cold, Naram-Sin,' said Suri-Yi.

'I learnt from the best, Suri-Yi.'

Adan became aware of the clerk studying Suri-Yi closely. She took a step back. The clerk was staring at her with those cold, hard eyes. She held his gaze, and he turned away.

Suri-Yi swirled around, striding for the vault door. Adan hurried after her. Naram-Sin remained stationary beside the clerk.

'Master Suri-Yi,' said the clerk.

She froze, turned slowly, and faced him. Adan did the same but was desperate to leave. 'Yes?'

He studied her face again. 'Nothing. You may go,' he said.

When Adan was back out in the corridor, his heart pounding, he realised Suri-Yi's hand had been around the hilt of her sword, Shamshir.

Extracted from *Last of the Tasburai* by Rehan Khan, independently published, 2014.

FIVE POEMS

Peter Stockton

God is Not an Elephant (but He is in the Room)

At the inter-faith conference
All hell was breaking loose
As men of faith failed to convince each other
Of which was God's preferred people
Or favourite Prophet
Or most desired form of worship
So,
One stood up and said,
I will tell you a story
And because they all liked stories
They shut up and let him speak and he said:
There were some men of faith in a room
And there was an elephant there but it was dark
So they could not see it
But they knew something was there
So they all said:
Describe it!

The Orthodox Christian said:
It is like a piece of rope,
To which the Catholic said:
No, not like rope but a snake.
Indeed not, said the Protestant,
Long and straight maybe
But not a snake or a rope but smooth
And it jabs my finger sharply;

It is like a sword.
The Orthodox Jew said:
No, it is not like that at all.
It is like a wall,
While the liberal Jew said:
Not so! 'Tis like a ball!
The Sunni Muslim said:
If you could see
You'd know like me
That it is like a tree.
The other Muslim said:
What nonsense!
It is like parchment!
He was Shia
And was, of course, holding the ear,
The Sunni, the leg,
The Jews, the side and the head,
And the Christians, respectively,
The tail, the trunk and tusk which,
If nothing else,
At least all began with 't'.

Like you perhaps
They recognised the tale –
The Jews, thinking of jokes about
Two Jews,
Three opinions
And four Prime Ministers,
Said:
It is a Jewish story
(Perhaps not actually but metaphorically)
The Christians could not agree naturally and said:
It is our story
And describes our curious trinity.
And a Muslim shouted out:
Actually, it is our story!

It is Sufi!
Which was met by a loud retort from another brother of that faith
(Salafi, probably)
That that meant the story was wrong absolutely
As it had not been recorded by Muslim or Bukhari

And so what happened to these men
Was that the conference ended there and then
Not only could they not agree
They could not even let the story be
And so went home
Quite angrily
(There but for the grace of God go we)

Rapping My Way to Islam

I had a dream
A crazy dream
Where things weren't really what they seemed
I drove a cart
Through a city
A Jewish man in the back behind me
Ringlets, coat-tails
Looked like JC
Crowds were shouting
'Bout World War III
A chance to blame it on world Jewry
I felt bad for him sitting there behind me
Cos way back in the 80s in the Galilee
I got lifts from loads of Israelis
They didn't give me
Milk and honey
But gave me cake and drinks all fizzy
So this here now it really got me
I wanted to give the guy some sympathy

So I stopped at a stall right next to a tree
And got him a bun
All pink and sticky
Turned to give it him
And say I'm sorry
But he'd changed to a guy from deepest Araby
Kaffiyeh and thobe all white and sparkly.

Three years later that guy was me.

Can You Keep a Secret?

A Palestinian child takes the good soldier a glass of tea,
and she tells you this only when she trusts you,
trusts you on pain of death
a massive vow of secrecy

An Israeli talks of a Palestinian family in Gaza
that she and hers are good friends with.
Visits aren't possible any more.

But it is not a war
though sometimes it seems so

Everyone here can find reason for hatred and fear.
Yet perhaps everyone has a moment
they have shared that they hold secret
hold dear
in their hearts,
A secret that may be deeply buried,
so deep that it is a secret even from the self.

They are dangerous, these secrets.
Illogical, and they seem to negate
whole sets of belief systems

by which people define themselves.

But we all need one,
at least one, good 'Other'.
And if we haven't met them
we will keep a place in our hearts for them,
for this mythical figure to enter our lives
and make us whole.

But if we have to wait too long
our hearts will ache and close,
and we will succumb
to something like madness
and we will declare war
In our numbness
on the other,
and hence on ourselves.
We will vow annihilation.
An end to all our fears

They hanged Eichmann here in '62
For what he'd done
But even he had once learned Hebrew for two years.

Who's Who?

On TV
You sit there and
I realise that
You are hollow
Your words echo
From the empty
Cavern of your chest
As you describe how best
To just be rid of the rest

I'd wondered before
How you'd been able
To dismiss with such ease
The one across the table
They'd sounded genuinely
In pain describing
Their suffering
At your hands
And I'd thought that you
If anyone
Would understand
Where they'd been and
What they'd seen
But no
You felt no echo
You have to choose
To be in someone else's shoes
But you choose
Not to

The Anatomy of Longing

I am going to be like a scientist
(She can cry
Not I)
We will take some numbers
This one tells us much
See how big it is
Compared to this one
Longer, rounder
(Do I smell food?)
Enough
Let us move one step away
And talk of names
The naming of parts

Of who we are
And where
(No, the oudh does not sound like a guitar)
We are from
And let us look at the term
That suffered collateral damage
No, it is a joke!
No-one died!
(Of course, they did
That's why they left
My grandmother for one)
From that book
(The curtain flaps in the breeze
Just like the one in my old room)

So, to conclude
What is in a name?
Nothing
It is dead
I have cut out the letters
Like bones
And now the soul is gone
It probably died in that place
Unfortunately, I do not belong
It is an interesting case
And what is that water on my face?

Dream On

I am sitting in a taxi,
Jerusalem to Gaza,
Dozing
On the radio, two Arab women are talking.
I understand next to nothing.

But as my eyes become heavy
I come to understand exactly
what they are saying.

'There will be peace,
and the guns will melt
into the sand.'
They elaborate, explaining how,
and it rings true.
I am sure I will remember the specifics
when I wake
and I drift into a deeper sleep,
comforted that there is peace
within and without.
from all this.

When I wake,
I want to write it down,
but have no pen,
the car is moving,
and, as I try to hold on to what they said
it slips through my fingers like sand
until I can't, for the life of me,
remember anything.

THREE POEMS

Hodan Yusuf

Utopia

Land of milk and honey
Streets paved with gold
Or so we were told,
Or so we were told.

A far cry from the truth
That came to light
And how it differed from the lies

When our fathers docked in northern cities
On merchant ships
Searching for a better way
When our cousins docked on the Windrush
Looking for their Motherland

They too soon learned that
Utopia is nowhere.
Ou' is Not
Topos, a Place.
Utopie in the sky.
Not eu.
Not good.
Not a tangible neighbourhood.
It is literally nowhere.

Some say it borders Achora,
Polyleritae or Macarenses.

But dear Hythlodaeus, pray tell me about this place.

If it's so real tell me about this place.
Tell me how to get there and what I am to find.
Tell me if my dreams will come true.
Tell me if there is a pot of gold at the end of the rainbow.
Tell me if there is a rainbow at all.
Tell me if I may have my daily bread and water
Or are we to fetch our water from the river Anydrus?

So where are we going?
And where are you going?
And for whom are you waiting while your life passes you?
While your hair goes grey and your children grow up.
Did you even notice?
Did you even know?

Utopia. Pff.
We need more than navel gazing and futile introspection.
This Utopia is more "you topia" not "my topia".

Nay, I want space to Breathe. To think. Critique.
One where the language is mine.
The politics too.
But until then, who will take the kids to school
and
What shall we have for dinner tonight?

Oh Hythlodaeus, tell me how to hustle this life.
Tell me how to survive this place.
Tell me how to raise my kids
And
How to fetch my water from a tap that is not poisoned.

Tell me how my sons can walk the road and not be killed by the men
They pay their taxes, to protect them.
Hythlodaeus, can you tell me how
My daughters can be judged instead for their intellect and character
Rather than their hue and the cloth that covers their skin?

What sin
Did we commit to be corralled,
Prevented,
Caged
And
Stripped of our humanity?
Does your Utopia save us from this modern day internment?

I need to know how to make it on out of here.
This Topos.
How to live in this topos.
How to thrive in this topos.
How to eat and sleep and fight for a justice denied.
There is much to do in this Topos.

So you can keep your Utopia.
I live here.

Where Can I Go?

Where else can I go
When all the doors seem closed
And minds are switched
Off
To what I have to say?

I never asked for their agreement
Endorsement
Or approval
Just for a chance to speak.

There was a time when we spoke
To one another
And others
Agreed to disagree
But we spoke.

Where else can I go
When I'm too something for the mainstream
When I'm too extreme to be humanised
Or too liberal to be trusted

Just too unconventional

My face too covered
Or my hair not covered enough
Too black and not Arab enough
Not desi enough
Too queer or misunderstood
Too revert and not schooled enough
Too sell out and not bold enough

Too something for someone.

Where else can I go?

In whose bosom can I sob my intellectual
tears
My philosophical pearls and questions
In whose space can I be held
And listened to

Even if every word I utter is dissent.

Where else can I go
If not here?

Innovation

The birth of a nation
The very motivation
For expansion
On information

Studying the causation
Of chemical Ionisation
Mathematical integration

The fascination
Borne of desperation
Of looking for hydration
To maintain the human civilisation

Leads to the negation
And accusation
Of deviation
Beyond salvation

And the insinuation
Is, without hesitation
That the revelation
Has made it an obligation

That you will be a considered a cancellation
From the population.
This normalisation
Of endless condemnation

Can only lead to stagnation
When interpretation
Should be open to participation
Or it becomes justification
For the devaluation
And subsequent subjugation
Are you following my argumentation?
Let me add a little quantification
For the purpose of prolongation

If the classification
And over simplification
Are a continuation

It is a misrepresentation
Of the proclamation
The Maker of this Creation
Deserving of Exaltation

We need the preservation
Of the diversification
Prolification
An augmentation
A confederation
For opposing observations

Allowing for one's affirmations
With respectful navigations
And careful examinations
Not alienating damnations

This location
Witnesses a congregation
Of varying vocations
And occupations

Travelling for lengthy durations
To exchange narrations
With those who don't share their associations
Or denominations
With differing ideas on salvation
And who is best for emulation
All of these the fruits of Innovation
And this here delegation,
Please continue these conversations.

REVIEWS

DISCOVERING PICKTHALL

Sarah Pickthall

There is very little trace of Muhammad Marmaduke Pickthall in my family. During my childhood that branch of our family tree was somewhat overshadowed by the other side of the family, which had an element of scandal about it. My Jewish grandmother had run away from the synagogue to marry a Catholic man, so that's where the focus tended to be.

I do remember as a child occasions when I would pick up the house phone before my parents got to it, and have a conversation with the adult on the other end. Often at some point they would ask me whether I was related to Marmaduke Pickthall, to which I would reply that I was. Even at an early age I knew that I was in some way connected to him, because of the row of books with that distinctive name on the spines that lay out of reach but not out of sight, on the top row of my father's bookshelf.

I also have an early memory of sitting with my father watching television. It was the Michael Parkinson show, and 'Parky' was interviewing satirist Barry Humphries in his Dame Edna Everage alter ego. He asked Dame Edna what 'her' favourite writer was, and upon Edna replying 'Pickthall, Marmaduke Pickthall' my father jumped out of the chair and shouted 'You see what I mean?! That's it! That's it!' So the name really meant something to my dad, but of course, I didn't understand its significance, or who this man was, or his relation to me.

Peter Clark, *Marmaduke Pickthall: British Muslim*, revised edition, Beacon Books, London, 2016; originally published by Quartet Books, London, 1986.

It's not that myself and my brothers, as we were growing up, were actively discouraged from going to the bookshelf and finding out about our ancestor; it was more that our upbringing was steeped in our father's devout Catholicism and my mother's Jewish heritage, making our Islamic antecedents somehow discordant and out of bounds.

Much later on my father started delving into family archives, but by then he was in the first throes of Parkinsons and found it increasingly difficult to continue. So, when he died in 2003 I decided to go through his collection of books to find out about Muhammad Marmaduke Pickthall for myself. I thought that by reading his work, I would somehow also find out more about my late father and what drove him. He was a very private man and none of us kids really knew him; except from the self-evident fact that he was an amazing pilot, and was only truly happy when he was up in the air.

By then of course I knew Marmaduke was my great-great uncle. On the bookshelf were copies of his numerous English and Middle Eastern fiction: *Said the Fisherman*, *VeiledWomen*, *Knights of Araby* and *All Fools* to name but a few. However, the first book I sat down to read in my father's study was Peter Clark's biography *Marmaduke Pickthall: British Muslim*. I should declare, that as Muhammad Marmaduke Pickthall's great-great niece, I am biased in my affection for Peter Clark and his biography that I first read in its original 1986 edition. Quite simply, without this book I may have spent a good deal longer trying to find out about the life of my esteemed relation, his literary works and the work for which he is most revered and well known – *The Meaning of the Glorious Qur'an*.

After reading Clark's biography I was left with the sense that there was something extraordinary about Muhammad Marmaduke Pickthall and the way in which he had fearlessly pushed the boundaries of what was considered appropriate for the time in which he lived, and had thereby achieved great things, but still retained a sense of humility to the end. I began to appreciate that which had been under my nose all the time, my blood relation – a man whose name I shared – who had stepped out of line and into the light of Islam.

Clark presented me with an accessible and easy narrative that unpacked Pickthall's trajectory and the shifts and changes that moulded his life, spiritual, moral and political beliefs and his extensive literary works. Clark's biography captured in detail Marmaduke's journey from his birth in 1875, the son of an Anglican rector, through his unhappy patch of public schooling at Harrow, his failure to enter the Levant Consular Service and onto his subsequent early travels; two years wandering through Palestine,

Egypt, Lebanon and Syria – where his linguistic capacity and knowledge flourished. Clark shared with the reader Pickthall's reflections of his awakening: 'Following the customs of the people of the land in all respects. I was amazed at the immense relief I found in such a life. In all my previous years I had not seen any happy people. These were happy people.' As Clark comments: 'The two years away determined the course of Pickthall's life. He left England a depressed boy, burdened with a sense of failure. He returned a man, not confident but buoyant and with a distinct identity.' I read of how the youthful Pickthall, during a stay in Damascus, had been dissuaded from converting to Islam by the Shaykh al-'ulama of the city's Umayyid mosque, on the basis that he should not upset his mother by taking such a step without her consent. Another two decades were to pass before Pickthall would publicly announce his embrace of the faith.

Reading the biography did add to my understanding of my late father. I realised that he had a real ethereal spiritual seeking quality to him. I recalled him saying at the end of his life that there was a time when he would have committed his life to faith if he hadn't married my mum. Reading Clark's biography convinced me I had to start to unpack for myself Marmaduke Pickthall and that side of the family.

There was not that much to go on, however. We had a copy of Anne Freemantle's 1938 account of Pickthall's life, commissioned after his death by his widow Muriel. Freemantle, a socialite, Fabian and Catholic convert who later became a New York-based journalist, had known Pickthall when she was a young girl, describing him in a letter she wrote to Peter Clark in the 1980s as 'my greatest friend from my father's death when I was 12 until his own death'.

Freemantle's book was titled *Loyal Enemy* and, whilst rich on detail, was floral, lurid and silly and put a lot of people's noses out of joint, including his extended family at the time, because it had speculated that he might have had held an affection for a cousin. She wrote in this fashion: '*L'homme moyen sensuel* that he was, that we all are, he transmuted, as few have succeeded in doing, into pilgrim and paladin.'

Overall the style of Freemantle's work in many ways distorted the reader's view of what Pickthall's life had really been all about – the pursuit of absolute truth and love of Islam, and how this quest had been central to everything he did.

Pickthall has often been described both by friends and enemies as a vehement Turcophile – a sentiment that had blossomed in a five-month period of time spent in Constantinople in 1913 which put him at odds with the British Government then preparing for war with Turkey. His spell at the centre of the disintegrating caliphate, described a year later in his book *With the Turk In Wartime*, also consolidated his commitment to Islam. He became one of a number of Anglo-Ottoman sympathisers who drew the attention of the British security services – hence the title of Freemantle's book. The authorities made sure that he was blocked from being offered a job with the Arab Bureau in Cairo (which given his expertise, should have been his), the post instead going to TE Lawrence; an appointment that subsequent events proved to have been a disaster for all concerned.

I was to discover later that along with the countless Muslims who revere Pickthall for being a pioneer of the modern Islamic community in Britain, and the many more English language speakers first introduced to the Glorious Qur'an through his transliteration, are an army of what I can only describe (affectionately) as Pickthall nerds. I learned that Barry Humphries is one of them – a voracious collector of Pickthall manuscripts and ephemera – as is Peter Clark.

I first made contact with Peter Clark in 2010, after searching for him online. He was clearly delighted that I had reached out to him, and invited me to visit the home he shares with his wife Theresa in Frome, Somerset. This was the first of many encounters discussing Marmaduke together for hours at a time.

I remember Peter, during one of our early conversations, spontaneously reading out loud the eyewitness account of Pickthall's public declaration of faith on 29 November 1917, during the course of a lecture on 'Islam and Progress' to the Muslim Literary Society in Notting Hill, west London, and how:

> It threw those who were not used to listening to such recitations from a Western's lips into ecstasies. From start to finish Mr Pickthall held his audience as if in a spell…With his hands folded on his breast, and an expression of serene contentment on his face, he recited that famous prayer which concludes the second chapter of the Holy Qur'an. When he sat down, every one of his

hearers felt that they had lived through, during that one short hour, the most remarkable period in his or her life.

The passage completely silenced me in its profundity; how Marmaduke had spent years hiding this truth within himself, and the beauty by which he finally revealed his faith, in a state of absolute conviction. It is with me to this day.

In 2011 I asked Peter Clark to arrange a three-day visit to Istanbul for myself and two friends. Guided by Peter and his deep knowledge of both Pickthall and the city he loved most of all, we retraced my great-great uncle's movements during his stay on the eve of World War One. It proved to be an amazing psycho-geographical trail, as we followed in Pickthall's footsteps from one place to another. We ended up in sleepy Erenkoy, a small town on the Anatolian side of the Bosporus, visiting the mosque he had attended and trying to identify the boarding house of 'Misket' (Miss Kate) Hanum, the German lady in whose garden he had found such peace, even as war hovered all around: 'Real Eastern cries were wafted from the distant roadway. I felt entirely comfortable and in place for the first time since leaving my own Sussex Farmhouse.'

Much of what we know about Muhammad Marmaduke's thoughts and opinions are taken from his letters to his wife Muriel. Sad to say, there is no trace of her in our family. We know that she followed him, she was by his side, and that she converted to Islam shortly after him. She joined him on his subsequent travels, including his extended stay in Hyderabad, India, at the invitation of the Nizam. In 1928 he was given a special two year leave of absence from his teaching duties by the Nizam, during which he produced the first translation of the Qur'an by a Muslim whose first language was English.

I do know that Muriel had a particularly hard time in India and she came back to England. I don't think it was particularly easy for her because Marmaduke was quite single minded, he had a job to do. I often think of Muriel, and how when her husband died in 1936, she was left on her own (they didn't have any children) – a Muslim convert in Cornwall, living in St Ives. We'll never know what she really felt about him.

The original edition of Peter Clark's biography is out of print. So this new and revised edition by Beacon Books is particularly welcome. Now more people can read this pioneering account that shares the wonderful trajectory of Pickthall's life alongside synopses of his English and Middle Eastern literary works. We all owe a debt of gratitude to Peter Clark, who has been instrumental in documenting the profound depths of Pickthall's life, and highlighting his invaluable contribution to literature, to our understanding of Islam and to the history of the Muslim community in Britain. He recently told me that he was 'bemused and gratified' by the new interest in Pickthall.

November 2017 will be the centenary of Muhammad Marmaduke Pickthall's public declaration of his faith in Notting Hill, London. It should be honoured in some way. These days conversion to Islam seems steeped in taboo and stigma and tainted with fanaticism and frenzy, which is why I feel that it is worth marking the nature of Marmaduke's conversion, that was, as it is for many, simple, undeniable and natural:

Soldier of the Faith, True servant of Islam.
To thee 'twas given to quit the shades of night
And onward move, aye onward into Light
With soul undaunted, heart assured and calm!

HAND OF FATIMA

Fatimah Ashrif

In early January, I visited Oxford's Ashmolean Museum to see their 'Power and Protection: Islamic Art and the Supernatural' exhibition. It was a crisp and sunny day, which I took as a good omen. As I stepped off the train and made my way to the exit, I spotted an image of the 'Hand of Fatima' pasted to the ticket barrier indicating the direction to the Museum. This image of the 'hand' has been the exhibition's 'frontispiece', which is perhaps fitting as its most likely use dated eighteenth to early nineteenth century was as a finial. Made of gold on a lac core, it is encrusted with rubies, emeralds, diamonds and small pearls outlining the fingers. The 'hand' has throughout the centuries been seen as a representation of the Prophet Muhammad's immediate family through his daughter Fatima through whom many believe his spiritual inheritance is continued. The *'khamsa'*, as it is also known, became one of the preferred shapes for battle and presentation standards under the Safavid Dynasty (1501–1736). As such it seemed a perfect introductory piece to the exhibition being a symbol of both power and protection.

'Power and Protection: Islamic Art and the Supernatural', Ashmolean Museum of Art and Archaeology, Oxford, 20 October 2016–15 January 2017.

I have always been drawn to the symbol of the 'hand' as a connection point to the Prophet's family, and as a reminder of the qualities of 'Fatima'. The Islamic spiritual tradition holds that 'the name and the named are one' the association with the Prophet's daughter, therefore, carries its own treasure and protection for me on a personal level.

The exhibition was arranged over three rooms, and I confess I felt all the excitement of a child in a toy shop as I pored over the rich treasures on view: over 100 exquisitely crafted objects, many on their first public display, on loan from private and public collections. 'Power and Protection' examines the divinatory arts and practices adopted and developed by Muslims, and the role and use of sacred words and symbols amongst Muslim communities. The artefacts hailed from areas ranging from North Africa to India, and from Sub-Saharan Africa, Southeast Asia and China spanning the twelfth century to the present day, taking one on a journey through the earthly, celestial and unseen spheres.

The first room was concerned with the arts of divination. The piece which first caught my imagination was an Iranian early-thirteenth-century jar of fritware, painted in lustre over the glaze, with a diameter of 18.5cm with the signs of the zodiac. These included signs which we would recognise in the western world and Chinese zodiac signs. It also carried the personification of the planets and importantly sacred Arabic inscriptions. It stood out for many reasons. I was not aware that there was a tradition of following horoscopes in the Muslim world. I wondered if the well-meaning aunts who had advised me that reading my horoscopes in the paper as a young person was *haram* knew about this. It confirmed that the Muslims of this period had, even in the area of astrology, taken knowledge from different traditions without paranoia over *bida* (innovation), reminding me of the Prophetic injunction to seek knowledge 'even as far as China'. As Islam spread from the seventh to eight century, advancing to the near east, Iran and North Africa, Muslims came across many new scientific and religious beliefs and practices. They integrated these into their own, though some divinatory customs were challenged as to their efficacy or on the basis that they were felt to challenge the omnipotent nature of the Divine. Though interestingly the jar I refer to, like most such items, was completed with a reference to the ultimate power of the Divine through Qur'anic and sacred inscriptions. In this case, '*La illaha il Allah*': there is no god but God.

As I wandered around the first room, admiring the astrolabes, the astrological and astronomical charts, horoscopes, everyday items inscribed with zodiac signs and sacred phrases, manuals and devices, I remembered a visit I had made as a young person to a Muslim healer with my mother. He was an elderly bearded Uncle Jee, an acupuncturist who also worked with colours and auras. I was captivated by his apparent insights and knowledge of what seemed magical and mysterious but for him sat easily with his Islamic faith. I recall on one visit he took out a pendant on a long string, and I was invited to ask questions which could be answered with a 'yes' and 'no' response, and through a series of these we figured out that I would be a teacher when I grew up. I am not one yet but then some might say that I am still not quite grown up! I am not sure exactly what brought the pendant on the string to mind or indeed Uncle Jee but maybe it was the description of the practice of 'geomancy', reading sand. There was an impressive Geomantic Tablet exhibited, thought to be from Damascus, dated 1241–2 of brass alloy and inlaid with silver and gold, measuring 26.8 x 33.6 cm. It's a very exciting looking tablet with various dials and inscriptions, and wouldn't look too out of place in a JK Rowling novel. It demonstrates how the art of creating and interpreting designs in the sand made up of clusters of dots and lines was transferred to a sophisticated mechanical device, which was used to answer questions about an individual's future using similar principles. The exhibition displays an image of the Prophet Idris, also using sand to read the future perhaps to give the practice the prophetic seal of approval. The image is taken from an illustrated copy of *Stories of the Prophets* by Ishaq ibn Ibrahim al-Nishapuri from Iran c.1570–80.

It was interesting, but perhaps unsurprising, to note that those engaged in the art of divination for the benefit of the royal courts they served, first studied the rational sciences. Masters of multiples practices, such as Al-Buni (d.1225), trained initially as mathematicians and he became known for developing the science of talismanic squares. The desire to read the future was not limited to royalty but ordinary people also availed themselves of horoscope reading and similar practices, and charlatans no doubt did operate in such contexts. Divinatory practices were not always for telling the future but also choosing the appropriate time for certain events such as entering battle, and assistance with making decisions such as proceeding with marital alliances. Muslim astrologers of the medieval period believed that celestial bodies impacted on the earth and its inhabitants, and therefore astrologers were consulted for the most auspicious timing for events.

Some of the practices I came across felt familiar as I also practise them in some form, not having ever thought about there being an 'Islamic precedent' for these. For example, dream journaling and bibliomancy. In the latter practice, one opens sacred, even literary texts (including the works of Rumi and Hafez!) and specially compiled '*falnamas*', books of omens with a question and taking guidance from the page at which the book opened. This art also became more sophisticated as tables were developed for asking the desired question using sacred numbers. I often open the Qur'an or an anthology of Rumi's poetry finding a response to a question formed in my heart. I discovered that dream journals were kept by noted individuals who would then look back at these for symbols and omens. The artefacts included the dream journal of Indian ruler Tipu Sultan from the eighteenth century. Rather surprisingly, in the first four centuries of Islam, sixty manuals of dream interpretation were compiled, which is equivalent to the number of Qur'anic commentaries produced in the same time frame!

Though I feel that a preoccupation with the future might be an unwarranted distraction from living life in the present with trust in the Divine, my personal feeling is that we live in a highly intelligent and interconnected universe through which God communicates with us. With a world view in which the Divine is intimately engaged in the unfolding of every aspect of creation and human existence, it seems natural and fitting that dreams — like other occurrences — might also carry signs, and bring guidance. Modern day psychoanalysis recognises them as key to working out the things that trouble our sub-conscious minds and thereby our conscious existence, and from a spiritual perspective they might be seen as an access point to the super, supra or collective consciousness. The Islamic and Judeo-Christian traditions document the dreams of the Prophet Joseph. The Qur'anic story of Joseph begins with his dream that the eleven stars and the sun and the moon prostrated before him. Muslims continue to practise *istikhara*, a form of prayer in which they seek guidance from God through dreams though some might argue that the guidance wouldn't come through a dream but rather things will simply unfold as they should as a result of the prayer. Direct guidance from God is not something that all Muslims are comfortable with, and there have always been those who have argued against this possibility. Perhaps because it is perceived as a potential challenge to religious authority.

The exhibition moved on in the second and third rooms to explore the protective power of sacred words, and devotional items. The rooms included the finial 'Hand of Fatima' I mentioned at the outset, beautiful amulets, talismans, swords, images of protective symbols relating to the Prophet, verbal portraits of the Prophet, coats of armour inscribed with protective inscriptions, and shirts covered fully with some or all of the following: amuletic formulas, magic squares, protective verses from the Qur'an, and the *asma al-Husnaa* (the names of God). The objects and their descriptions conjure a world of magic and mystery to rival even Tolkien's imagination.

One of the items which caught my attention was a talismanic shirt attributed to the Ottoman Empire dated seventeenth century. It is made of cotton and inscribed with coloured inks. Historical references suggest a range of possible uses for such shirts. In a written source from the 1530s, the wife of the Ottoman Sultan Suleyman (r. 1520–66) begs him to wear the shirt she has sent him because it would 'turn aside bullets' and protect him from death. The shirt she bestowed to her husband is clearly intended to be worn for the cause of God and is decorated with the sacred Names of God from which it derives its protection. It is thought that such shirts were likely to also have been worn during illness, as protective amulets or for ceremonial purposes. The shirt on display is unlikely to have been worn and the folds in it suggest that it was carried in a container less than a quarter of its size, which indicates it was most likely transported and used as a protective amulet. It is decorated with a combination of Qur'anic passages and invocations also featuring the names of God, including *al-Hayy al-Qayyum*, the everlasting, self-subsisting source of all being. The types of invocation used on the shirt exalting God's power and calling for His assistance in difficult times also indicate its likely ceremonial use. The shirt brought to mind an oral tradition in which the Prophet Muhammad is said to have been given a symbolic coat of armour covered in the Names of God to help in one of his military campaigns. Though I believe in the power of words and symbols, I wonder if the tradition in the form of the shirts (and the body armour) might be taken too literally or indeed if it ought to be worn to remind oneself that the names of God, as per Islamic spiritual tradition, are inscribed within the heart ultimately leading to the abandonment of the need for the shirt for what is written in invisible ink into every heart beat! The question the talismans and amulets raised for me was, how do we become or realise our own talismanic power?

The exhibition examines the practice of the use of Qur'anic words, verses letters and phrases for healing and protective purposes. The Qur'an itself refers to its healing and protective properties, and related practices continue to this day. It occurred to me that I myself do not leave the house without reciting the *Ayat al Kursi* (the Throne verses). The science of letters, *ilm al huruf*, which involved deciphering the hidden meanings of words appears to have developed from the ninth century onwards, and there are manuals speaking of the hidden meanings of verses and phrases in the Qur'an and healing and other effects. I would have loved to read some of these. Many manuals and treatises document these practices over time. *Al-Buni (Brilliant Lights)* dated 1425, a volume (also exhibited) relating to the properties of the names of God, advises that believers who wish to avoid injury and gain victory should carry a copy of *Surat al Nasr* on a blue cloth or paper during 'the exaltation of the sun and Mars'. The text through diagrams and verbal recipes such as that aforementioned offers instructions on how to harness and channel the powers of the Names of God through amulets and talismans.

Specialist literature refers to the astrological conditions which are necessary for the production and use of talismans. What these texts highlight is the breadth in scope and relevance of divinatory skills to this, and also the level of expertise required to undertake such practices in the Islamic tradition. One needed not only astrological knowledge but also knowledge of celestial bodies and their habits, associated earthly creatures, compounds and resources, knowledge of sacred words, letters and numbers. Verses were broken down into letters, which along with free standing letters from opening *Surahs* (Chapters) of the Qur'an were often also used to fill 'magic squares'. It is not clear how much the specialist literature was referred to at different levels of society, and likely that much knowledge of creating and wearing talismans was passed down orally.

The exhibition includes a range of magico-medicinal bowls ranging from the twelfth to the nineteenth centuries. These are inscribed with instructions as to their use and various talismanic healing formula. This part of the exhibition brought to mind experiments undertaken by the Japanese photographer Masaru Emoto in the 1980s–90s. He took photographs of water which had been prayed over and water which had not. In another related experiment, he placed water in glass jars and attached the name of each of the world's major religions to each jar for a number of hours. With both the photographs of the water which had been prayed over and the water which had been labelled with the name of a religion (a single word), the water created beautifully formed geometrical crystals. I am aware within my family of the practice of praying over water and drinking it for healing, though of course such practices do not sit comfortably with all Muslims. It resonates with Tibetan prayer flags and wheels. The wheels are definitely reminiscent of talismans for me. The prayers are disseminated through the world through the flags coming into contact with the wind, and the turning of the prayer wheels by devotees. It is interesting that those people of faith who might be sceptical of the energy of the written word or symbol or the impact of prayer on water, are however, comfortable with verbal supplications.

Moving into the final room of the exhibition, I found more inscriptions on body armour and swords, and their encasings. I was particularly impacted by the sight of holy inscriptions on swords. There is a particularly beautiful eighteenth-century sabre hilt from India inscribed with the ninety-nine names of God, iron, cast and pierced, with gold damascening. Also a central section from a banner with the sword of Dhulfiqar dated seventeenth century made in Turkey on silk with metal thread. The sword was given to Ali by the Prophet Muhammad and saw action in the battle of Badr, which the early Muslims won. The win was seen very much as a result of divine intervention as the Muslim fighters were outnumbered. The sword is depicted on the banner as inscribed with verses from the Qur'an. Ali's sword was seen as a symbol of invincibility and the banner would have been carried into battle. For me these inscriptions and holy words are difficult as they relate to bloodshed and one does not wish for religion to be connected to that. However, I like to think that the inscriptions might be there not only for protection but also as a reminder that the sword ought only be wielded in service of God, i.e. not for self-serving purposes but solely in the defence of the innocent. The sight of Ali's sword reminded me of a related story at the end of Volume 1 of the *Mathnawi* of Rumi, the thirteenth century Muslim jurist and mystic in which he describes an incident in which Ali is in battle and at the very moment Ali could have taken the life of his opponent, he spat on Ali. Ali threw down his sword. The man was confused and he asked Ali why he had thrown down his sword when he could have easily just taken his life. Ali explained that when the man had spat at him, it had made Ali angry and he threw down his sword because he knew in that moment that if he killed him it would not have been out of service to his God but to his own anger, his own ego. There is much in Islamic spiritual literature which asks the seeker to take the sword metaphorically to his or her own ego in order that he or she may act always from a place of service to the Divine will. Perhaps as Muslims we need to rediscover this spiritual heritage and in doing so connect with the humble mind and heart-set of the earliest Muslims.

The exhibition demonstrated our shared human frailty in the face of Divine power. My sense was that the curators ought perhaps to have enlarged the exhibition to show by means of a small selection of objects methods and means of divination and protection in other faith traditions too. In many ways for me that would have made for a more balanced exploration of the human relationship with Divine power. The exhibition risks the possibility of fetishising Muslim practices and portraying Islam as backward – which I don't believe is the intention of the curators – because it doesn't attempt to set the inter-faith context.

The objects shared in this exhibition and their histories provide a wonderful lens through which to view the complex landscape of devotion and religious practice of the Muslim world. Many of the practices particularly related to amulets, talismans, reverence of Prophetic relics and healing prayers continue to this day amongst various groups of Muslims and in certain parts of the world. It is felt by some that they reflect inherited cultural practices and not 'orthodoxy'. Of course this depends very much on who is defining the orthodoxy. To me it seems that historically Muslim communities have viewed knowledge as of universal value and demonstrated a willingness to integrate new learning whilst staying true to a belief in God's omnipotence and ultimate power over all things. I am particularly drawn to practices which recognise the integrated intelligence of the universe. For me the universe is filled with wonder and meaning and it seems that earlier Muslim communities were perhaps more attuned to this. So called 'orthodoxy' and rationalism devoid of the search for meaning, can deprive us of the wonder, mystery and connectedness to creation.

The exhibition ended for me with the symbol of the Prophet's sandal. It's not a symbol that has drawn me before but reflecting on the idea of the Prophet ascending through the heavens in his sandals, gives a new perspective to the possibility of walking in the shoes (sandals) of the Messenger of God.

BRAVE NEW HOUSE

Halima Gosai Hussain

We all know what Muslim utopia looks like – it's the 'Happy Muslims' video by Honesty Policy, the enigmatic British Muslim collective, available on YouTube. And it lasts all of four minutes and 13 seconds.

Now, thankfully due to finger-on-the-pulse BBC commissioning, we have a reality TV experiment in British Muslim dystopia. *Muslims Like Us* brought ten Muslims together for ten days, and as my favourite housemate Naila summarised, 'I feel like we're in a zoo, day after day – I'm overloaded with the same horseshit.' To make sure the dichotomy was truly striking, the city of York was chosen as the backdrop – calm, historical and cultured to ensure a proper clash with the volatile, alien Muslims, mainly hailing from KFC wrapper-strewn London. The show turns out to be two hours of largely painful viewing designed to ensure that people at home stay worried about the Muslims (who might move in) next door.

> *Muslims Like Us*, produced by Love Productions, BBC2, Broadcast on 12–13 December 2016.

The first housemate we meet is Mehreen ('like a submarine'), who only a die-hard Islamist could dislike. She is intelligent, opinionated and beautiful and would have looked perfect in the 'Happy Muslims' video. Cue resident number two, Abdul Haqq, our caricature villain that every drama must have, who is instantly concerned by Mehreen – her clothes, her make-up and her non-existent hijab. She is not someone that he intends to mix with. In fact, the former boxer and convert doesn't want to mix with any women regardless of their dress code. So, he goes about educating his fellow housemates about the dangers of free mixing by handing out leaflets. Yes, like you, I thought that at the very least the Abdul Haqqs of this world had moved on from leaflets and onto social media. But he doesn't stop there. Not content with simply preaching to his already Muslim but deviant household, we learn about his desire to spread the message of al-Islam to the 'Grade A *kufar* (infidel)' residents of York. Lucky them.

As the housemates introduce themselves, I can't help but fall for all of them. They are like the Muslims I have met and interacted with my whole life (and I know two of them personally). I find myself moved as the housemates gather for their first prayer. Naila, who doesn't take part, says she has her own ways to pray and believes there is space for everyone to find that. I am even more excited. The space seems to have an openness and warmth. I can immediately see that the participants have taken part in the programme to help dispel negative stereotypes about Islam and Muslims – I can't help but admire their bravery.

Yet early on during their stay the Nice attacks take place and the British public, probably for the first time, get to see a group of Muslims respond with genuine anger and grief up close. The housemates speculate on what the tragedy will mean for Muslim communities, how it will fuel Islamophobia and exacerbate radicalisation. This all reminds me of the Young Muslim camps I attended as a teenager. I remember my own naivety, believing that by smiling and showing Muslims to be the harmonious 'best nation', we would win over the wider British population. Not yet seeing the patriarchy, misogyny, homophobia, anti-blackness, and discrimination in favour of able-bodied people within my own community.

Cut back to Abdul Haqq, whom the show essentially revolves around and who is a card- (sorry leaflet-) carrying supporter of Anjem Choudary, the infamous convicted terrorist. He next discovers that he doesn't just have to protect his virtue from his female housemates, but from Ferhan, too, who comes out to household and nation as gay. The response to this announcement is completely mediated through Abdul Haqq's reaction – which is, of course, disgust. The rest of the house are either supportive or decide to follow the golden rule according to Nabil, 'When in doubt, don't be a dick,' – a slogan that is probably being made into bumper stickers by Honesty Policy as you read. But the household which had dealt so swiftly and decisively with the question of gender segregation initially posed by Abdul Haqq now largely brushes off concerns about the visibility of queer people in the Muslim community. There are attempts to get the discussion going again – Naila says that 'the Muslim community drowns in shame'

when it comes to sexuality and conformity to gender norms and roles –
but nothing goes further.

Instead, almost every point in every debate seems to be made in
opposition to Abdul Haqq's perspective – staying on the surface, probing
no further. The best we get is a discussion on dress code, instigated by
Abdul Haqq's leaflets, that has the household questioning the importance
of what a Muslim looks like vis-à-vis what being Muslim means. The
consensus is that Muslims judge each other far too harshly. But the
discussion stops short again, with the housemates singularly directing
themselves at Abdul Haqq and being wholly unsuccessful in what amounts
to their ad hoc de-radicalisation programme.

This point about judgement almost results in group consensus about a
level of pluralism that could exist within the house and by extension the
wider *ummah*. We may not be able to accept the choices of other Muslims,
which may not be choices we would make ourselves, but at the very least
we can leave others to practise in a way that allows them to connect (or
not connect) with the divine as they best see fit. As the chair of the
Inclusive Mosque Initiative, I know that some (or indeed many) Muslims
may struggle with the idea of women as imams in mixed-gender
congregations or attendees who identify as lesbian, gay, bisexual or
transgender. However, my hope is that if they can't understand and accept
these perspectives, then they can at least suspend their judgements and
allow other Muslims to exist and explore these alternatives.

If the goings on in the house have not been enough to scare viewers so
far, a faction begins to emerge. Our star residents Naila and Mehreen
decide to lead and spread their liberal version of Islam in York via the
medium of karaoke. Viewers are forced to witness the group sing 'Let It
Go', the treacly earworm from Disney's *Frozen*, which helps to prove the
point that, like everyone else, Muslims are atrocious at karaoke.

Later, to purge themselves of their singing misdeeds the group volunteer
at a homeless shelter. Prior to this noble event, Bara, our Syrian resident,
already attempted pre-emptive absolution by hugging a member of the
far-right English Defence League (EDL). The household jury is out as to
whether this was a praiseworthy attempt to disarm a misguided young man
or an unwitting endorsement of fascism.

Besides encounters with EDL members, karaoke warblers and visitors to Abdul Haqq's *da'wah* (preaching) stall, our diverse Muslims are also subjected to visits by members of the York (read: white English and/or non-Muslim) community who each have a five-day, VIP, all-access pass to the house. And boy are these visitors baffling in their arrogance. One asks Ferhan if he can rename him Ferdinand – so much easier to pronounce, you see, despite the extra syllable.

These York emissaries not only wear bow ties and play the piano – they also want to take the group out into the world to experience British culture. They choose a trip to the York World War II memorial. The Muslims are forced to decide between two obnoxious choices – staying in the house with Abdul Haqq (who is first to declare he will not be going) or traipsing to the memorial. They split down the middle.

The inclusion of the York residents is cringeworthy. Has it not been enough for the housemates to become social experiments for our television screens? Did the producers seriously need to bring in 'local' folk to convince us of their humanity?

The group left behind in the house now starts discussing white privilege. Nabil, a black Muslim comedian, challenges Saba, an older white convert, on negating his experiences of racism. Finally, a discussion that doesn't have Abdul Haqq in the frame! Nabil accepts that he has certain privileges as a man, but says that Saba has her own privileges as a white woman and needs to acknowledge this instead of shutting down discussions on racism. (What would Abdul Haqq – who is also black – have said to this?) Saba struggles to engage with Nabil and instead storms off, voicing her disappointment at Humaira, the hipster hijabi, for not standing up for her. Humaira quips to the camera, 'I didn't realise being accused of racism was worse than actually experiencing racism.' Holding up a mirror to anti-blackness within Muslim communities, it's one of the better interactions in the house – honest, difficult and with both sides showing their vulnerabilities.

Still, it's not long before The Abdul Haqq Show returns, this time focusing on his views about Shia Islam. This is where descent into dystopia reaches its nadir, with Abdul Haqq all but condemning Shias to their death in front of Zohra, the household's lone Shia. Zohra is speechless, leaves the discussion and breaks down. This is followed by a beautifully warm moment in which the housemates comfort her, having witnessed the devastating impact of Abdul Haqq's words. A light is held up to sectarianism in Muslim communities – but with only its most extreme form being tackled by the housemates.

Having Abdul Haqq in the picture does repeatedly make the point that the rest of the household disagrees with the majority of what he says. But his presence makes it impossible for us to hear perspectives that are truly introspective on difficult topics like gender segregation, homosexuality and sectarianism. These discussions probably happened – how could they not have? – but the editorial choices leave us wondering if these were not considered viewer worthy.

Instead, ten days of footage culminate in 'onion-gate'. It's a moment in which we see how the unresolved hostilities about anti-blackness and homophobia come together and explode when Nabil and Ferhan confront each other over an onion. 'Onion-gate' illuminates how all the residents carry both privileges and prejudices, and how all have the power to hurt and the vulnerability to be hurt.

Yet all is not lost in the Big Muslim House. During their last supper, Mehreen finally dons a hijab and a blushing Abdul Haqq certifies her dress as 'much better from an Islamic point of view'. Yeah, even hijabis can be hot. In the residents' final reflections on their experience, they speak with a disparate yet unified voice. They have been unable to define what a Muslim is – and from my recollection they barely even talked about it. They come across as a group of varied and contrasting personalities who never really shared the deeper aspects of their faith. Still, as Mani concludes, 'We are not the enemy.' And Mehreen says, 'We are just people who want normal things from life, we are people who fall short and we are people who try our best, just like everyone else.'

The clincher comes from Zohra when she concludes, 'Next time you see a Muslim, maybe say "Hi" and see what happens.' This makes me think that it's not inside the Big Muslim House that the dystopia is taking hold. Dystopias are often characterised by dehumanisation, and *Muslims Like Us* is an attempt to humanise. By doing so, it acknowledges and validates the dehumanisation of Muslims by wider society and the dehumanisation of Others within Muslim communities. That's an uncomfortable thought to come away with.

Muslims can't wave a magic wand and reverse this tide, but we do have a role to play in acknowledging the dehumanisation that takes place within our communities. How do we deal with anti-blackness, homophobia, sectarianism and patriarchy? How do we have discussions about the issues raised in the house in an honest and just way? Humaira puts it beautifully but heartbreakingly: 'We are intellectually dishonest.' If a utopia requires an emphasis on egalitarian principles of equality, which we at the very least accept to be a Qur'anic ideal, how would we go about nurturing a community that values gender justice, includes people of all races and sexualities, and is open enough to accept Muslims from different sects and with different theologies? As someone who chairs an organisation aiming to do just that, I can tell you the answer isn't easy. To me, at its most basic, it comes down to judgement. And the housemates settled on the point early on – that Muslims judge each other far too harshly. I agree. So, the first step along the road – as the Muslims (Who Sing Karaoke) Like Us and Disney's *Frozen* remind us – is to 'Let It Go'.

ET CETERA

ON UTOPIAN MELODIES

Merryl Wyn Davies

What is the distinction between simple profundity and being profoundly simple? This is not exactly the last word in semantics, rather a niggling thought about the way we think. Most particularly it is the question about how we conceive of and search for answers about what is for the best. What makes the world a better place is always at stake, on a knife's edge, teetering on the brink … etc., etc., as, in the musical, the King of Siam was apt to opine. The desire for a perfect world is always with us. Making the transformation from where we are to what we long for, dream of and devoutly wish – there's the rub! Is it all simple profundity or profoundly simple?

I will admit that my musing on the aforementioned question has taken a musical turn. It all began with a stray recollection. In my mind's eye I had a flashback of La Stupenda, as the opera singer Dame Joan Sutherland was known to devotees, statuesque before a glitterati audience rendering not some soaring trilling aria but that quintessentially sentimental Victorian melody 'There's no place like home'. To be sure this incongruous juxtaposition probably explains why it stuck in my mind. However, I have to admit that almost everything else I thought I remembered about this incident turned out to be horribly garbled and, in short, wrong.

I got the occasion wrong, the opera incorrect and presumed it happened way back in time. It all goes to demonstrate that what I thought conforms to the most common conventions of historic memory – of which more later.

My trick of memory was conflating the encore Australia's finest, Sydney-born Dame Joan, delivered after her farewell performance at the city's iconic Opera House with her last public performance a few months later at London's Covent Garden. The gala event was broadcast on New Year's Eve 1990. Is it increasing age, mine, that makes that seem just yesterday rather than the eons earlier memory assigned to the event? Presumably the BBC's coverage of the gala included reference to or footage of the Sydney encore. Q.E.D false memory. I thought I saw (no, not a pussy cat) a diva triumphantly stonking humility with the simplest hummable melody.

The lyric to that plaintive tune is all important for the question at hand. 'There's no place like home' is the most memorable line of 'Home Sweet Home' which began life as part of the 1823 opera, *Clari, Maid of Milan*, by the American John Howard Payne. The music was provided by the Englishman Sir Henry Bishop. It became an immediate hit selling 100,000 copies when issued as sheet music. In 1852 Bishop relaunched the piece as a popular ballad and the rest is history.

So let's think about that unforgettable line: there is no place like home. As we know, another term for 'no place' is utopia. With this in mind the ballad sets up a tricky conundrum. Home as it exists is not the conceptual utopian vision of the perfect world. Utopics as a vision of the future would not exist were the here and now ideal. To exist utopia implies something other, better, something beyond the home we know. The selling point of the ballad however is an idyllic vision of the irreplaceable lure and nature of 'home' which has overtones of hallowed ground, a sacred bond 'ne'er met with elsewhere'.

It's a toughie. Two senses and potential meanings of utopia as a much desired place and condition could be said to collide in the song. Two senses of scale are also involved. The utopian vision is always broadcast, an ideal of perfection for all, setting the world to rights for everyone. The utopian vision of home sweet home is a personal sanctuary where all cares are soothed in the bosom of family providing, as the lyric says 'that peace of mind, dearer than all'.

The ballad sets the grand vision of 'pleasures and palaces' of splendour that 'dazzles in vain' against a humble thatched cottage set amidst natural beauties that is hearth and family home. It is one of the reasons it was banned during the American Civil War lest it inspire desertion from the Great Cause. Presumably its imagery was as dangerous to the endeavour of both armies battling for their different interpretations of the future. The ballad offers a quiescent vision of a disengaged personal utopia that is actual and available now, not pie in someone else's sky and without the possibility, most often the probability, that one may need to die to achieve it– which would you choose?

There is another vital question lurking behind the two implicit meanings of utopia. One finds it encapsulated in another ravishing ballad: Stephen Sondhiem's 'Somewhere' in Leonard Bernstein's classic musical *West Side Story*. This song was conceived and written with decided utopian purpose. There is an abundance of home and family in *West Side Story*, but it is a dystopian vision desperately in need of what waits somewhere. It is not just a vision of 'peace and quiet and open air' but 'a new way of living' founded on 'a way of forgiving'. It is utopia indeed for the doomed couple living in the world of the Jets and the Sharks.

West Side Story is a retelling of Romeo and Juliet, a family tragedy. The Montagues and Capulets of Shakespeare's fair Verona are transmuted into the ethnically distinct gangs, the white Jets and the Puerto Rican Sharks inhabiting the crowded airless back streets of New York's upper west side. The opening number, the wonderful 'Officer Krupke', defines the 'social disease' that underlies the racial tensions that will doom the star crossed lovers Tony and Maria. Home for the Jets is a world of drugs, drink, violence and disaffection offering limited jobs and no uplifting prospects. In this environment the gang becomes the effective family. Later, in the rousing number 'America' upper West Side New York may be no utopia for the Puerto Rican immigrant sweat shop workers yet it is infinitely better than the tropical idyll idea of 'back home' that means even worse poverty and overcrowding. In the face of racial prejudice the Puerto Ricans stick together and stick up for themselves and are ever ready to rumble.

What the scenario of a world of struggle and strife makes clear is that a new way of living is only available in another place: somewhere, some day, somehow. Utopia is not here – it is yet to be identified and achieved. As the choreography of the final scene makes clear – when the body of the slain Tony is raised like a crucifix and carried away, his bearers members of both gangs – attaining the somewhere of their dreams comes through sacrifice. Utopia is a revolution in the world we know. And as so often has been proved revolutions eat their children and entail the slaughter of innocents; it is par for the course.

So why pause over the thought that there is no place like home? Is it the concern that our most prevalent conception of utopia is in reality anywhere but home? Home, our current condition and circumstances, generates the problem that the utopic master plan is to resolve. Release from what ails our present home world demands dedication to the new utopian order that must be constructed, dragged into being, forced into life, imposed against all odds because it is for the best. What happens then is the Bolshevik curse at the heart of Boris Pasternak's novel *Doctor Zhivago*. (Thankfully, not yet made into a musical!) Come the revolution its characters face the simple profundity that the life of the personal is over. Individual comforts and contentment are bourgeois indulgence anathema to the utopian grand scheme of remaking the world by creating and serving the ideal state for the disembodied idealised collective.

Having a problem with the Bolshevik kind of utopian vision is not difficult precisely because it eradicates the home grown benevolence and comforts explicit in 'Home Sweet Home'. It is redolent of the master plan that makes the individual a cypher, a cog rather than the object of the exercise. It instils and demands a depersonalised utter dedication to the grand end that allows for no humane accommodation to the peculiarities, peccadillos and personality of people as individuals in their infinite variety. Such an outlook gives utopia every justification to be brutal in its means to the end.

On reflection I have just as deep seated an objection to the somewhere vision of utopia. It concedes home ground. Somewhere, someday somehow is not just an incapacity to define the means by which the utopia of a new way of living will be made a reality. It implies a not here, not with the material we have to work with; a 'no redemption on my turf' capitulation – but in another place all things may be possible approaches. What such a vision lacks is rootedness as much in people as place. Home is both a populated concept, a cultural artefact, as well as a location. Home is the microcosm of society and humanity from which we begin and by which we come to know our circumstances and the world at large. Home is context: history, tradition and present reality. In understanding what would, should and ought to be better context is all. Only context can inform the vision of what improvements must, should and ought to be made. Without context there is no yardstick to assess whether change is meaningful, if it is indeed substantive and quantifiable betterment or mere surface difference. As a very wise man once said to me, 'Things have changed many times, they just haven't improved'. There's simple profundity for you!

Present reality and home grown solutions – these are the only bedrock, rationale and means to utopia I can acknowledge. I have seen grand visions come and wither on the vine. They always seem to pass by my home place, make a detour to avoid our convenience and inclusion. So you keep your grand visions I say. I'll take the hard slog of small increments of making things better here and now. At least in this way I can be sure there is improvement that is meaningful and ministers to real people in their actual need according to their infinite diversity. There never will be any place like home by this autochthonous – grand word for home grown rather than grand vision – procedure. Everywhere can participate and all can share in betterment 'ne'er met with elsewhere'. Meaningful improvements enhance human life, human dignity and respect for the diversity of humanity. When we are all in a better home there may be nothing simple about the descriptive vision but it will be profound change for all that.

When I recall Dame Joan singing 'Home Sweet Home' I am not thinking of nostalgia or sentimentality, though I am conscious of a deep irony. First, the choice was inspired and profoundly appropriate on many levels. Context is all to appreciate the point. Singing a tribute to home in one's home town can never go amiss, of course. Choosing something utterly humble and homely certainly fits Dame Joan, famously a game Aussie girl without the vanities and self-importance of a diva despite decades of huge international stardom. Apparently she used to sit in the wings quietly stitching tapestry before strutting her stuff on the stage. And then there is the melody, the musical theme of 'Home Sweet Home' has been appropriated and recurs in many places such as in Sir Henry Wood's *Fantasia on British Sea Songs*, played every year at the Last Night of the Proms. I grew up watching the annual television broadcast of this particular concert that concludes the summer season of Promenade Concerts bringing fine music to the masses. The theme was also picked up by Donizetti and included in his opera *Anna Bolena*. His operas fell out of fashion until the special match between Donizetti's style and the amazing coloratura range, the incredible high notes Dame Joan sang so purely, revived this repertoire. Dame Joan performed Anna Bolena. The careful selection of the Donizetti repertoire was the inspired vision of Richard Bonynge, who was Dame Joan's husband and conducted so many of her performances including her Sydney farewell. There is indeed no place like home!

The irony is that the context of a full opera is quite beyond me. I would thank you to permit me never to have to endure an entire performance of an art form to which I simply cannot respond, beyond cringing and toe curling at the dreadful device of singing operas in English so one hears and understands the awful recitative – the sung dialogue bits. Gala concerts, great voices, great arias shorn of context – now we are talking my language. The beauty of the human voice and the raptures of emotion it can occasion can transport me to a state of bliss for hours on end. Therefore we can be absolutely sure I did not sit through the broadcast of *Die Fledermaus*, the opera during which Dame Joan made her final public appearance. I guarantee I decontextualised the event and only watched the party scene, the device which allowed Dame Joan, Pavarotti and Marilyn Horne as special guests to sing a selection of their greatest hits. It is also true that just as Placido Domingo is my personal preference over Luciano Pavarotti so Dame Kiri Te Kanawa is my preference over Dame Joan.

Lack of context, foreshortening or expanding time spans and wrong attribution – the litany of the frailty of historic memory – is part and parcel of the tale I have laid before you. It is impossible to escape from history but it is endlessly possible to manipulate what is history or what one thinks history is. This is as true of manufacturing utopic visions as it is of recruiting people to utopian causes. History is deeply entwined with human frailty in its making and remembering – and sometimes it is just a good story.

The simple profundity of the issue is: context is all – with the profoundly simple exception that there are instances when one is better without it. In which case I shall continue to hear Dame Joan and Marilyn Horne incomparably singing the flower duet from *Lakme* and call myself blessed until I no longer have ears to hear. Simply marvellous.

REEM KELANI'S TOP TEN PALESTINIAN INSPIRATIONS

There is a scene in Hany Abu-Assad's *The Idol* (2015) which would make even the most hardened curmudgeon blub. A multitude of hopefuls are auditioning in Cairo for the Middle-Eastern version of the *Pop Idol*-inspired television franchise. Among them is Mohammed Assaf, a wedding singer from a Gazan refugee camp, who has risked life and limb crossing the border into Egypt for this one shot at stardom. He almost does not make it into the audition because of bureaucratic red tape but gets given a chance because of the surprising kindness of a stranger – as the film's title succinctly reveals, Assaf goes on to win the 2013 *Arab Idol* competition.

Abu-Assad, an Israeli-born Palestinian, has won recognition for his films that address 'hard' issues – suicide bombers (2006's *Paradise Now*) and the fate of Palestinian collaborators with the Israeli regime (2013's *Omar*). Both were nominated for Best Foreign Language Film at the Academy Awards, while *The Idol* was submitted as Palestine's official entry in 2015 but was not nominated. Abu-Assad says, 'The story of this young man, Mohammad Assaf, is such an incredible story that even somebody like me who, just three weeks earlier had won the Jury Prize of Certain Regard at the Cannes Film Festival, was more excited for Assaf to win *Arab Idol* than for myself. I was caught on camera between thousands of people gathered in the square in Nazareth to hear the final results for *Arab Idol*; I was jumping in excitement like a little kid, and I have not had this kind of excitement for a very long time. When Ali Jaafar (the film producer with Quinta Communications) offered for me to direct Mohammad Assaf's story, my arms were covered in goosebumps. I knew immediately that I would do everything to make this story a movie.' Such was Abu-Assad's commitment that he insisted on shooting the film in Gaza, despite confronting formidable challenges, and chose first-time Gazan child actors to play four pivotal roles.

Art and culture are integral to the collective self-worth of entire peoples. This is why Palestinian culture is so often made invisible by those who support the Israeli occupation. It leaves the rest of the world with images of Palestinians as barbaric suicide bombers and aeroplane hijackers who threaten the very existence of Israel as the Middle East's only democratic utopia. And this is not a religious struggle between Muslims and Jews, however much the countless mass media reports reduce it in this way. More recently, even the Christian Palestinian dance troupe Baqoun nearly did not make it for their British tour in 2016 due to 'difficulties with travel and obtaining visas' – cryptic reasons indeed.

Where does one start, though, to uncover and celebrate the numerous examples of art and culture that capture the complexity of Palestine? We asked singer-composer and musicologist Reem Kelani if she would compile a list of her own inspirations. The result is highly personal and that's why we love it. You will not find Edward Said and Mahmoud Darwish listed here – as monumental as they are – because they are familiar figures already. Instead, get ready for a Top Ten of Palestinian cultural inspirations to delight and excite the uninitiated.

1. Za'atar

Kelani says, 'I eat Palestinian Za'atar, therefore I exist.' This aromatic herb mix of thyme, sumac, toasted sesame and sea salt is also often described as 'Israeli'. And what's the problem with this if nearly everyone in Israel consumes it too? The issue is that this kind of national labelling is not limited to za'atar – hummus is now being claimed as 'Israeli' too. And the choice of national adjective has serious geopolitical ramifications. Cuisines are products of the land – herbs, spices, meats, water, soil – and downplaying the Palestinian origins of certain foods is inextricable from the occupation of Palestinian land and the erasure of its national identity. This is not to say that everyone should stop referring to za'atar as 'Israeli' (or 'Palestinian'). But it does mean that the consumption of za'atar is deeply political. The celebrated poet Mahmoud Darwish has a poem, 'Ahmad al-Za'atar', that demonstrates the deep connections between agriculture, cuisine and identity for Palestinians. And no, this does not mean everyone should stop buying za'atar from the famed British Israeli chef Yotam Ottolenghi either. He does, after all, explicitly market it as *Palestinian* za'atar. But why not try the za'atar sold by Zaytoun, a social enterprise and community interest company that was set up in 2004 to develop a British market for artisanal Palestinian produce? Be warned, though – za'atar is addictive!

2. Palestinian 'Big Mamas'

The term 'Palestinian Big Mama' might be a Reem-ism, but it's easy to understand why she coined it. Kelani is enamoured by everything to do with these powerful women – their sense of humour, musicality, politics, feistiness, piety and sheer size. And for the past twenty years, these Big Mamas have been teaching Kelani their most cherished songs which she has lovingly studied, performed and recorded. In the liner notes of her album *Sprinting Gazelle*, she recounts a story of how a group of Big Mamas in a refugee camp in South Lebanon erupted into the title track when they learnt of her first name – '*reem*' translates as 'addax' or 'white antelope', but can also be used generically for 'gazelle'. The lyrics went: 'My eyes flooded with tears / I cried over our parting / I've taken a vow of silence / I've forbidden myself to dance the *dabkeh* / I've dyed my clothes dark and gone into mourning.' Profoundly moved, Kelani asked when they sang this song. They replied, 'We're Palestinian – at weddings, of course!'

3. Traditional Palestinian Cooking

Tying together the magic of za'atar (which Kelani stresses needs its own entry and must lead the list) and the irrepressibility of the Big Mamas is the cuisine of Palestine, specifically Gazan cuisine. Every news report about an Israeli bombardment or Hamas's controversial governance should be balanced by a Gazan recipe to remind people of what this embattled region also represents. According to Laila El-Haddad and Maggie Schmitt, authors of *The Gaza Kitchen*, Gaza's unique cuisine combines Levantine and Egyptian elements in such a way that its very history can be traced through its recipes. They write: 'And even in Gaza, that most tortured little strip of land, hundreds of thousands of women every day find ways to sustain their families and friends in body and spirit. They make the kitchen a stronghold against despair, and there craft necessity into pleasure and dignity.' Their book contains 130 sumptuous recipes, photographs and in-kitchen interviews and has been acclaimed by none other than Ottolenghi and Anthony Bourdain. So why not invite Gaza into your kitchen, too?

4.   Salma Khadra Jayyusi

Born in Jordan to a Palestinian father and Lebanese mother, poet and literary historian Salma Khadra Jayyusi (born 1926 or 1927) grew up in Palestine surrounded by Arab/Islamic and Western literature. After graduating from the American University of Beirut with honours in Arabic and English literature, she married a Jordanian diplomat and followed him all around the world. She began her academic career in earnest after raising three children, obtaining a doctorate in Arabic literature from the University of London. Eventually, she came to the conclusion that the misrepresentation of Arab culture and Islam in the West was in no small part due to the paucity of Arabic literature in other languages and decided to take the bull by the horns. She therefore left university teaching to found the Project of Translation from Arabic (PROTA), which aimed to introduce some of the best examples of Arabic literature to the English-speaking world. Realising that it was equally important to take on the discipline of cultural studies, Jayyusi then founded East-West Nexus. Through this, she spearheaded *The Legacy of Muslim Spain*, a 1,100-page tome written by forty-two scholars that was acknowledged as a bestseller by its publisher, Brill.

5.   Naji al-Ali

Political cartoonist Al-Ali (1938–1987) was known for his witty and satirical cartoons criticising the Israeli occupation but he also lampooned the Palestinian leadership, including Yasser Arafat. His most famous creation was the character Handala, who first appeared in 1969 in a Kuwaiti publication. After the 1973 Arab-Israeli War, the ten-year old Handala turned his back to viewers and had his hands clasped behind his back. Al-Ali explained that Handala's age represented the moment when he was forced to leave his homeland and he would not grow up until he was allowed to return. Al-Ali was shot in the face outside the London office of the Kuwaiti newspaper *Al Qabas* and died a few weeks later. The circumstances of the assassination are shrouded in mystery – at one point, it was suspected that the killer was a Palestinian double agent working for the Mossad. This incident plunged relations between the British and Israeli intelligence services to a historic low, with Prime Minister Margaret Thatcher expelling three Israeli diplomats in consequence. Handala lives on, however, and remains an icon of Palestinian identity and defiance. At one point, he even became the online mascot of the 2009 Iranian Green Movement.

6. Ghassan Kanafani

Born into a middle-class Muslim family in the British Mandate of Palestine, Ghassan Kanafani (1936–1972) is Kelani's favourite writer and novelist. His father, a lawyer, was active in the opposition to the British occupation. The family was forced into exile upon the outbreak of the 1948 Arab-Israeli war and Kanafani eventually became a leading figure in the secular, revolutionary socialist Popular Front for the Liberation of Palestine (PFLP) when it was founded in 1967. The PFLP is the second largest of the groups forming the Palestinian Liberation Organisation (PLO), the largest being Fatah. Kanafani was killed in a car bomb attack in Beirut, together with his seventeen-year-old niece Lamees Najim. The Mossad claimed responsibility but there were rumours that the Lebanese security forces had also been complicit. Like the cartoonist Al-Ali, however, Kanafani's enduring legacy is his art. He wrote stirring short stories, seen through the eyes of children, when he was working in Palestinian refugee camps and went on to produce several acclaimed novels. Throughout his short life, Kanafani's dualistic worldview as expressed in his writing gradually evolved into a more nuanced analysis of the Palestinian struggle and emphasised the importance of empathising with the Other. Upon his death, several uncompleted novels were found among his collected manuscripts and notes.

7. Palestinian embroidery

According to Kelani, some of the patterns that are used in Palestinian embroidery go back to Canaanite times, much like the Mesopotamian origins of some Palestinian song forms. Until the creation of the State of Israel in 1948, embroidery, or *al-tatreez*, was a communal activity – women in the countryside would gather together after finishing their chores to chat and stitch. In the decades after 1948, this activity increasingly became a luxury that many families could not afford and slowly died away. Non-governmental organisations played a pivotal role in ensuring that this art form has stayed alive, especially through programmes that continue being run in various refugee camps. This is important because *al-tatreez* is an integral part of the geographical and cultural Palestinian landscape – each town has its own unique pattern. You can tell where a Palestinian woman comes from just by looking at the patterns on her dress. Palestinian embroidery is also non-sectarian – Christians and Muslims engage in it and do not incorporate religious symbolism as a mark of separation. An excellent resource for further reading is the book *Palestinian Costume* by Shelagh Weir, the independent researcher and former Middle East curator for the British Museum.

8. Before Their Diaspora

What is your mental image of pre-1948 Palestine? What did homes, marketplaces, churches and mosques look like and what did people wear? What did a typical Palestinian family look like? *Before Their Diaspora* brings all these aspects of Palestinian society (and more) to life through 500 carefully selected photographs from 1876 to 1948. First published by the Institute of Palestine Studies in 1984, the book is by Walid Khalidi, a Jerusalem-born scholar who has taught at Oxford, the American University of Beirut and Harvard. A digital version of the book can be viewed online.

9. Mohammed Bushnaq

Bushnaq (born in 1934) is a Palestinian visual artist of Bosnian origin who was based in Kuwait when Kelani was growing up there. He was an immense influence on her, and taught his own daughter Suzan Bushnaq who is now also a visual artist. Father and daughter produce works that are impressionistic and slightly surreal, although Suzan's work focuses more on feminine vitality and beauty. They are also examples of the diversity within Palestinian society, including the contemporary diaspora. Partly because of Mohammed's influence, Kelani also pays meticulous attention to the artwork in her albums and to the resonances between Palestinian performing and visual arts.

10. Palestinian proverbs

There is a universal reverence in Arab culture for poetic language and so it is hardly surprising that proverbs play a central role in everyday Palestinian conversation. Knowing some popular Palestinian proverbs can offer an illuminating glimpse into their collective beliefs, values and concerns – past and present. Some evocative examples include: 'Your tongue is your horse – if you take care of it, it will take care of you and if you offend it, it will offend you.' 'The ignorant are their own enemy.' 'The eye does not get over the eyebrow.' (Spoken as a mark of respect. The brows are higher up in the face than the eyes and so the person who utters this proverb is one who feels less important than the person being addressed.)

CITATIONS

Introduction: The Coast of Utopia by Boyd Tonkin

On the history of South Africa, see Martin Meredith's *Diamonds, Gold and war: the making of South Africa* (Simon & Schuster, 2007), and on the enduring legacy of Rhodes, Brian Roberts's *Cecil Rhodes: Flawed Colossus* (Hamish Hamilton, 1987). Nigel Worden, Elizabeth van Heyningen and Vivian Bickford-Smith trace Cape Town's development in *Cape Town: the Making of a City* (David Philips, 1998), while David Johnson explores the settlement's significance as a place of dream as well as fact in *Imagining the Cape Colony: history, literature and the South African nation* (Edinburgh University Press, 2013). RW Johnson's *South Africa's Brave New World: the beloved country since the end of apartheid* (Penguin, 2011) is a well-informed, but utterly bleak, account of post-liberation politics and society. Alec Russell's *After Mandela: the battle for the soul of South Africa* (Hutchinson, 2009) sees stronger grounds for hope. As does Albie Sachs, freedom fighter-turned-constitution builder, in *We the People: insights of an activist judge* (Wits University Press, 2016).

Lyndall Gordon remembers a Jewish childhood in the post-war city in her memoir *Shared Lives: growing up in 50s Cape Town* (Virago, 2005). Shaun Viljoen investigates the life of its greatest 'Coloured' writer in *Richard Rive: a partial biography* (Wits University Press, 2013). *Noor's Story: my life in District Six* by Noor Ebrahim (District Six Museum, 1999) recalls the kind of mixed community that apartheid's ethnic cleansing destroyed, while Cariema Isaacs's *My Cape Malay Kitchen* (Struik Lifestyle, 2016) evokes a way of life as much as a cuisine. John Muir's *Walking Cape Town* (Struik, 2013) is an invaluable, and charming, guide to the past and present of the city's varied neighbourhoods. For the history of division beneath Kirstenbosch Botanical Gardens, see sanbi.org/gardens/kirstenbosch/history-kirstenbosch-nbg. The Oude Molen Eco-Village website, oudemolenecovillage.co.za, gives an account of its history and aims. 'A Guide to the Kramats of the Western Cape' can be downloaded from the website of the Cape Mazaar Society, capemazaarsociety.com.

Among many editions of Thomas More's *Utopia*, George M Logan's (Norton Critical Editions, 2011) stands out for its illuminating extracts from More's correspondence with his fellow-humanists in addition to an anthology of critical interpretations. More's transition from intellectual to statesman, free-thinker to hard-liner, is chronicled by Peter Ackroyd in *The Life of Thomas More* (Chatto & Windus, 1998), and, through the prism of his relationship with his daughter Margaret, by John Guy in *A Daughter's Love* (Fourth Estate, 2008). From Plato's *Republic* to Orwell's *Nineteen Eighty-Four*, a variety of readily-available editions gives access to the Utopian tradition. Those less easy to locate may include Evgeny Zamyatin's *We* (translated by Natasha Randall; Vintage Classics, 2007) and Edward Bellamy's *Looking Backwards: 2000-1887* (Oxford World's Classics, 2009). The text of Tom Stoppard's trilogy *The Coast of Utopia* is published by Faber & Faber (2007). Boualem Sansal's *2084: the End of the World* appears in Alison Anderson's translation (Europa Editions, 2017). Ursula Le Guin's essays on modern utopianism serve as an afterword to the Verso quincentennial edition of More's *Utopia* (2016). Lyman Tower Sargent's *Utopianism: a very short introduction* (Oxford, 2010) looks far beyond Europe for examples of the theory and practice of 'intentional communities'. For hard-core speculators, Frank E Manuel and Fritzie P Manuel's *Utopian Thought in the Western World* (Harvard University Press, 1979) remains the most detailed map of this vast terrain.

Findhorn by Hasan Mahamdallie

The Findhorn Foundation can be found at www.findhorn.org. Peter Caddy's autobiography, *Perfect Timing: Memoirs of a Man for the New Millennium* (Findhorn Press Ltd.1996), provides interesting insight into both Findhorn's and Caddy's own history. A full list of Findhorn publications by the Caddy's, Dorothy Maclean and others is on their website at https://www.findhorn.org/aboutus/vision/history/. See also *The Findhorn Community: Creating a Human Identity for the 21st Century* by Carol Riddell (Findhorn 1997). A critical account of Findhorn can be

found at http://citizeninitiative.com/the_findhorn-foundation.htm#
rosicrucian

The polemical essay 'Whither The New Age?' by J. Gordon Melton can be
downloaded   at   http://www.theway.org.uk/Back/33Melton.pdf.
Nicholas Goodrick-Clarke's *The Western Esoteric Traditions: A Historical
Introduction:* (OUP, 2008) includes chapters on Rosicrucianism and
Theosophy. The best overall account of the tangled history of twentieth-
century western esoteric traditions is Stephen J Sutcliffe's *Children of the
New Age: A History of Spiritual Practice* (Routledge, 2002).

By Oneself, Together by Marco Lauri

Main translations of cited works: Lenn Evan Goodman, translator, Ibn
Tufayl's *Hayy ibn Yaqzan. A Philosophical Tale* (Chicago: The University of
Chicago Press, 2009); Joseph Schacht and Max Meyerhof, editors and
translators, *The Theologus Autodidactus of Ibn al-Nafis* (Oxford: Clarendon
Press, 1968); Ralph Lerner, editor and translator, *Averroes on Plato's Republic*
(Ithaca: Cornell University Press, 2005). On Arabic Science fiction: Ada
Barbaro, *La Fantascienza nella Letteratura Araba* (Roma: Carocci 2013).

For an introduction to Ibn Tufayl, see Taneli Kukkonen, *Ibn Tufayl: Living the
Life of Reason* (London: Oneworld Publications, 2014); regarding its
reception, see: Avner Ben-Zaken, *Reading Hayy Ibn Yaqzan: A Cross-Cultural
History of Autodidacticism* (Baltimore: John Hopkins University Press, 2011);
Gül Russel, 'The Impact of the Philosophus autodidactus: the Pocockes,
Locke, and the Society of Friends', in *The Interest of the Natural Philosophers
in 'Arabick' in Seventeenth-Century England* (Leiden: Brill, 1994: 224-66).

For its utopian dimensions: Fedwa Malti-Douglas, Hayy Ibn Yaqzan as a
Male Utopia in *The World of Ibn Tufayl* (Leiden: Brill, 1996: 52-68) and my
article 'Utopias in the Islamic Middle Ages: Ibn Tufayl and Ibn al-Nafis'
(*Utopian Studies*, 24, 1: 23-40).

On Ibn al-Nafis see Nahyan Fancy, *Science and Religion in Mamluk Egypt: Ibn al-Nafis, Pulmonary Transit and Bodily Resurrection* (London, Routledge, 2013).

Escape to Andalusia by Medina Tenour Whiteman

The fascinating history of the Sufi community of Norwich is yet to be written. The authoritarian leader of the community, Ian Dallas, was born in Scotland, attended University of London, trained as an actor at RADA, and worked in film with the celebrated Italian Director Federico Fellini. Later, he worked as playwright for the BBC and wrote a number of novels, including *The Book of Strangers* (Pantheon Books, New York, 1972), which is semi-autobiographical. After converting to Islam, he changed his name to Abdal Qadir – adding new appellations over time: Abdalqadir as-Sufi, Abdalqadir as-Sufi al-Darqawi, Abdalqadir as-Sufi al-Darqawi al-Murabat. The essence of his – rather extremists – views on Islam can be found in *Jihad: A Ground Plan* (Diwan Press, 1978) and *Root Islamic Education* (Medina Press, 1993).

The spiritual Moroccan music that inspired Abdal-Lateef Whiteman can be heard at: ianwhiteman.blog (Diwan singing tab).

For the Islamic history of Andalusia, and the impact of Islam on contemporary Spain, see *Critical Muslim 6: Reclaiming Al-Andalus* (Hurst, London, 2013).

Islamic Utopianism by Nazry Bahrawi

The ibn 'Arabi quotation is from Abdullah Saeed, *Islamic Thought: An Introduction*. (London: Routledge, 2006), p81. The Rumi quote is from Afzal Iqbal, *The Life and Work of Jalal ad-Din Rumi*, sixth ed. (Islamabad: Pakistan National Council of the Arts, 1991), p 207; for Annemarie Schimmel quotes see her , 'Muhammad Iqbal 1873-1938: The Ascension of the Poet'. *Die Welt des Islams* 3. 3-4 (1954): 145-157, 150; the Roy Jackson quote is from *Fifty Key Figures in Islam* (Routledge, London, 2006), p71; and, finally, quotes from Muhammad 'Abduh are from *The Theology of Unity*, translated by Ishaq Musa'ad and Kenneth Craig (Kuala Lumpur: Islamic Book Trust, 2004), p107 and p133.

See also: Abdullah Saeed, *Islamic Thought: An Introduction.* (London: Routledge, 2006); Titus Burckhardt, *Introduction to Sufi* Doctrine. (Indiana, Bloomington: World Wisdom, 2008), and Majid Fakhry, *A History of Islamic Philosophy.* (Columbia: Columbia UP, 1970), 283.

Searching for Khilafatopia by Sadek Hamid

This article is on based on my book, *Sufis, Salafis and Islamists: The Contested Ground of British Islamic Activism* (IB Taurus, London, 2016). See also: Hugh Kennedy, *The Caliphate* (Pelican, London, 2016) and Mohammed Nawab Osman, 'The Caliphate of Hizb-ut-Tahrir' *Critical Muslim 10: Sects*, edited by Ziauddin Sardar and Robin Yassin-Kassab (Hurst, London, 2014, pp75-86).

Unravelling Utopia by Yasmin Khan

Sinbad Sci-Fi: Reimagining Arab Science Fiction can be found at http://sindbadscifi.com/.

Ahmed Khaled Towfik's *Utopia* was published by Merit in 2008, and in an English translation by Chip Rossetti by Bloomsbury Qatar in 2011. Sofia Samatar's review is at http://strangehorizons.com/non-fiction/reviews/utopia-by-ahmed-khaled-towfik/.

Larissa Sansour's work can be found at her website http://www.larissasansour.com/. A curatorial overview of Sansour is at www.lawrieshabibi.com/exhibitions/45/overview/.

Ahmed Saadawi's *Frankenstein in Baghdad*, which won the International Prize for Arabic Fiction (IPAF) for 2014, will be published by Penguin early in 2018.

Sophia Al-Maria's essay 'Sci-Fi Wahabi' is at http://scifiwahabi.blogspot. com/. Al-Maria and fellow artist Fatima Al Qadiri discuss 'Gulf Futurism' in a 2012 *Dazed* magazine interview by Karen Orton http://www. dazeddigital.com/artsandculture/article/15040/1/the-desert -of-the-unreal.

Rokheya Shekhawat Hossain's *Sultana's Dream* has been published by the Feminist Press, Delhi, 1988; Charlotte Perkins Gilman's *Herland* is available as a Vintage Classic. There are numerous editions of both novels; and both are available as a single volume in Kindle edition.

The Never-Ending Journey by Colin Tudge

I have been thinking about the ideas in this article for the past half century. The expression 'Enlightened Agriculture', later also known as 'Real Farming', first appeared in my book, *So Shall We Reap* (Penguin, London, 2004). Other ideas can be explored in more detail in my recent books, *Why Genes are Not Selfish and People are Nice* (Floris Books, Edinburgh, 2013) and *Six Steps Back to the Land* (Green Books, Cambridge, 2016).

A year or so ago with a few like-minded chums we set up our College for Real Farming and Food Culture – with the goal of re-thinking all the things that need re-thinking, each in the light of all the others, focused on food and farming (though it could be focused on architecture, or medicine, or what you will) and rooted firmly in metaphysics. If you want to know more and join in the fun please tune in to the College website (http:// collegeforrealfarming.org/).

Cancer: Key to Utopia by Naomi Foyle

This essay is indebted to the following books and articles: Siddhartha Mukherjee, *The Emperor of All Maladies: A Biography of Cancer* (Fourth Estate, London, 2011), pp 388, 18, 120, 38, 130-31, 125, 225; Simeon Nelson, 'Cancer and Complexity in an Unfolding World' in *Anarchy in the Organism* (Black Dog Publishing, London, 2012), p 33; Eva Saulitis, *Becoming Earth* (Boreal Books, Pasadena, 2016), p79; Rebecca Solnit, *Hope in the Dark*

(Canongate, Edinburgh, 2016), pp 85, 4, 1; Susan Sontag, 'Illness as Metaphor', in *Illness as Metaphor & Aids and its Metaphors* (Penguin Classics, London, 2002), pp 3, 83, 87, 14, 77.

The verses from the Qur'an are taken from *The Meaning of The Glorious Qur'an: An Explanatory Translation* by Muhammad Marmaduke Pickthall (Islamic Dawah Centre International, Birmingham, 2004).

The essay also quotes Samuel Broder as quoted by Mukherjee (op cit) p135; Eduardo Galeneo as quoted by Rebecca Solnit (op cit), p 77; Kent Meyers from http://redhen.org/authors/eva-saulitis/; Gloria Steinem from https://www.theguardian.com/commentisfree/2016/nov/10/after-donald-trump-win-americans-organizing-us-politics [both accessed Jan 25th 2017]; David Westley from an article by Ann Robinson: https://www.theguardian.com/lifeandstyle/2016/jun/06/coping-with-catastrophe-what-keeps-us-going-in-face-adversity; and makes reference to the work of Ziauddin Sardar in *How Do you Know? Reading Ziauddin Sardar on Islam, Science and Cultural Relations* (Pluto Press, London, 2006).

All cancer statistics are taken from Cancer Research UK at cancerresearchuk.org. Substantial information on integrative medicine, including clinical trials, is available at the Memorial Sloan Kettering Cancer Care website: https://www.mskcc.org/cancer-care/diagnosis-treatment/symptom-management/integrative-medicine.

Further information on the political context of breast cancer treatment can be found at: https://electronicintifada.net/content/israel-blocks-gaza-women-breast-cancer-treatment/18761, 'Breast Cancer Often "More Advanced" in Black Women', http://www.bbc.co.uk/news/health-37991460 (Nov 16 2016); 'Woman wins Herceptin court fight', http://news.bbc.co.uk/1/hi/health/4902150.stm (April 12 2006) and the website of Breast Cancer Action: http://www.bcaction.org/ [All accessed Jan 25 2017].

Standing up For Palestine by Shanon Shah

Details about Reem Kelani's albums and performances can be found at her website: http://www.reemkelani.com/.

On *Mawtini*, see http://www.nationalanthems.me/iraq-mawtini/. For a brief yet nuanced biography of Layla Murad, see https://www.library. cornell.edu/colldev/mideast/llmurd.htm.

Northern Women for Palestine has a Facebook page at https://www. facebook.com/NorthernWomenforPalestine/. Lionel Shriver's full speech on cultural appropriation can be found at https://www.theguardian.com/ commentisfree/2016/sep/13/lionel-shrivers-full-speech-i-hope -the-concept-of-cultural-appropriation-is-a-passing-fad.

An interview with Ottolenghi where he discusses the role of cuisine in the Palestinian-Israeli conflict can be found at http://www.wbur.org/ hereandnow/2015/05/18/plenty-jerusalem-yotam-ottolenghi.

The List: Reem Kelani's Top Ten Palestinian Inspirations

An in-depth interview with Hany Abu-Assad on *The Idol* can be found at http://www.indiewire.com/2016/05/the-idol-director-hany-abu-assad- on-making-a-movie-without-cultural-barriers-170321/. Information on Baqoun's 2016 British tour can be partly gleaned from http://www. westyorkshiredales.anglican.org/content/visit-palestinian -dance-group-confirmed.

The Gaza Kitchen has its own website – http://www.gazakitchen.com/. – and the book can be purchased at http://justworldbooks.com/books/ the-gaza-kitchen-2nd-ed/. One way to get ethical za'atar is from http:// www.zaytoun.org/zaytoun_zaatar.html.

A video of Palestinian Big Mamas in action that is bound to put a smile on your face is at https://www.youtube.com/watch?v=0kB82s4-0tw.

Learn more about Salma Khadra Jayyusi at http://archive.
thisweekinpalestine.com/details.php?catid=9&id=2283&edid=146 and
Naji Al-Ali at https://en.wikipedia.org/w/index.php?title=Naji_
al-Ali&oldid=754761507. The shocking details of Al-Ali's assassination and
the tensions it sparked off between Britain and Israel can be found at
http://www.independent.co.uk/news/world/mi5-was-feuding-with-
mossad-while-known-terrorists-struck-in-london-1101024.html.

The Wikipedia entry for Ghassan Kanafani contains excellent references
for further reading: https://en.wikipedia.org/w/index.php?title=
Ghassan_Kanafani&oldid=759246500.

The Ladah Foundation maintains a website on Palestinian embroidery at
http://palestinianembroider.tripod.com/

The Institute of Palestine Studies has an excellent website on Walid
Khalidi's *Before Their Diaspora* at http://btd.palestine-studies.org/.

Mohammed Bushnaq's work is extremely hard to come by online, but
there are some arresting magazine covers that he has done which can be
found at http://palestineposterproject.org/artist/mohammed-bushnaq.

Of the vast treasury of Palestinian proverbs, the ones chosen in this list are
from http://abualkam1982.ahlamontada.com/t55-a-collection-of-palest-
inian-proverbs and http://www.barghouti.com/folklore/proverbs/.

CONTRIBUTORS

Sharbari Z Ahmed is a writer of screenplays, stage and fiction ● **Fatimah Ashrif** works as a consultant advising on philanthropy projects; she currently works for the University of Cambridge as Project Lead on Coexist House ● **Nazry Bahrawi** teaches at the Singapore University of Technology and Design ● **Merryl Wyn Davies** is a writer based in Merthyr Tydfil ● **Naomi Foyle**, a lecturer at Chichester University, is a science fiction writer; her *Stained Light: The Gaia Chronicles Book 4* has just been published by Jo Fletcher Books ● **Sadek Hamid**, an academic with research interests in Islam in Britain, America and Europe, is the author of *Sufis, Salafis and Islamists: The Contested Ground of British Islamic Activism* ● **Halima Gosai Hussain** is Chair of the Inclusive Mosque Initiative ● **Noor Iskandar** is an award-winning, multidisciplinary artist based in Singapore ● **Rehan Khan,** a Regional Consulting Director in the MENA region for a FTSE 100 corporation and Professor of Management at HULT International Business School, has just completed the second book in his Tasburai trilogy ● **Yasmin Khan** is an independent curator, cultural consultant and founder producer of Sindbad Scifi ● **Marco Lauri** is adjunct professor of Arabic Literature, Arabic Philology and Islamic Studies at the universities of Macerata and Urbino, Italy ● **Hassan Mahamdallie**, Director of the Muslim Institute, is a playwright ● **Sarah Pickthall**, a writer and performer, studied Kabuki Theatre at Kokuritsu Gekijo, Toyko, Japan ● **Shanon Shah,** Deputy Editor of *Critical Muslim*, used to be a pop star in Malaysia ● **Peter Stockton** is a poet as well as teacher of English language, Art and Gardening at Cambridge Regional College ● **Boyd Tonkin** is an independent journalist, columnist and writer ● **Colin Tudge** is a biologist by education, a writer by trade, and founder of the College for Real Farming and Food Culture by necessity ● **Bruce Wannell**, an independent scholar, is a specialist on Persian and Arab cultures ● **Medina Tenour Whiteman** is a writer, musician, singer and an occasional permaculturist ● **Hodan Yusuf**, writer, poet, and photographer, is currently working on her debut collection of poems.